Classics and the Bible

Classical Literature and Society
Series Editor: David Taylor

Classics and the Bible: Hospitality and Recognition
John Taylor

Culture and Philosophy in the Age of Plotinus
Mark Edwards

Homer: The Resonance of Epic
Barbara Graziosi & Johannes Haubold

Ovid and His Love Poetry
Rebecca Armstrong

**Pastoral Inscriptions:
Reading and Writing Virgil's *Eclogues***
Brian Breed

Pausanias: Travel Writing in Ancient Greece
Maria Pretzler

Silent Eloquence: Lucian and Pantomime Dancing
Ismene Lada-Richards

Thucydides and the Shaping of History
Emily Greenwood

CLASSICAL LITERATURE AND SOCIETY

Classics and the Bible

Hospitality and Recognition

John Taylor

Duckworth

This impression 2009
First published in 2007 by
Gerald Duckworth & Co. Ltd.
90-93 Cowcross Street, London EC1M 6BF
Tel: 020 7490 7300
Fax: 020 7490 0080
info@duckworth-publishers.co.uk
www.ducknet.co.uk

A catalogue record for this book is available
from the British Library

ISBN 978 0 7156 3481 3

Typeset by Ray Davies

Contents

For Martin and Jane Hammond

Editor's Foreword

The aim of this series is to consider Greek and Roman literature primarily in relation to genre and theme. Its authors hope to break new ground in doing so but with no intention of dismissing current interpretation where this is sound; they will be more concerned to engage closely with text, subtext and context. The series therefore adopts a homologous approach in looking at classical writers, one of whose major achievements was the fashioning of distinct modes of thought and utterance in poetry and prose. This led them to create a number of literary genres evolving their own particular forms, conventions and rules – genres which live on today in contemporary culture.

Although studied within a literary tradition, these writers are also considered within their social and historical context, and the themes they explore are often both highly specific to that context and yet universal and everlasting. The ideas they conceive and formulate and the issues they debate find expression in a particular language, Latin or Greek, and belong to their particular era in the classical past. But they are also fully translatable into a form that is accessible as well as intelligible to those living in later centuries, in their own vernacular. Hence all quoted passages are rendered into clear, modern English.

These are books, then, which are equally for readers with or without knowledge of the Greek and Latin languages and with or without an acquaintance with the civilisation of the ancient world. They have plenty to offer the classical scholar, and are ideally suited to students reading for a degree in classical subjects. Yet they will interest too those studying European and contemporary literature, history and culture who wish to discover the roots and springs of our classical inheritance.

The series owes a special indebtedness and thanks to Pat Easterling, who from the start was a constant source of advice and encouragement. Others whose help has been invaluable are Robin Osborne who, if ever we were at a loss to think of an author for a particular topic, almost always came up with a suitable name or two and was never stinting of his time or opinion, and Tony Woodman, now at Virginia. The unfailing assistance of the late John W. Roberts, editor of the *Oxford Dictionary of the Classical World*, is also gratefully acknowledged. Deborah Blake, Duckworth's indefatigable Editorial Director, has throughout offered full support, boundless enthusiasm and wise advice.

vii

Finally, I pay tribute to the inspirational genius which Michael Gunningham, *fons et origo* of the series and an editor of consummate skill and phenomenal energy, brought to the enterprise. His imprint is everywhere: *sine quo, non.*

David Taylor

Preface

This is an amateur sketch of a big subject. In reading and teaching Greek and Latin literature I am constantly struck by biblical parallels. These have received surprisingly little attention in recent times, though a glance at the history of art (or at Milton) shows that acknowledgement of affinity was once usual. Classical literature and the Bible are nowadays conventionally studied in separate compartments, but this is a curious and constricting orthodoxy. The time span of the two sets of texts is roughly the same, beginning in perhaps the eighth century BC (though incorporating earlier material) and extending for about a thousand years. Both are products of a Mediterranean world influenced by older cultures of the Near East. Resemblance between stories can sometimes be explained by a common source, but my concern here is with analogy rather than genealogy. The Trojan War has a role in classical literature comparable to that of the Exodus in the Bible as an endlessly rich source of reference and allusion. Authors in both traditions are concerned with a heroic past and its bearing on the present, and they rewrite earlier texts because they see earlier events re-enacted. In Virgil and in the New Testament alike we find (within a century or so, spanning the turn of the era) a particularly influential reworking, a radical re-appropriation of a revered past. Styles of interpretation and criticism have often been closely parallel. We depend still on the results of nineteenth-century analytical scholarship, yet its practitioners often murdered to dissect. Both classicists and biblical critics are now typically more concerned with what happens in front of a text (reception history and reader response) than with trying to peer behind it. A new humility assumes, in the absence of compelling contrary evidence, that texts have the form their authors planned, so that (for example) an apparently abrupt and unresolved ending is read as an effect deliberately created.

I offer a series of connected essays. The first three chapters consider the subject from the classical side: Homer, the literature of classical Athens, and Virgil; the fourth turns to the New Testament; and the fifth more briefly to aspects of later reception. The themes of hospitality and recognition (often in combination) provide an extended test case for comparison of the two traditions. I hope to show that they are important in both, but they are intended also as metaphors about the relation between the two sets of texts and our perception of it.

Experience of discussing the subjects treated here suggests I should forestall two misconceptions. This is not a quest for what Simone Weil called 'intimations of Christianity' in classical authors. Conversely, however, I hope that the juxtaposition of scriptural and pagan texts will not seem inappropriately reductionist. The theologian David Brown in his acclaimed *Tradition and Imagination* observes the paradox that an ecumenical age open to revelatory insight from other world religions implicitly denies it to the classical past: studies both in comparative religion and in comparative literature flourish, but this most obvious comparison is neglected. We now generally accept that texts can be read in a variety of ways, and this acceptance I hope may extend to respect for different understandings of inspiration (a concept whose history shows how closely theology and literary criticism are intertwined). Except perhaps on the most narrowly fundamentalist view, books of the Old and New Testaments are the work of ancient human hands and can be approached as such, irrespective of the further status that may be attributed to them by confessional allegiance.

This is a book about reading, and I hope also an invitation to read. The Bible and classical literature long enjoyed a joint hegemony in our culture, but both are now much less widely known than they once were. An attempt to read the Bible all through is liable to founder somewhere in the middle of Leviticus. Help is at hand in two recent books with telling titles. John Dancy in *The Divine Drama* presents the main story of the Old Testament with an illuminating commentary. Philip Law in *Testament: The Bible Odyssey* contracts the whole Bible to be read like a novel. For major classical authors translations are easily available in the Penguin Classics and Oxford World's Classics series.

Bible passages are usually quoted in the Revised Standard Version, occasionally in other versions to make a particular point. Translations of classical authors are mostly my own. References to ancient sources are given in the text, and at the back of the book there is a full list of passages. Most of the notes are simply references to secondary literature: I have tried to attribute specific borrowings, though it is not always easy to trace where a particular idea first occurs and I hope in these cases a generalised acknowledgement may serve. I hope too that the range of material justifies the fact that an incidental reference to (say) Pope or Coleridge may be cited from a secondary source where the passage is quoted and discussed, rather than overloading the book with full detail of its original context.

The commentaries of A.S. Hollis on Callimachus and Ovid first alerted me to the wide resonance of the theoxeny theme, and Terence Cave's *Recognitions* provided the fundamental insight that the Aristotelian plot device of *anagnôrisis* is also a description of literary experience. Beverley Matthews, librarian of Tonbridge School, has been unfailingly efficient in tracking down elusive books. I am grateful to the series editors: to Michael

Gunningham for the invitation to contribute to it, and to David Taylor for his comments on the text. Deborah Blake and Ray Davies at Duckworth have provided patient and helpful guidance.

Tonbridge School
June 2007

1

Homer

'Life is warfare, and a visit in a strange land' wrote the Roman emperor Marcus Aurelius about AD 170 (*Meditations* 2.17.1), referring implicitly to the two Homeric epics. The *Iliad* and the *Odyssey* embody our most basic spiritual metaphors: life as a battle, and life as a journey. The hero of each is in some sense a representative man. The *Odyssey* comes after the *Iliad* (by subtle allusion presupposing it[1]), but in this chapter I look first and more fully at the later epic because of its firmer narrative shape and its striking biblical parallels.

The two poems stand at the beginning of Greek literature but have a long tradition of storytelling behind them. The *Odyssey* is already a sophisticated variant of a more obvious narrative. Many of the experiences of Odysseus seem naturally those of a hero seeking a wife and a home: in the scenes with the princess Nausicaa we almost believe he might settle among the hospitable Phaeacians; yet we know that the loyal Penelope and rocky Ithaca represent his true destination, explicitly preferred to more glittering alternatives. Returning home in disguise, Odysseus wins again the woman to whom he is married already. He regains what he lost at the beginning of the larger story which the epic assumes: this is a boomerang quest. The Bible repeatedly uses the same narrative pattern. The Promised Land is the place where Abraham had precariously established a foothold long before. The accounts of Jacob and of Job, the history of the Babylonian Exile, the parable of the Prodigal Son: all these are stories of absence and return, of loss and restoration. Above all this model shapes the grand structure created by combining the Hebrew scriptures and the New Testament ('from the first days of our disobedience unto the glorious Redemption'[2]). Its archetypal resonance, both Homeric and biblical, gave T.S. Eliot the powerful lines in the last canto of 'Little Gidding':

> And the end of all our exploring
> Will be to arrive where we started
> And know the place for the first time.[3]

Heavenly visitors

While Odysseus is away from Ithaca many proprieties lapse, but hospitality remains the decisive social litmus. Telemachus is sitting disconsolately

1

among the Suitors and thinking about his absent father when he sees someone approaching:

> He went straight to the outer door, for he was ashamed in his heart that a stranger should stand long at the gates. (*Od.* 1.119-20)

Homer has told us that this is the goddess Athene disguised as his father's friend Mentes. A council of the gods has preceded this visit, but the first human words in the poem are spoken by Telemachus:

> Greetings, stranger. You will be entertained in our house, and then when you have tasted food you can tell us what your need is. (1.123-4)

The Suitors are preoccupied with their feasting, a grimly ironic parody of the wedding to which each of them aspires. Yet even they, when later confronted with the beggar who is the returned Odysseus, acknowledge that a visitor may be a god in disguise. Their aggressive leader Antinous is reproached by one of his companions for throwing a stool at the unrecognised hero:

> You are a doomed man if he turns out to be some god from heaven. And the gods do disguise themselves as strangers from afar, and move from city to city in every shape, observing the violence and the justice of men. (17.484-7)

That belief constantly colours Homeric hospitality. We meet here the widespread folktale theme of a divine or royal visitor, testing people by coming among them in disguise to see how he will be treated when self-interested deference is stripped away. We shall see versions of this idea in many different contexts.

Connections between religion and hospitality are pervasive in Homer. Odysseus when newly arrived in an unfamiliar place speculates, in a repeated pair of formulaic lines, whether the inhabitants are 'wild, savage and unjust' or 'hospitable to strangers and of god-fearing mind' (for example 6.120-1). In the latter and desired case, the qualities of hospitality and piety go naturally together. In a world with no legal system and no hotels or consulates, newly arrived strangers are vulnerable, and so come under the special protection of Zeus.[4] In this role the father of gods and men is Zeus *Xenios*, overseeing the behaviour and needs of the *xenos*, who is according to context *stranger*, *foreigner*, *host* or *guest*. The semantic range of the word expresses the reciprocity ideally present in the relationship which the newcomer establishes with the person who receives him.

The religious obligation is especially binding when the stranger comes in the intensified form of a suppliant (*hiketês*, literally 'arriver') seeking sanctuary, or a beggar seeking sustenance. Every visitor has a claim on those to whom he comes, but the heightened vulnerability of a suppliant or beggar puts him particularly in need of divine protection, and makes any breach of appropriate treatment correspondingly culpable. The well-bred Nausicaa knows that 'all *xenoi* and beggars are from Zeus' (6.207-8), and is sensitive to the possibility that the brine-encrusted stranger before her may be himself a god. When Odysseus confronts the Cyclops Polyphemus, he knows in his heart that the giant is a savage monster, but nonetheless urges him:

> Be respectful, good sir, of the gods: we are your suppliants.
> Zeus is the avenger of suppliants and *xenoi*,
> Zeus *Xenios*, who accompanies *xenoi* who deserve respect. (9.269-71)

Zeus, perhaps in origin a god of the sky and weather, is already in the *Odyssey* envisaged as the guardian of morality. Later poets and thinkers will make of him a quasi-monotheist universal deity. It is plausible to see in this development a steady broadening of his role as the god of host and guest, and protector of the weak. Greek religion imposed virtually no absolute divine commands, but the law of hospitality to strangers was universally observed.[5] It can properly be called a sacrament.

The stranger himself is an ambiguous figure, potentially threatening as well as vulnerable. In a society which divides people into friends and enemies, he is put into quarantine by the formalities of hospitality until he can be suitably categorised. He is a welcome source of information and diversion in a world without broadcasting or newspapers. Reciprocity, a central organising principle in early Greek society,[6] applies to the entertainment of strangers in two ways. At best you may hope to begin a relationship of guest-friendship which will be lasting, and even hereditary: that is what Athene here claims (1.187-8). Such an arrangement, ensuring that you are entertained in the other person's house when you visit his city, is of obvious utility in the Homeric world. But even if that link is never forged, reciprocity is more immediately achieved because the stranger sings for his supper: he entertains the company, and tells of the outside world.

Homeric hospitality is governed by strict rules. Physical needs must first be met: roads were hot and dusty, and seaways hazardous. Only when food and drink have been provided are questions allowed, though they can then be very direct. Telemachus enquires about his visitor's ship with the favourite Ithacan pleasantry that he is unlikely to have come to the island on foot (1.173). The disguised Athene, who fashions herself as a man in the mould of Odysseus, a traveller full of worldly wisdom, tells him that his father still lives, and that the time has come to go in search of him; and so 'the hand of divinity begins to move and work amid the chaos'.[7] Athene leaves 'flying upward like a bird' (1.320), presumably to the smoke-vent in the roof. It is left expressively unclear whether we are to think of this uncannily quick departure as a metamorphosis or only a simile, but it is enough to make Telemachus aware that he has been entertaining a god.

This recognition is programmatic for all later ones in the poem. Telemachus will himself be recognised as his father's son by Helen in Sparta (4.143), and Odysseus when he has returned to Ithaca will identify himself to Telemachus (16.187-8) as part of a carefully arranged sequence of revelations. Aristotle in the *Poetics* (1459b) comments that the *Odyssey* uses *anagnôrisis* ('recognition') throughout, unifying its complex plot. In the *Odyssey* and in later Greek literature recognitions of people (and internalised recognitions, moments of self-knowledge and of insight into the workings of the world) are modelled on scenes where a god is recognised and retain something of the atmosphere of those encounters.[8] The scene with Athene shows how hospitality expresses morality. It has also provided the context for recognition. The two themes are constantly linked.[9] Bystanders can remain in ignorance when a recognition takes place, as the Suitors do here. Their lack of perception is bound up with their disregard for the rules of hospitality. Not only have they ignored the visitor Mentes, but they are themselves unwelcome guests in the palace, improperly aiming to win the wife of their absent host. We are reminded of the Trojan prince Paris eloping with Helen, the wife of his host Menelaus, and of all that flowed from that initial transgression.

The meeting between Telemachus and Athene is marked by friendly familiarity. Entertaining a goddess is to him no more surprising than other new experiences of late adolescence. The encounter nonetheless has a numinous quality. A scene which describes the entertaining of a god is now usually referred to as a theoxeny.[10] This modern critical term was used in classical Greece for a religious ritual which enacted such entertainment (we might in broad terms compare the Roman *lectisternium*, where couches were prepared for the gods as banqueters, or the later custom of laying an extra place at table for the returning Christ). This first theoxeny in the *Odyssey* is a significant beginning, instinct with promise: Telemachus will take up his adult responsibilities, and Odysseus will indeed return. Mentes is the guise of Athene only here, but as Mentor (a similar name for a similar role) or in her own person she will repeatedly intervene, to help the cause of Odysseus and to police the plot. Mentor accompanies Telemachus on the first part of his travels, when he is welcomed by old Nestor at Pylos (*Od.* 3.4-372), and in that pious setting initiated into the traditions of peacetime heroic society functioning as it properly should. Its exemplary hospitality is offered to young man and disguised goddess alike: this again is a theoxeny.[11] But so too, as Emily Kearns shows in an important essay, is the reception of the disguised Odysseus in Ithaca.[12] As in the underlying folktale, the unknown but important guest may be a heroic or royal but still human figure. Scenes of hospitality in human contexts (as well as scenes of recognition) draw repeatedly on a basic story pattern where the guest is a god. The moral worth of other characters is tested by their response to the beggar: accepting or rejecting this humble visitor is tantamount to accepting or rejecting Odysseus himself.

1. Homer

Homer and Genesis make a natural pair, as foundational texts in their respective traditions. More broadly the whole Pentateuch (Genesis to Deuteronomy), though formally in prose with poetic interludes, has in its presentation of a heroic past compelling similarities to early Greek epic. Homer has often been described as the Bible of the Greeks: the epics were not indeed sacred texts (Greek religion had none), but the tag aptly evokes a cultural centrality for which we may see parallels both in ancient Israel and in the influence of the English Bible from the seventeenth century until the twentieth. The parallel extends to the history of criticism. The first discussion of the Homeric Question in the eighteenth century was inspired by pioneering study of the Old Testament.[13] In the nineteenth century much scholarly effort was in both cases directed towards reconstructing earlier documents thought to lie behind the texts we have. For the Homeric poems (particularly the *Iliad*) many elaborate schemes of literary stratigraphy were devised, but none won general assent. Modern understanding of oral composition sees this failure as significant: the epics are indeed the product of a long and rich tradition, but we do not now assume written versions prior to the extant texts (composed perhaps in the eighth century BC). For the Pentateuch in contrast the hypothesis of four main pre-existing documents woven into the finished texts has been widely accepted since the late nineteenth century. Modern readings which stress the coherence and unity of the texts still generally acknowledge this, but give a more important role than formerly to the final editor or redactor (now usually thought to post-date the sixth-century Babylonian Exile). In one respect this puts them close to modern critics of Homer, who likewise typically see evidence of an organising intelligence in the very sophisticated poems we have. But whereas in the Greek epics the incorporation of traditional material into something of greater spirituality and depth is usually seen as the final stage of composition (perhaps indeed the achievement of Homer himself), in the Pentateuch much of the most profound and powerful material comes from the oldest source, the document called J (from its author the Jahwist or Yahwist, who used the name Yahweh for God). The broad human interest which we find here contrasts with the ritual and priestly preoccupations characteristic of later strands in the tradition: it appeals most readily to modern readers, and seems frequently Homeric (or even Herodotean) in character.

Entirely from this source comes the story of the hospitality of Abraham in Genesis 18. Much travelled, aged and prosperous but as yet without legitimate offspring, the patriarch has settled in the hills of Canaan.

And the Lord appeared to him by the oaks of Mamre, as he sat at the door of his tent in the heat of the day. He lifted up his eyes and looked, and behold, three men stood in front of him. When he saw them, he ran from the tent door to meet them, and bowed himself to the earth, and said, 'My lord, if I have found favour in your sight, do not pass by your servant. Let a little water be brought, and wash your feet, and rest yourselves under the tree, while I fetch a morsel of bread, that you may refresh yourselves, and after that you may pass on – since you have come to your servant.' So they said, 'Do as you have said.' (Gen. 18:1-5)

This passage has a programmatic importance for later biblical theoxenies analogous to the encounter of Telemachus with Athene in the *Odyssey*. Perception of a similarity between the two stories can be traced back a long way. The Hellenistic Jewish scholar Philo commenting on Genesis cited Homer for the idea of gods appearing as strangers from far-off lands.[14] In seventeenth-century Oxford, the classical and biblical scholar Zachary Bogan wrote his *Homerus Hebraizon* (1658) as a diversion when ill-health forced him to discontinue a more severe treatise on Greek particles: ostensibly a comparison only of linguistic idiom, it provides also a rich collection of thematic parallels between the epics and the Bible. The foot-washing and feeding of the stranger (*Od.* 1.310, Gen. 18:4) are for Bogan the specific point of comparison here.[15] But there are several other parallels, as well as significant differences. Like Homer, the narrator in Genesis has signalled to the reader that this is to be a divine encounter. Abraham realises that one of the visitors is God, and so in reading the story do we: recognition experienced simultaneously by character and reader is a phenomenon we shall see repeatedly. Yet Piero Boitani in *The Bible and its Rewritings* points out that this scene is also in many respects unlike the kind of recognition scene familiar from Greek epic and tragedy, and from its analysis by Aristotle: there is here no moment of insight through token or detection, no reversal or denouement.[16] Much is left unsaid. In contrast to the familiar atmosphere of the Homeric story, this one seems to come from a more remote and mysterious world.[17]

In Genesis and Homer alike, strangers are respectfully welcomed. The code of hospitality, and the reasons for it, applied throughout the ancient Near East: the claims of the stranger within the gates are referred to more than thirty times in the Old Testament. After a hasty whispered conversation between Abraham and his wife Sarah, and some flurry and delay, a meal is provided on a more elaborate scale than initially offered (18:6-8). As Athene brought information and encouragement to Telemachus, this story too is about reciprocal generosity, for now comes the promise that by the following spring Sarah (whose name the spokesman mysteriously knows) will have a son (18:10). This scene sets a pattern for later biblical annunciations, in the Old Testament and on into the New, heralding the births of Samson (Judg. 13:2-5), of Samuel (1 Sam. 1:11-20), and of John the Baptist (Luke 1:13-17). Robert Alter in *The Art of Biblical Narrative* shows how the story of 'a woman long barren … vouchsafed a divine promise of progeny' recurs with repeated elements, making it akin to a 'type scene' in Homer (a repeated narrative pattern such as arrival in a new place, or a hero putting on his armour).[18] The message of Gabriel to the young Mary echoes

6

but significantly varies this traditional pattern, heralding what Luke (1:26-38) presents as a yet more dramatic divine intervention.

Generalised promises of future greatness have already been made to Abraham, but it is specifically through Isaac that he will be the father of a great nation, and it is perhaps because of these combined literal and extended senses of fatherhood that the message is delivered to him rather than to his wife. Like the *Odyssey* passage, this is a story about a significant beginning. As Abraham recognises his divine visitor, the reader with the benefit of hindsight recognises a pattern in later history. But before any of this, Abraham himself has been recognised and appointed as the instrument of the divine purpose.[19] Listening from inside the tent, the aged prospective mother laughs. This mild breach of etiquette prompts a gentle reprimand: with God all things are possible. Sarah denies that she laughed, but is benignly corrected: 'No, but you did laugh' (Gen. 18:15). The narrator here casts God in a warm and human light, not unlike Athene with Telemachus, though still far above the indignities to which Homeric gods sometimes descend. There are here no special effects like the Burning Bush (Exod. 3:2).[20] Homeric theophanies are typically more informal and intimate than the grand ones of the Old Testament: Jacob's Ladder (Gen. 28:10-22), or Isaiah's vision in the Temple (Isa. 6:1-13). But on both sides there are exceptions. We later hear how 'the Lord would speak to Moses face to face, as a man speaks with his friend' (Exod. 33:11). Conversely the angry Apollo at the beginning of the *Iliad* (1.43-52) shows that the appearance of a Homeric god can be a fearful thing, and we shall see in Chapter 5 the description of Poseidon later in the epic (13.18-31) praised by Longinus for its majestic sublimity.

In the *Tale of Aqhat*, a Ugaritic epic poem surviving in substantial fragments on clay tablets excavated in the 1930s, the hero's pious father Dan'el as he sits before his gate beneath a mighty tree encounters the craftsman god Kothar, and calls to his wife to prepare a meal. Another fragment describes the childlessness of Dan'el, and the divine promise of a son.[21] The two episodes probably belong together, providing a close parallel with the biblical passage. Critics have seen the story of Abraham at Mamre as a 'monotheistic adaptation'[22] of this text or of a shared Near Eastern source: it seems therefore paradoxical that the modified version should introduce not one but three visitors. Abraham's initial 'my lord' can in Hebrew be vocalised as either singular or plural, but is natural to assume that he begins in the singular (identifying the leader of the three), then switches to the plural in dealing with the practicalities of welcome.[23] Philo envisaged God accompanied by personifications of his creative and kingly powers (*On Abraham* 121); more influentially, the very ambiguity of one and three was a felicitous legacy to early Christianity, making the three heavenly visitors a type or foreshadowing of the Trinity. Hence their prominence in Christian art: witness the sixteenth-century icon reproduced on the cover of this book, or the great mosaics in the church of San Vitale in Ravenna.

The theoxeny scenes in classical literature similar in other respects to the story of Abraham at Mamre are not typically announcements of a coming birth, but one interesting exception is an obscure story related by Ovid (*Fasti* 5.493-544) and mentioned before him in a fragment of the Hellenistic poet Euphorion of Chalcis.[24] It is a local myth from rustic Boeotia in central Greece, telling of the birth of the hero (and subsequently constellation) Orion. The three gods Jupiter, Neptune and Mercury in the guise of mortal travellers visit the tiny farm of the childless and impoverished widower Hyrieus. To feed them he slaughters his only animal, an ox. Granted a wish in return, he asks for a son. The hide of the ox is somehow impregnated (Ovid is coy about the details), and buried in the ground: in due course Orion is born. This account resembles the story in Genesis in several respects, not least by having a male recipient of the annunciation. It also resembles a more famous Ovidian theoxeny, the account of Baucis and Philemon in the *Metamorphoses* (discussed in Chapter 3): there too we find Jupiter and Mercury as visitors, the readiness of an impoverished host to kill his only animal, and the granting of a wish. The network of narrative connections with the scene at Mamre may plausibly be seen to exemplify the shared debt of classical literature and the Old Testament to the rich traditions of the Near East.[25]

Jewish tradition made Abraham a model of hospitality.[26] The author of the Epistle to the Hebrews commends the reception of strangers by observing with implicit reference to this story that 'thereby some have entertained angels unawares' (Heb. 13:1), a passage compared by Zachary Bogan to the warning given to Antinous in *Odyssey* 17.[27] That is a perceptive juxtaposition, for as his two envoys proceed from Abraham's tent to the cities of the plain, God takes his host more candidly into his confidence (Gen. 18:17-33), and we discover that they are to become angels of destruction. The reception of the two visitors in Sodom is cast as a series of comparisons and contrasts with the welcome at Mamre.[28] Abraham's nephew Lot is also sitting at an entrance as the strangers approach (19:1), but this time it is the city gate: the values of a still semi-nomadic world suggest urban danger in contrast to rural security. Lot himself is indeed initially hospitable, and is rewarded with a warning of the coming destruction, though he will later suffer for the rash if well-intentioned offer of his own daughters to dissuade the city mob from their apparent purpose of homosexual gang rape (19:8). He at least escapes, but his wife is turned into a pillar of salt (19:26) for breaking (like Orpheus leaving the Underworld) a primitive taboo against looking back at a scene of doom. This story is about the perversion of hospitality. Sodom, like Troy, is destroyed for breaking its rules. We shall see that the *Odyssey* likewise includes episodes where the relation of host and guest goes badly wrong: in both texts the offence is underlined as the narrative conventions of proper hospitality are elegantly but grimly recast.

8

1. Homer

Odysseus among the Phaeacians

After his visitor leaves, Telemachus listens to the bard Phemius entertaining the company with a song about the homecoming of the Greeks from Troy (*Od.* 1.325-7), made difficult by the anger of Athene over the desecration of her temple in the sacked city: there is irony in the Suitors hearing about the goddess who has just been unrecognised among them, and a hint that they too will attract her wrath. Penelope finds the song distressing, but Telemachus defends the bard: the latest story always has most appeal. Recent events have already become the subject of heroic song (we shall meet this theme again), and the poet implicitly defends artistic freedom and originality.

The *Odyssey* gives a warm picture of bards: Homer celebrates his own profession, and offers a poetics of his craft. This is seen more fully in Book 8 when Odysseus is entertained at the court of Alcinous. The blind bard Demodocus sings three songs, two of them about the Trojan War. The hedonistic Phaeacians are genuinely hospitable, and indeed claim a special intimacy with the gods, whom they regularly entertain (*Od.* 7.201-6). But their experience excludes both the horror and the glory of war, hence their rapt interest. The quarrel between Achilles and Odysseus in the first song (8.73-82) comes from the world of the *Iliad* though does not occur within it (the *Odyssey* as usual avoiding direct repetition of material from the earlier poem): Homer perhaps invented this story to contrast two ideals of heroism, or even as a figure for the relation of the two epics. Odysseus (as yet unidentified) weeps when he recognises himself in the story, a motif that will be repeated. Its immediate effect is to prompt his observant and kindly host to suggest a diversion (8.94-103), illustrating a reticence characteristic of Homeric courtesy. When songs and feasting resume, Demodocus recounts the adultery of Aphrodite with Ares (8.266-366): her husband, the lame craftsman Hephaestus, retaliates by trapping the red-handed lovers in a net for the other gods to mock. This apparently light interlude both resembles and contrasts with the situation of Odysseus himself: he will have his revenge on the Suitors, but only after confirming that Penelope has remained resolutely loyal. There are echoes of the story of Agamemnon (a counterpoint to Odysseus throughout the epic), and again we think back to the original adultery of Paris and Helen.

As in the earlier description of Phemius, there is a self-referential element. Hephaestus as a lame blacksmith is a divine counterpart of the blind bard: both (along with doctors, carpenters, and diviners) were *dêmiourgoi*, workers for the people. They are a significant group, described by Walter Burkert as 'craftsmen of the sacred':[29] all of them itinerant, and with a quality bordering on the uncanny in their activities of healing, creating and communicating. In a society where most men were farmers, and at need warriors, simple service industries were provided by those whose talent elevated or whose debility debarred them from the common

9

course of life. The skills of Hephaestus and Demodocus are implicitly equated. A principle of compensation applies: the Muse gave the bard the gift of song even as she took away his sight (8.63-4). This can readily be rationalised (the other senses are sharpened), but physical blindness accompanied by spiritual insight will be an important theme in later literature. Cut off from his immediate surroundings, Demodocus is taken into another world of the imagination. By tradition Homer was himself blind: equivalence of detail should not be pressed, but his portrayal of Demodocus was rightly perceived as in some sense autobiographical. Throughout early Greek literature, poet and prophet have a special closeness to the gods: it was believed that Homer had privileged insight into the divine world, and Neoplatonist critics saw in his depiction of Demodocus the self-portrait of a religious visionary at work.[30]

The culmination of this Phaeacian scene comes with the third song, of the Wooden Horse (8.499-520). Again Odysseus is told a story about himself. Again it is an incident from the Trojan War, but after the end of the *Iliad*. Its theme is cunning intelligence, the defining characteristic of Odysseus. George Steiner called this 'one of the great moments of divided focus in all literature',[31] comparable to the scene where Don Giovanni hears a piece from *Figaro* during his last supper. Again Odysseus weeps as he re-lives the experience described, and Homer uses an arresting simile to describe the power of his reaction: he resembles a woman weeping over the body of her husband who has died defending his city (8.523-31). More obviously applicable to a Trojan context and evoking in particular the widowed Andromache, this image expresses again the humanity shown by the poet of the *Iliad* to both sides in the war. Alcinous once more stops the performance, but this time asks his guest directly to reveal who he is. The stranger identifies himself as the subject of the heroic song the Phaeacians have just heard, illustrating what Terence Cave shows is the recurrent association of recognition with retrospective narrative.[32] This reorientation of roles has an uncanny quality, for the self-revelation of Odysseus resembles a divine epiphany.[33] The episode attests the power of poetry, and it is tempting to see in it an ambitious metaphor for literary experience. The Phaeacians are entertained by a story which to Odysseus is painfully moving: we as readers partake of both reactions, and this account of response to a story reflects our perception of the epic which contains it. Odysseus is moved by narratives about himself; we as readers are moved by stories about people whose experiences are like our own, and in this sense we recognise ourselves within them.

Many of the themes here have biblical parallels. For the power of a minstrel's performance we may think of the young David playing his harp for the unquiet Saul (1 Sam. 16:23). When David much later is reprimanded by Nathan for his treatment of Uriah the Hittite through the story of the rich man stealing the poor man's lamb to entertain his guests (2 Sam. 12:1-4), he too is told a story about himself, though this narrative

10

about a perversion of hospitality is contrived deliberately as a parable whereas Demodocus is crucially unaware of the identity of Odysseus. The identification of a person present with a character in a narrative just heard has a parallel in Luke's account of Jesus in the synagogue at Nazareth: after reading from Isaiah about the one sent to preach good news to the poor, freedom for prisoners, and recovery of sight for the blind, he ends 'Today this scripture has been fulfilled in your hearing' (Luke 4:16-21, quoting Isa. 61:1-2). The parables in the gospels repeatedly and designedly prompt the reader to ask, like the Lost Boy in *Peter Pan*, 'Am I in this story?'[34] We shall see in Chapter 4 that recognition linked to revelatory narrative and hospitality is central to the story of the supper at Emmaus (Luke 24:13-35).

Odysseus is both the subject and the teller of stories. He does not literally become a bard (no lyre is mentioned), but his long narrative to the Phaeacians about his adventures is explicitly praised for resembling a bardic performance (*Od.* 11.368). The adventures are carefully ordered. The initial raid on the Cicones (9.39-61) is deliberately low-key and realistic, evoking again the world of the *Iliad*. As Odysseus sails off the map of identifiable places we are lulled gradually into suspending disbelief. The supernatural features more prominently in the narrated adventures than in Homer's main story, but even here it has a lesser role than in the broad epic tradition to which the poet had access: it gains from being used with restraint. The Lotus-eaters dangerously though without malice offer a fabulous food which brings forgetfulness and makes the recipient want to stay with them indefinitely (9.83-104). This theme is programmatic for what follows. Throughout the *Odyssey* inappropriate eating is linked to the loss of homecoming. Forgetfulness of the past is forgetfulness also of the destination, and failure to return means the dissolving of identity.[35]

Allegorical interpretation of Homer began at an early date and took many forms.[36] Some of them seem to a modern reader impossibly strained or mechanical: narrow focus on particular passages and preoccupation with the physical universe mean that trivial details are elaborated and the majestic action of the gods is reduced to an elaborate way of talking about the weather. Reading the *Odyssey* as a Pilgrim's Progress (to us its most obvious figurative sense) seems to have taken longer to become established: traceable to the second-century BC Platonist philosopher Antiochus of Ascalon,[37] it was important in Stoicism, endorsed by Horace (*Epistles* 1.2.17-26), and a critical commonplace in later antiquity.[38] It is particularly familiar in its Neoplatonist form: Plotinus has a fine passage (*Enneads* 1.6.8) on the homecoming of Odysseus as a figure for the spiritual journey of every individual. If the soul forgets its divine origin we risk being turned aside from a destination which is explicitly eschatological: Ithaca here stands for eternity. The theologian Rudolf Bultmann suggests that Odyssean stories about hazardous consumption are more specifically the

11

origin of a recurrent myth in Gnosticism, the syncretistic religious movement roughly contemporary with the rise of Christianity. According to its
dualistic world-view, the demonic powers of darkness watch over sparks
of light which they have stolen, now enclosed in man and representing his
innermost self: 'the demons endeavour to stupefy them and make them
drunk, sending them to sleep and making them forget their heavenly
home'.[39] In a broader sense Cavafy's poem 'Ithaca' attests the vitality in a
later age of a reading which surely accounts in part for the continuing
appeal of the epic itself. *Allêgoria* literally means 'speaking about other
things': all serious literature is perhaps in a loose sense allegorical, simply
by investing its immediate subject with larger meaning.[40]

The narrated adventures of Odysseus differ from the main story not
only in their handling of the supernatural but in their presentation of the
hero. The unscrupulous element in his cunning led to his unsympathetic
portrayal on the tragic stage, notably by Sophocles in *Philoctetes*. But
already in his own narrative Odysseus is recognisably a trickster, that
stock character of folktale represented by Old Testament figures such as
Jacob and Samson. Much later treatments (for example by Dante and
Tennyson) show him driven by restless and disinterested curiosity,
spurred to adventure like the man who must climb a mountain because it
is there. This characteristic is indeed for Sophocles (as we shall see in
Chapter 2) part of the legacy from Odysseus to Oedipus, but it is not
prominent in the *Odyssey* itself except in the one adventure where the
trickster comes most fully into his own: the encounter with the Cyclops
Polyphemus. Odysseus wants to see what the Cyclops is like (*Od.* 9.229).
He and his men put themselves in the wrong by entering his cave as
uninvited guests, but it is an excessive chastisement when six of them are
eaten before the rest escape clinging underneath sheep, in a manoeuvre of
Odyssean cunning which echoes the story of the Wooden Horse.

Homeric hospitality is a triangle, whose points are host, guest, and food.
When it works properly, benevolent hosts ply welcome guests with wholesome food. When it goes wrong, each element turns into a dark obverse (so
for example the guest becomes a prisoner), or the triangle disturbingly
rotates: the elements themselves change places and become confused. In
Ithaca the Suitors behave like bad hosts when they are in fact intrusive
and uninvited guests. The returned and disguised Odysseus is ill-treated
as an unwelcome guest though he is the true host. But the most dramatic
perversion of proper hospitality is when guests become food, as they do in
the Cyclops episode (9.288-93, 311, 344) and again with the Laestrygones
(10.116). Lesser breaches of the code (the presumptuous entry of Odysseus
and his men into the cave of Polyphemus, the excessively abrupt questions
of their involuntary host ahead of the social niceties) are insignificant in
comparison.

Polyphemus at the end of the episode experiences a moment of recognition: like the Phaeacians, he links the man in front of him to someone he

has heard about, in an old prophecy that Odysseus would one day come and rob him of his sight (9.507-12). Similarly in the next book the enchantress Circe immediately realises it is Odysseus she is entertaining when, forearmed with an antidote from Hermes, he proves impervious to her potion (10.330-2). The Sirens too know at once who Odysseus is (12.184). Enemies and unexpected people quickly recognise the hero whilst his benign Phaeacian hosts do not. This theme has a parallel in Mark's gospel, a text similarly concerned with the themes of disguise and revelation.[41] Demons and evil spirits habitually recognise Jesus while his own companions remain unaware of his true identity. The possessed man in the synagogue at Capernaum cries out 'I know who you are, the Holy One of God' (Mark 1:24). When Jesus carries out healings he 'would not permit the demons to speak, because they knew him' (1:34). The man called Legion (because of the multitude of spirits tormenting him) asks 'What have you to do with me, Jesus, Son of the Most High God?' (5:7). Mark's distinctive idea of the 'Messianic secret' (expressing the real but deliberately hidden nature of Jesus) uses dramatic irony about the identity of the central character in a way which is curiously reminiscent of the *Odyssey*. Denis MacDonald in *The Homeric Epics and the Gospel of Mark* argues that such parallels attest a direct debt.[42] Many readers may in contrast conclude that whilst the claimed echoes in wording are no more than trivial coincidence, the thematic similarity is the more remarkable for occurring independently.

The episode with the Sirens (showing a dangerous side to the enchanting power of song) lent itself readily to allegorical interpretation, and became popular in early Christian art. A fourth-century sarcophagus (discussed alongside many other examples by Hugo Rahner in *Greek Myth and Christian Mystery*) shows Odysseus bound to the mast, represented as a cross: safe in the ship which is the church, resisting the blandishments of the world.[43] At this point his surviving companions are responsible and obedient, but shortly afterwards they fall prey to their own stupidity. Motivated by hardship and discontent, and spurred on by one of their own number, they kill and eat the Cattle of the Sun in the absence of their leader and in direct contravention of his warning. Here again is disastrously inappropriate eating, singled out and foretold in the opening lines of the epic (*Od.* 1.7-9). The incident is a necessary plot device: the narrative requires Odysseus to be alone when he reaches Ithaca, but he must not be portrayed as a careless or irresponsible leader. It also however illustrates larger themes. The characterisation of a hero through followers who persistently misunderstand him takes us again to Mark's presentation of the disciples. They in turn evoke the Israelites in the Exodus story. Disobedience in the leader's absence has a parallel in the making and veneration of the Golden Calf while Moses is on Mount Sinai (Exod. 32:1-20). Inappropriate eating is to the *Odyssey* what inappropriate religion is to the Old Testament.

Odysseus in Ithaca

The Byzantine Homeric commentator Eustathius applied to the recognition scenes in the *Odyssey* the formulaic adjective *polutropos* ('of many turns') which the poet uses of Odysseus himself: they share his many-sided cleverness and versatility.[44] A fine example comes in Book 13 when Odysseus is delivered asleep by his Phaeacian escorts to Ithaca, to wake up alone and disorientated: this is to be the recognition not of a person but of a place. The scene is set for the reader by a description of the Cave of the Nymphs, in ten lines of evocative detail (*Od.* 13.103-12). The cave stands at the head of a harbour which the Phaeacians seem mysteriously to know already. The whole scene gives the reader a sense both of a benignly numinous presence, and of familiarity with a place which Odysseus himself will initially fail to recognise. The passage is famous because the Neoplatonist philosopher Porphyry made the cave the basis of an elaborate allegory, as an image of the cosmos and the basis of a whole mystical system.[45] For the modern reader this may seem an example of ancient exegesis misguided in its ingenuity, building much on little: Homer's eighteenth-century translator Alexander Pope already described it as 'a labour'd and distant Allegory'.[46] Yet Robert Lamberton in *Homer the Theologian* treats the philosophical allegorists with new seriousness: Porphyry's essay is interesting for its relation to Plato's Parable of the Cave (discussed in Chapter 2) as a meditation on the connection between this world and another, a theme suggested by Homer's description of the two entrances to the cave, one for men and one for the gods.

In a divine interlude Poseidon, implacably angry over the blinding of his son Polyphemus, expresses to Zeus his resentment that Odysseus has reached home, then relieves his feelings by turning the Phaeacian ship to stone on its return. After this heady dose of the supernatural comes the awakening of Odysseus and his simple human failure to know his own country (13.188). As often in Homer, this is explained on two levels: he had been long absent, and Athene poured a thick mist around him. Odysseus has lost during his travels the identity conferred and represented by Ithaca. Its own identity is revealed to him by the goddess, disguised as a shepherd boy. His prompted recognition of the land stands at the head of a great climactic sequence of prompted and unprompted recognitions of Odysseus himself.[47] The wily hero himself here gives nothing away in return, but replies with the first version of his Cretan story, weaving a false identity for himself. Here alone it fails: the deceiver is deceived, but the goddess (herself also now recognised) is pleased that her favourite shows a cunning akin to her own (13.287 and 296-7). This quality will be needed in Ithaca no less than in more exotic settings, and we sense that the returned Odysseus has passed a first test.

Athene now sends him, his appearance transformed to that of an old beggar, to the hut of the loyal swineherd Eumaeus who entertains his master unawares. As we shall see in Chapter 3, this scene became the prototype for accounts of rustic hospitality in later classical poets. Eumaeus reluctantly supplies the table of the prodigal Suitors, but his own farmstead is a model of modest good order (14.3-20): we think back to the welcome of Athene by Telemachus, where courtesy was maintained against the background of the Suitors' rowdiness. Eumaeus calls off the dogs from the approaching visitor, tells him that food and wine will precede questions, and improvises a comfortable seat: his disguised master wishes him the blessing of the gods (14.29-54). Like Nausicaa, Eumaeus knows that *xenoi* and beggars are from Zeus (14.57-8). Odysseus receives from him disinterested kindness, unpretentiously generous entertainment, and much information. In the extended sequence of scenes in Eumaeus' hut we have the first statement of major literary themes: the paradox of the courtly, that the best manners are learned in simple life (a little lessened by our later discovery that Eumaeus is of noble birth: 15.413-14), and the idea of a pastoral setting for an epiphany (coloured in later tradition by the story of the shepherds in Luke 2, as well as by Psalm 23).

We have seen that recognition or revelation of the hero is in the *Odyssey* repeatedly reminiscent of a theoxeny or epiphany. This association of ideas becomes more explicit when Odysseus reveals himself to his son in Book 16. Telemachus returns from his travels having failed to find his father, though by learning of his father's world he has in a sense found himself. He too goes first to the swineherd's hut, showing proper courtesy and a new confidence in conversation with Eumaeus and the beggar (16.1-153). While the host is temporarily absent Athene (taking an increasingly direct role in the story) arranges the restoration of Odysseus to his normal appearance. Telemachus, seeing him uncannily transfigured, exclaims that he is surely a god. In a fine example of wordplay (characteristic of the *Odyssey* but almost totally absent from the *Iliad*) Homer has Odysseus reply: 'I am not a god (*theos*) ... but I am your (*teos*) father' (16.187-8). The human is here shown as paradoxically more miraculous than the divine.

This is a great moment in the *Odyssey*, but Pope declared it inferior to the revelation of Joseph to his brothers in Genesis 45.[48] Regardless of the specific judgement, this is a suggestive juxtaposition. The story of Joseph (Gen. 37-46) has many similarities to the *Odyssey*: a trickster hero, picaresque adventures, the tone of a romance, and the psychological interest later characteristic of the novel. Joseph's brothers, resenting his precocious ability and his special position in their father's favour, plot to kill him. Spared at the intercession of Reuben and Judah, he falls into the hands of traders and is sold to Potiphar, captain of Pharaoh's guard in Egypt, who in due course puts him in charge of his household. The narrator's delight in description of another culture has something of Herodotus as well as the *Odyssey*. The incident with Potiphar's wife (who tries to seduce the handsome employee) resembles the story of Hippolytus: a scorned woman retaliates with an accusation of attempted rape. Joseph seems like Oedipus in his combination of extraordinary knowledge and self-centred ignorance.

Robert Alter rightly describes recognition as the leitmotif of the story:[49] the theme of *anagnôrisis* has the same recurrent centrality as in the *Odyssey*. Joseph is governor of Egypt superintending arrangements for the years of famine when his brothers (strictly half-brothers: the ten sons of Jacob by Leah) make their first visit to buy grain (Gen. 42:1-7). He knows them immediately, but recognition is not mutual. Curious about his full brother Benjamin (like him the son of Jacob by Rachel) who has stayed behind in Canaan, he accuses them of spying, and they are imprisoned. He then suggests one should stay as a hostage while the others take the grain home and return with Benjamin. The brothers confer in their own language, unaware that the governor can understand it. When they recognise in their misfortunes a nemesis for their treatment of Joseph, he turns away to conceal his tears (42:24). Like Odysseus in Scherie, he is moved by a story about the past, his own role in it unknown to those with him.

The pace quickens as Simeon is left as a hostage whilst the others leave, their donkeys laden with grain. Stopping at an inn they are disturbed to find the purchase money (restored at Joseph's instigation) in one of the sacks. At home all this is told to Jacob, who is induced by worsening famine to allow Benjamin to accompany a second visit. The atmosphere is tense: they are welcomed by Joseph, explanation of the apparently incriminating silver is brushed aside, and they are summoned to dinner (but disconcerted to recognise that they are seated in exact order of age). Again they depart: the trick is repeated, this time with the addition in Benjamin's sack of a silver cup used by Joseph for divination (foreshadowing the next part of the story by giving him a supernatural aura). This time Joseph sends his steward to overtake and accuse them. They return and prostrate themselves, begging him not to enslave Benjamin and force them to return with news that would kill Jacob. No longer able to control himself, he reveals: 'I am Joseph' (45:3).

As in the *Odyssey*, the narrative is retarded for dramatic effect: Joseph like Odysseus in Scherie reveals himself only at the second moment of high emotion. There are parallels with other Homeric scenes. Joseph plays cat and mouse with his father and brothers as Odysseus does before revealing himself to his father Laertes (*Od.* 24.205-329). When at the end of the story Jacob too comes to Egypt, he (like Laertes) is happy that a son thought dead has been restored to life: we shall see that this sense of a return from death is a recurrent element of recognition scenes.[50] Joseph is more arrogant than Telemachus, but like him matures through adversity. Joseph's self-revelation resembles that of Odysseus to Telemachus in being almost a theophany. Unlike most of Genesis, this story gives little direct role to God, but suggests a way of recognising him indirectly in people and events.[51] In contrast to the account of Abraham at Mamre, the Joseph story fits closely the Aristotelian pattern of recognition leading to denouement. Gabriel Josipovici in *The Book of God* points out that it nonetheless resists neat closure: descent and narrative continuity will be through the line of Judah rather than Joseph.[52] The *Odyssey* has a similarly unsettling pendent: Teiresias in the Underworld prophesies that Odysseus will not rest in Ithaca but will undertake an enigmatic further journey (11.119-37).

From the hut of Eumaeus Odysseus goes to try his luck as a beggar, and to see how things stand, in his own palace. This is the context for the sequence of recognitions of the hero, steadily increasing in tension, and involving people of progressively greater closeness and emotional importance to him. But before any human character comes the dog Argus (17.291-327). This famous scene is handled with moving economy and lack of sentimentality. The dog Odysseus had reared before going to Troy, but had not stayed to enjoy, now lies neglected on a dung-heap. Recognising his master he wags his tail and drops his ears but is unable to move. Odysseus in turn cannot show the dog overt affection but diverts Eumaeus with conversation as he wipes away a tear. So Argus dies, having seen the long awaited Odysseus. If small things can be compared to great, this passage has a parallel in the story of Simeon, who had been told he would not die before seeing the promised Messiah: 'Lord now lettest thou thy servant depart in peace' (Luke 2:29).

Just before this scene, Telemachus himself has returned to the palace and has introduced to his mother the exiled prophet Theoclymenus, a mysterious figure, whom he brought as a passenger and suppliant on his return from Pylos. Penelope has heard from strangers numerous accounts of supposed meetings with Odysseus and predictions of his return, but Theoclymenus makes a more dramatic claim, swearing by Zeus and by the hospitable hearth to which he has come that 'Odysseus is already here in his native land, sitting still or on the move, learning of these evil deeds, and sowing the seeds of destruction for all the Suitors' (*Od.* 17.157-9). Though Penelope wishes this were true, her conviction of it lies far ahead. But the words of Theoclymenus give a powerful frisson, and introduce a theme of which we shall hear repeated echoes in later chapters: that what is sought is somehow here already.

The next recognition is another celebrated passage. In Book 19 the stranger (casting himself as a Cretan prince fallen on hard times) has been giving Penelope a fictitious account of his entertainment of Odysseus. This conversation itself provokes a veiled and vicarious recognition, for she recognises (from the tokens of his accurately described clothing) not the stranger himself but the absent figure he claims to have met (19.250).[53] With rich dramatic irony his speech ends with a ringing prophecy of the imminent return of Odysseus (19.300-2). Penelope is unconvinced by this, but sufficiently impressed to offer hospitable comforts including maidservants to wash his feet. In response to his request for an older servant, the nurse Eurycleia is summoned. While at work she recognises a scar on his leg, and a long digression (19.393-466) describes how he acquired it on a hunting expedition in adolescence: only then does the narrative resume. Eurycleia lets go of his foot in shock, his leg knocks over the washing-bowl (Athene diverting Penelope's attention), and Odysseus grabs the old woman by the throat and swears her to secrecy (19.477-502).

This fine account has caused commentators anxiety: it seems implausible that Odysseus should not remember his scar until the last moment, or foresee that Eurycleia will recognise him. A particular focus of critical attention has been the placing of the digression. In the influential first chapter of *Mimesis* (1953) Erich Auerbach set the story of Odysseus and his scar against the account of Abraham and the command to sacrifice Isaac in Genesis 22.[54] He was concerned not with any similarity of theme, but with a contrast of narrative method, expressing two different ways of representing reality. His contention was that the Old Testament is (in his much-quoted phrase) 'fraught with background' whilst Homer is all foreground. The one deals in mystery, hint and suggestion, whilst the other sees everything in a strong vertical light: we saw something of that contrast in the theoxeny stories of Telemachus and Abraham. Auerbach further claimed that the placing of the digression about the scar showed that Homer had no sense of suspense. Most readers will instinctively reject this. The natural reaction is surely that leaving the main narrative at the very moment of Eurycleia's recognition shows a fine (if daring) handling of suspense: we want to know about the scar (its importance attested by the attention it receives), but at the same time we become increasingly impatient to discover how great a crisis the recognition will precipitate. Many would now challenge Auerbach on a wider front. The Old Testament is indeed fraught with background, but is this not frequently true of Homer too?

Even though it is now accepted that the Homeric poems are the products of an oral tradition, there is room for a variety of views about how and when they assumed written form: it is plausible (though unprovable) that their length and their sophisticated plots, full of echoes and cross-references, attest a poet trained in the oral tradition but inspired by the new scope for ambitious composition made possible by writing, or perhaps dictation. Older debates between Analysts (claiming to detect separate layers in the poems) and Unitarians (claiming to detect a master hand) are thus largely superseded: the larger perspective offered by understanding the nature of oral tradition allows us to see that both approaches were partly right, though each was limited. More recent Neoanalyst criticism reverts to some of the observations of the older Analysts to suggest that other stories or versions familiar within the broader epic tradition leave their impress on the texts we have, or are implicitly alluded to within them. This insight, developed since Auerbach wrote, offers an important argument against his thesis. Thus the scene where the scar is recognised may have been heard with awareness of a version where Penelope was indeed alerted by Eurycleia's reaction, or one where the woman washing the feet of Odysseus was Penelope herself. As it is, the expected recognition and reunion are deliberately delayed.

Similarly the bow contest for the hand of Penelope would be more easily explained if she and Odysseus planned it together, but again Homer has eschewed that form of the story (though we can see its influence) in order to postpone the most important recognition scene. The contest takes place in a faintly uncanny atmosphere, giving the feeling of a religious rite as well as a sport. Telemachus seems to know already (in an almost Platonist way) how the axes are set up, though he has never seen it done (21.120-3). After the Suitors have abandoned their attempts and the contest seems finished, Homer marks the climactic moment when the disguised Odysseus strings the bow by a memorable simile: he is like a skilled bard stringing his lyre (21.406-9). Bow and lyre are alike as stringed instruments requiring special skill, and both are under the patronage of Apollo on whose festival day these events are taking place. At the crucial point where Odysseus strings the bow, hero and bard are juxtaposed because they are mutually dependent. In a culture where fame and repute are supremely important, and the afterlife shadowy, heroic deeds must be commemorated. The hero seeks recognition in the broadest sense: of his achievements on the battlefield, and of his legitimacy in a position of privilege and power.[55] The bard in turn needs heroic prowess as the theme of his song. As in the Phaeacian scene, Homer seems at a crucial moment in the narrative to reflect on the nature of his poetic craft. When Odysseus later spares the life of the bard Phemius, who had sung for the Suitors against his will (22.351-3), it is as if he ensures thereby the immortality of his own story.

When the triumphant hero reveals himself, competitive sport gives way to warfare: having fired one arrow successfully through the serried axes, Odysseus levels the next at Antinous. His victim is about to take a draught of wine when the arrow passes through his throat: he drops the cup, and as his life-blood gushes from his nostrils he kicks the table from him, scattering the food in the dirt (22.1-21). Improper feasting is ended, and the hall becomes an Iliadic battlefield. With the help of Telemachus, the loyal servants Eumaeus and Philoetius, and not least Athene in the guise of Mentor, the Suitors are dispatched. The climactic recognition scene (leaving the encounter with Laertes as a coda) comes with the reunion of Odysseus and Penelope. Like the scene with the dog Argus it is the more powerful for being understated. Penelope is shown as worthy of Odysseus in her wary scepticism. She finally proves his identity to her own satisfaction by tricking the trickster. When he reproaches her for cool lack of response and suggests a bed should be made up for him to sleep alone, Penelope tells Eurycleia to move from the bedroom the bed which Odysseus himself had constructed. This stings him into describing how it is immovable because built around the trunk of a living olive tree (23.166-204). The bed symbolises the rooted and living quality, and also the uniqueness, of their marriage: Odysseus will be once again fully known to Penelope only in their bodily union.

The rejected beggar, who had suffered insult and violence at the hands of the Suitors, has been revealed as the rightful owner of the palace. The type of theoxeny story where the divine or royal visitor comes in disguise specifically to his own domain is of course also biblical. The prologue of John's gospel applies it to the Incarnation: 'He came unto his own, and his own received him not' (John 1:11), and we shall see in Chapter 4 several variations on this theme. The Tractarian theologian and poet Isaac Williams in *The Christian Scholar* (1849) translated passages from classical authors which he saw as illustrating Christian doctrine, with versified commentary. Of the returned Odysseus he says this:

> Something I read of higher mysteries,
> Of One who hath descended from the skies,
> And wanders here in His own kingly hall,
> A stranger, and in prison often lies,
> And on His brethren's charities doth call,
> Yet weighs and watches each, the God and Judge of all.[56]

The vision of the *Iliad*

Many features of the *Odyssey* can be seen already in the *Iliad*. Each epic starts near the end of the story it tells. Each is rigorously selective yet suggests something larger: Aristotle praises Homer for constructing the *Iliad* around the single action of the wrath of Achilles (*Poetics* 1451a) rather than including the whole Trojan War. Achilles withdraws from the fighting after an affront to his honour by Agamemnon, leader of the Greek army at Troy. Each epic is therefore the story of an absent hero and his return: Odysseus to Ithaca, Achilles to the battlefield. Each treats time in a complex way, and re-enacts earlier parts of the story: the duel between Menelaus and Paris (*Il.* 3.15-380) gives us again the start of the war, and Odysseus wins once more the hand of Penelope. This technique enables the *Iliad* to give a sense of the whole war: the catalogue of Greek ships (2.484-779) and the scene where Helen identifies the Greek heroes for the old men of Troy (3.161-244) belong properly at the beginning of the conflict, but by a sleight of hand Homer makes us accept them in its tenth year. The heroes are introduced not for Priam and his companions but for us: this is in effect the start of the war because it is the start of our reading. Likewise the funeral games at the end of the epic (23.257-897) act as a curtain-call for many of the main characters. We gain the sense of a long war in part simply by reading a long poem. We shall see again in tragedy, in Virgil, and in the gospels how the experience of the audience is drawn into and becomes part of the presentation of events: this important meta-poetic feature is already present in Homer.

Like the *Odyssey*, the *Iliad* reflects on the nature of epic poetry. Helen envisages a time when she and the other characters will be a theme of song (6.357-8), and the ambassadors who go to Achilles in the hope of persuading him to return to the battlefield discover him in his tent singing of *klea andrôn*, the glorious deeds of men (9.189): here in embryo is the Odyssean theme of the hero acting as a bard. The nature of the epic reflects its subject. The concentrated description of a few days of conflict mirrors on a smaller scale the way in which war itself is presented as a concentrated version of life.[57] Achilles will have a short and glorious life rather than a long and inglorious one. It is unclear whether the choice still remains open at the time of the self-questioning provoked by the embassy from Agamemnon (9. 410-16), but in one sense it is fixed by our knowledge of the story: Achilles has chosen Troy and death as Odysseus has chosen Ithaca and Penelope.

The case for seeing Homer as a serious thinker about man's place in the world was influentially restated a quarter of a century ago by a number of critics, in particular Jasper Griffin and Colin Macleod.[58] Awareness of the oral and formulaic nature of Homeric verse had in the preceding decades often led to an arid style of interpretation, and even to a doctrinaire denial that the poems could be evaluated by the same criteria as other literature, but Homer was now shown as the master rather than the servant of the tradition he inherited. It is striking that new literary readings of biblical texts (especially the Pentateuch and the gospels) gained currency at about the same time, in the works of Robert Alter, John Drury, Gabriel Josipovici and others.[59] This was likewise in reaction to an excessive stress on oral tradition, in this case by the exponents of Form Criticism who had broken down the texts into tiny units and insisted that they could not be read as continuous narrative with an overall design. The more recent movements in both Homeric and biblical scholarship accept many of the insights about how the texts may have originated, but nonetheless have returned to a high estimation of the skill and creativity of their authors, and a renewed emphasis on narrative unity. Rediscovery of stylistic richness was rediscovery also of moral seriousness. Griffin and Macleod showed how the *Iliad* presents human life as grand and tragic precisely because of its limitations. Men aspire to be godlike, yet paradoxically the life of the gods is not enviable. Living for ever, they are immune from real suffering: their life is unrewarding because it lacks urgency, challenge, and the capacity for tragedy. The *Iliad* thus reconciles us to mortality.

These Oxford critics of Homer were influenced by an essay of Simone Weil 'The *Iliad*, Poem of Might' (in her collection *Intimations of Christianity among the Ancient Greeks*[60]). Like Auerbach's piece on Odysseus and his scar, Weil's essay on the *Iliad* is both an influential contribution to Homeric criticism by a non-specialist and a curious combination of insight and distortion. She expounds movingly the tragedy of war: our reading is inevitably coloured by knowledge of her own heroism as a Jewish Frenchwoman in the Second World War, and the sense of loss is indeed a major element of the *Iliad*. But the epic has a complex attitude to its central subject: it expresses the glory and exhilaration of war no less than the pathos. Vera Brittain, an English contemporary of Simone Weil and later a prominent peace campaigner, wrote from her experience of service in Malta in the First World War about an 'incomparable keying-up of the spirit in a time of mortal conflict ... the intense sharpening of all the senses ... that element of sanctified loveliness which from time to time glorifies war.'[61] This dimension is at least as important in Homer as the sense of tragic waste.

In the vision of the *Iliad*, war is more intense and real than ordinary life, but ordinary life itself is more intense and real than the life of the gods: we recognise value through fragility, transience and loss (here is the germ of a central idea in Romanticism). The real religious content of the epic lies not in its depiction of the gods and their actions: indeed they point to it only by contrast with its study of the hero treading a lonely path towards death. If Homer showed a sureness of touch in starting near the end of the story, he shows the perversity of genius in stopping short of the two climactic events which at the end of the poem lie inevitably ahead: the death of Achilles and the fall of Troy. Much has been written about the concept of fate in Homer and its relation to the will of Zeus, but an important simple observation is that fate is in practice the way we already know the story ends, and that the real but limited freedom of Zeus to alter the course of events reflects the real but limited freedom of the bard to alter the story: here once more, the subject of the epic is bound up with its own nature, and the activity of the king of the gods (like that of the human heroes) is analogous to the activity of the poet. Homer's eighth-century society regained things the Mycenaean world had enjoyed: prosperity, overseas trade, writing, and confidence. But the perspective of the epics remained characteristic of the intervening Dark Age, even though the justification for this modesty was disappearing: the present falls far short of the past, where heroes easily lift stones it would take two men of today to lift (5.302-4), and old Nestor looks back to the still greater heroes of an earlier generation (1.260-1). The glorious deeds of the distant heroic world are nonetheless there to be emulated, and that is made possible because the bard has given them an immortality otherwise beyond human reach.

Fighting in the *Iliad* has a role analogous to hospitality in the peacetime world of the *Odyssey*, as the central activity by which men are judged. But many of the same values are seen in both, and hospitality is important in the *Iliad* too. Diomedes has in the absence of Achilles dominated the fighting in Book 5. At the beginning of the next book he kills an otherwise unknown Trojan, who like many Homeric victims is characterised by a brief portrait as he dies:

And Diomedes good at the war cry killed Axylus, the son of Teuthras, who lived in well-built Arisbe, a man rich in substance, who was beloved by all

22

men: his house was by the road, and he used to show hospitality to all who passed. (6.12-14)

The poet comments that none of his guests was there to help him now, and the narrative moves on. Axylus has however something of the host who in later literature receives a divine guest, and it has been suggested that a theoxeny story may lie behind this abbreviated tribute.[62] A little later Diomedes confronts the Lycian Glaucus. Their encounter ends not in fighting and death but in handshaking and the exchange of armour, because the Greek hero and the Trojan ally discover through the exchange of genealogies that they are hereditary guest-friends: this recognition comes once again in the context of a story about the past.

When asked by Diomedes about his family, Glaucus prefaces his answer with a poignant reflection:

Why do you ask about my lineage? The generation of men is just like that of leaves. The wind scatters some on the ground, but the burgeoning forest puts out others, as the season of spring comes round. So with men: one generation grows up, and another passes away. (6.145-9)

Appropriately for an aristocrat boasting of his family tree, Glaucus emphasises the stock that survives to produce more leaves as well as the leaves that fall to the ground like dead warriors. Richard Jenkyns shows how this famous simile relates to others with a similar theme, creating a powerfully complex overall effect.[63] In Book 2 when the Greek forces muster, just before the catalogue of ships, Homer tells how they stand in the flowery meadow by the river Scamander in their tens of thousands, as many as the leaves and flowers in springtime (2.467-8). Here the main point of comparison is quantity, but there is a sense too of burgeoning energy, as well as of transience. In Book 21 Apollo tells Poseidon it would not be worth the gods fighting for the sake of wretched mortals, who like leaves flourish for a time in a blaze of glory, then perish lifeless (21.463-6). This time the brevity of life is the main focus, though Apollo acknowledges also its splendour. Transience and heroism are closely linked: the Greek word *hêrôs* is probably related etymologically to *hôrê*, a season or crucial time,[64] and the hero comes into his prime only to be cut down.

All these similes in different ways express the characteristic vision of the *Iliad*. They also have familiar biblical parallels. Psalm 103 sets up a picture of individual transience, but suggests that on a longer view there is a consoling continuity:

As for man, his days are like grass; he flourishes like a flower of the field; for the wind passes over it and it is gone, and its place knows it no more. But the steadfast love of the Lord is from everlasting to everlasting upon those who fear him, and his righteousness to children's children. (Ps. 103:15-17)

Psalm 90 contrasts the perspective of God ('a thousand years in thy sight are but as yesterday') with men who are like grass: 'in the morning it flourishes and is renewed; in the evening it fades and withers' (Ps. 90:4-6). Most famously in Isaiah we read 'All flesh is as grass ... the grass withers, the flower fades; but the word of our God will stand for ever' (Isa. 40:6-8). The word here is something more than a text, but it is embodied in one and thus is broadly analogous to the Homeric idea of immortality vested in epic poetry. Both traditions use and develop further the image of the leaves: Mimnermus in the seventh century (probably alluding directly to the *Iliad*) refocuses it to express the brevity of each man's youth before the miseries of old age.[65] Ecclesiasticus (written perhaps in the second century BC) provides an early example of a biblical text directly influenced by classical literature:

> Like flourishing leaves on a spreading tree which sheds some and puts forth others, so are the generations of flesh and blood: one dies and another is born. (Ecclus. 14:18)

Meditation on wisdom is here recommended in mitigation of an uncompromising truth, but this passage is perhaps the most pessimistic in overall flavour. Jenkyns shows how the tradition continues: to Virgil, with the dead spirits by the river in the Underworld 'as many as the leaves in the woods which loosen and fall at the first frost of autumn' (*Aen.* 6.309-10), and eventually to Gerard Manley Hopkins in his poem 'Spring and Fall: to a young child': the little girl grieves for the falling autumn leaves, but is told 'It is the blight man was born for, It is Margaret you mourn for'. That in mourning we mourn in part for ourselves is an Iliadic theme: Briseis and her companions join in lamentation for Patroclus, 'but each of them wept over her own sorrows' (*Il.* 19.302), and Achilles in proleptically lamenting the father he will never see again mourns also for himself, the only son doomed to an untimely fate (24.540).

Epic battles

Many stretches of Old Testament narrative both in the Pentateuch and in the historical books from Joshua to Chronicles are broadly similar to Homeric epic in their story-telling conventions. Wars and journeys are central subjects, with an important role for divine intervention and guidance. Speeches, genealogies and incantatory lists punctuate and shape the story. Instructions are given, and similar wording describes them being carried out. The narrator intervenes with judgements that are brief and formulaic in expression but nonetheless devastating: Homeric castigation of people as *nêpios* ('rashly thoughtless') creates an inauspicious effect analogous to hearing that someone 'did evil in the sight of the Lord', though without so clear a moral dimension. The focus on successive heroes

24

in the book of Judges has something in common with Iliadic narrative technique: Gideon has his *aristeia*, his period of glory when he carries all before him (Judg. 6-9), no less than Diomedes does. Goliath (though he is an isolated example) is introduced with a recital of his battle equipment, Homeric both in giving emphasis through detailed specification and in creating the ominous irony that none of it will help him against the young hero David (1 Sam. 17:4-7).[66]

Nonetheless for full and convincing military narrative we have to wait until the books of Maccabees, dating from the very end of the Old Testament period and admitted only to the Apocrypha. In the battles of Joshua and Judges the narrator normally rushes ahead to the outcome, though in a few memorably exceptional passages we are given Homeric physicality and goriness. In Judges 3 the Lord raises up Ehud to deliver the people of Israel from Eglon king of Moab, who has been exacting from them heavy tribute. Important pieces of information are planted early, to prepare us for the climax of the story: Ehud is left-handed, and Eglon a very fat man. Ehud straps a short sword to his right thigh under his clothes (emphasis on the implement and technique of killing seems again Homeric[67]). He presents the tribute to the king, and everyone leaves. But then he returns alone, claiming he has important secret information to deliver. Eglon dismisses his attendants.

> And Ehud said, 'I have a message from God for you'. And he arose from his seat. And Ehud reached with his left hand, took the sword from his right thigh, and thrust it into his belly; and the hilt also went in after the blade, for he did not draw the sword out of his belly; and the dirt came out. (Judg. 3:20-2)

Ehud locks the door and escapes through the window: the servants seeing the door shut assume the king is relieving himself, and fear to disturb him. When they do finally enter, they find their royal master dead on the floor. Ehud musters the Israelite fighting men and inflicts a crushing defeat on the Moabites: 'And the land had rest for eighty years' (3:30). The cunning intelligence which achieved that end is commended by the narrator as the same quality is admired by Homer.

Both similarity and contrast to the *Iliad* can be seen in the story of the Canaanite leader Sisera in Judges 4-5. Sisera has the innovatory advantage of iron-clad chariots (Judg. 4:3): the *Iliad* too depicts a time of transition between bronze and iron weaponry. But after the prophetess Deborah has roused the Israelites to rally their tribes and fight him under the command of Barak, Sisera is defeated at the Kishon river and flees northwards on foot. Arriving at the tent of a Kenite woman he is invited in. He asks for water and she gives him milk, but this is to be a scene of grimly perverted hospitality comparable to those of the *Odyssey*, for when he falls asleep she kills him by driving a tent peg through his head (4:21). Barak is shown the results: the narrator seems equally satisfied with the outcome, and there follows Deborah's great song of victory, perhaps the earliest complete Hebrew poem we have (5:2-31).

It is often said that Old Testament war stories are in black and white, in contrast to the catholic humanity of Homer who tells his story from the Greek side yet sympathises with both, and makes the Trojan Hector one of his most attractive characters. The distinction is broadly fair: the Israelites are not of course presented in a uniformly favourable light, but when their enemies are portrayed warmly it is usually because of their value in teaching recalcitrant Israel a lesson rather than because of generous human sympathy. Does Deborah's song offer an exception? After recounting the killing of Sisera, it continues:

> Out of the window she peered, the mother of Sisera gazed through the lattice: 'Why is his chariot so long in coming? Why tarry the hoofbeats of his chariots?' Her wisest ladies make answer, nay, she gives answer to herself. 'Are they not finding and dividing the spoil?' (Judg. 5:28-30)

This is a moving picture: Sisera's mother anticipates his arrival when we know he is dead, and her maids try to divert her by chattering about the booty he will bring. Gabriel Josipovici aptly compares the scene in the *Iliad* where Andromache and her handmaids prepare a hot bath for Hector just after Homer has described his death at the hands of Achilles (*Il.* 22.442-6). How similar is the tone? Many commentators have assumed the singer in Judges invokes Sisera's mother and her attendants only ironically, in order to gloat over them, and this seems a world away from the *Iliad*. Josipovici however argues convincingly that this is not the effect when we read: the sudden switch to this vignette makes us aware 'that for every victor there is also a vanquished'.[68]

Homeric fighting is typically individual combat, whether because it better demonstrates aristocratic values, or because it was easier for an oral poet to handle and makes a more exciting story: large-scale movements of the two armies are sketched in only lightly. Combat is typically between two heroes of comparable status (like Diomedes and Glaucus), if not always of comparable prowess. But in Book 21 Achilles fights not with a mortal warrior but with the river Xanthus: he has just killed and exulted arrogantly over Asteropaeus, the son of another river-god; and Xanthus is angry that his channel is being choked by corpses (21.233-345). The fight is a great set piece, gaining its effect from Xanthus being simultaneously both river and god: the story invites yet resists being rationalised as a struggle to tackle a raging torrent. Achilles finally prevails only with the help of Poseidon and Athene. The passage shows Homer's carefully controlled use of the supernatural: as the epic moves to its climax, Achilles seems to enter another world and to transcend human limitations. It provides an illuminating comparison with the story in Genesis of Jacob at the Jabbok (Gen. 32:22-30).

Jacob is returning home from Haran to Canaan, anxious because he must confront his wronged brother Esau. His family and retainers cross at the ford before sunset, but Jacob lingers behind and suddenly finds himself wrestling in the dark with a mysterious stranger. The struggle continues until daybreak: the stranger tries to get away, but Jacob holds on to him until he obtains his blessing. The stranger then gives him the new name of Israel ('who prevails with God'). Like the story of Abraham and the heavenly visitors in Genesis 18, this is a narrative of great resonance. Somewhere in its past is a folktale about a river god who accosts travellers but must vanish before dawn. Israel is the name both of an individual and of a nation, and the life of each has the pattern of exile and return. We shall see that later reception of the story is importantly shaped by Luke: the returning Prodigal recalls Jacob, and the mysterious stranger with power to bless (Charles Wesley's 'Traveller unknown') becomes a figure for the risen Christ at Emmaus.

So richly enigmatic is the story that it seems almost a parable about our engagement with the text.[69] It is the subject of an influential essay by Roland Barthes, which like those of Erich Auerbach and Simone Weil on Homer stimulates even if it does not fully convince.[70] This piece has become a stock example of the application of the methods of Vladimir Propp, the Russian theoretician of narrative who in his *Morphology of the Folktale* (1928) attempted to show that all characters could be reduced to a finite number of roles (such for example as that of trickster), and all plots to their interaction in predictable ways.[71] In this story Jacob is the Hero on a Quest, God stands behind the narrative as the Originator of the quest, and the stranger with whom Jacob wrestles is the Opponent, who aims to prevent the hero from accomplishing his mission. Narrative syntax allows various combinations of these: the originator can aid the hero, in person or through helpers; the originator can be present again at the end, for example by offering marriage as a prize. The frisson in Genesis 32 comes from the realisation at the moment of recognition that originator and opponent are one. The syntactical rules have been broken, to disturbing effect (something similar happens with the triangle of hospitality in the *Odyssey*). Barthes claims that this dislocation occurs for a theological reason: so keen is the narrator to avoid diluting monotheism that he can countenance no other power strong enough to hinder God's servant. That is perhaps imponderable, and we may suspect a complicating desire to see a precedent for the subversive activity of a structuralist writer, exploiting and exposing convention. Nevertheless this analysis accounts in part for the powerful effect of the story in Genesis, and its paradoxical merging of two roles is a theme we shall consider in Chapter 2 in stories of the hunter hunted, the priest sacrificed, or the detective revealed as murderer.

The shadow of death

The scenes on the new shield given by his mother Thetis to Achilles in *Iliad* 18 (483-608) are poignant because they depict in its manifold richness the world he will soon leave. If Achilles in taking his destined course seems to move onto another plane in his final hours, the *Iliad* itself rises to new heights in its final book. Colin Macleod's commentary demonstrates how here above all the poet enriches and deepens the material he has inherited. Here too the Neoanalyst insight about implicit allusion to other stories and versions seems particularly fruitful. The aged Priam, prompted by Iris but in defiance of prudence and convention, goes out from Troy and across the battlefield by night to the Greek ships, to offer ransom to Achilles for the return of Hector's body. Homer stresses that Priam has suffered like no man before him: his suffering acquires a representative, exemplary quality. He stands for all the bereaved fathers, on both sides in the war, of whom Homer has given us brief pictures when their sons were killed: alone at home, the family property to be divided among distant kin (for example 5.158).

The old king sets off accompanied by Hermes, the patron of travellers (24.281-2).[72] We reflect however that this god of boundaries is also *psychopompos*, the shepherd of the dead.[73] As Priam leaves Troy, his family follow 'wailing aloud as if for one going to his death' (24.327-8). The eerie journey to the enemy camp is proleptically a *katabasis*, a journey down to the Underworld. It has been suggested that we are invited to map the story onto a whole mythical paradigm: the bereft father journeys as if to bring his son back from the dead, with Achilles cast as the death god who must be placated.[74] Such an interpretation though tantalising can only be speculative. What is undeniably central to the design of the *Iliad* is that decisive future events cast a strong forward shadow. Achilles has long known that he will not return home. Both attackers and defenders have long acknowledged that Troy is doomed: a repeated pair of lines, used by Agamemnon and later by Hector in a poignantly different context, tells how 'the day will come when sacred Ilium will be destroyed, and Priam, and the people of Priam of the fine ash spear' (4.164-5 and 6.448-9).

In Book 24 we almost have the sense that those things are already accomplished. It is a recurrent narrative device in the *Iliad* that what is said of a lesser character anticipates on a small scale what will happen to a greater one. Thus the passing reference to the wife and baby son of Sarpedon (5.480) foreshadows the more fully developed scene where Hector in effect says goodbye to Andromache and Astyanax (6.369-495), with the powerful pathos given by our knowledge of his impending death. It is by an extension of this same principle that the funeral games for Patroclus implicitly evoke also the similar ceremony for Achilles which will take place after the poem ends. Traditional accounts of the one have probably indeed furnished the poet with material for the other, but this bardic economy subserves bold and deliberate design. The fact that the death of

Achilles is beyond the end of the *Iliad* enables it to be generalised, and to become in effect ours: we are invited in heart and mind to follow the hero and to share his sufferings.

Priam enters the tent of Achilles unseen and immediately supplicates him, kissing his hands: 'those terrible, murderous hands, which had killed so many of his sons' (24.478-9). In describing someone coming to an unfamiliar place Homer usually gives us the reaction of the visitor. For this dramatic entry the focalisation is reversed and the poet describes instead the amazement of Achilles and his attendants (24.483-4): it is perhaps indeed as if Priam himself has appeared from the dead. The old king's speech makes Achilles weep for his own father, and for Patroclus; Priam weeps again for Hector (24.485-512). Over the course of the epic, supplications have been rejected with increasing violence, but this final one is accepted. The recurrent Iliadic theme of doomed son and grieving father has its culminating expression in this paradoxical scene of shared lamentation and understanding. Achilles has learned finally the importance of what he shares with other mortals, rather than what separates him from them. The two eat together, Achilles agrees to hold back the fighting until after Hector's funeral, and on the prompting of Hermes Priam quietly leaves. The fact of death has throughout the *Iliad* given the life of men its distinctive character. The imminence of death here brings a new and fuller humanity.

In Mark 14, as the gospel narrative moves towards its climax, Jesus is at Bethany: it is two days before the Passover. A woman comes into the house with an alabaster jar of expensive ointment: she breaks it, and pours the contents over his head. Onlookers protest at the waste, saying it could have been sold and the proceeds given to the poor. Jesus admonishes them and applauds her action (constantly in the gospels reckless spontaneity is commended and cautious calculation scorned):

> For you always have the poor with you, and whenever you will, you can do good to them; but you will not always have me. She has done what she could: she has anointed my body beforehand for burying. And truly I say to you, wherever the gospel is preached in the whole world, what she has done will be told in memory of her. (Mark 14:7-9)

Here is the Homeric theme of anticipatory mourning: Andromache is described lamenting Hector while he is still alive (*Il.* 6.500); and here again also (in more optimistic form) is the envisaging of future commemoration which we saw in the words of Helen. All through Mark's narrative the shadow of approaching death is cast forward.[75] We can see parallels to this narrative device in art. Raphael's *Madonna of the Goldfinch* (1507) shows Mary watching two small boys at play: the young Jesus lovingly strokes a goldfinch given to him by his companion John the Baptist. But the bird is also a symbol of the Passion: legend related how it acquired its red spot when it drew a thorn from the brow of Jesus on his way to Calvary and was splashed with a drop of his blood. In the nineteenth century similar devices were famously employed by the heavier hands of the Pre-Raphaelites: Millais in *Christ in the House of his Parents* (1850) shows the boy surrounded by symbols of his destined Passion, and Holman Hunt in *The Shadow of Death* (1873) shows Jesus as a young adult in the carpenter's shop casting on the wall in the morning sunlight an image of the cross.[76]

Like the *Iliad*, the gospel story moves towards a death which lesser ones foreshadow: in John's version this is particularly true of the death of Lazarus (John 11:1-27). Like the *Iliad*, the gospel story tells of a young man on a lonely course to a death which he foresees and accepts. The hero of Homer's poem is indeed a flawed and in many respects an unappealing figure, but that is irrelevant to his existential seriousness. The greatness of Achilles, indeed the profound religious insight of the *Iliad*, is that (in the words of Jasper Griffin) 'accepting destiny ennobles and transforms the mere necessity of enduring it'.[77]

In later chapters we shall see many examples of internalised recognition: moments of realisation, insight or self-knowledge. Although these are not explicitly discussed in the *Poetics*, Richard Rutherford shows that they fall clearly within Aristotle's general definition of *anagnôrisis* as a change from ignorance to knowledge, and are alluded to more specifically by his listing among versions of recognition the way in which 'one can recognise whether or not one has done something' (*Poetics* 1452a).[78] The theme of recognition in general is an important legacy from Homeric epic to tragedy. The *Iliad* contains many scenes where gods are recognised by mortals who penetrate the human disguise in which they customarily communicate: thus Ajax recognises Poseidon (*Il.* 13.66) and Aeneas recognises Apollo (17.333-4).[79] Such encounters indeed form an important part of the background to the Odyssean exploration of recognition in human contexts which we have considered already. But the theme of internalised recognition (a different trajectory from the same model of recognising a god) comes specifically from the *Iliad*.

Patroclus, Hector and Achilles all show a tragic pattern of error, recognition, and reversal of fortune: 'each ... realises too late how much his conduct has cost him'.[80] They do so however with significant differences, and in an ascending tricolon. Recognition of a god fighting on the enemy side is for a Homeric warrior an essential condition of survival.[81] The imminent death of Patroclus is heralded by the entry into battle against him of the unrecognised Apollo (16.786-92). Caught unawares, he has time only to recognise the role of the god in his death and to prophesy Hector's own (16.844-54). Hector in a general way acknowledged the approach of death (6.367-8), but it is only when he is abandoned by Apollo and deceived by Athene in the guise of his brother Deiphobus that he achieves a greater degree of insight, realising (in a moment paradigmatic for the tragic sense of 'late learning') that the support of the gods is withdrawn when their purpose is fulfilled (22.297-305).[82] Achilles in contrast immediately on learning of the death of Patroclus sees the whole picture: his own responsibility, the bitter and ironic cost of his wrath, and the doom that is now inevitable but of his own choosing,[83] a theme emphasised by the postponement of his death to beyond the end of the poem. Hector is in obvious ways a more attractive character than Achilles, but is less great because Achilles understands more fully than he does the principle of accepting destiny: 'as for my death, I will accept it whenever Zeus and the other immortal gods are minded to bring it to pass' (18.115-16). It is an idea with a long and influential history. The Stoics later taught that we should identify our will with the will of God revealed in what happens to us: Seneca famously wrote that 'Fate guides the willing, drags the unwilling' (*Epistles* 107.11). Much later still, soldier poets in and after the First World War looked to the great contrasting exemplars of premature death knowingly chosen. Thus Patrick Shaw-Stewart at Gallipoli: 'Stand in the trench, Achilles, flame-capped, and shout for me.'[84] And John Arkwright in 1919:

> Still through the Veil, the Victor's pitying eyes
> Look down and bless our lesser Calvaries.[85]

Hesiod and the *Homeric Hymn to Demeter*

I turn finally and briefly in this chapter to two other parts of early Greek literature, often considered together with Homer because they consist of hexameter poetry in a similar formulaic style and reflect a world-view in many respects akin to his, though with important differences: Hesiod, and the *Homeric Hymns*. The *Theogony* and *Works and Days* (dating perhaps from the early seventh century BC) are conventionally called didactic poems: later exponents of this type of writing look back to Hesiod as a model, but it was regarded by the Greeks as a version of epic rather than a separate genre. The Hesiodic poems can be categorised also as Wisdom literature: that rich tradition of the Near East, represented by Old Testament books such as Proverbs, Job and Ecclesiastes.[86] The *Theogony*, describing the Greek gods and their genealogy, also has broad similarities to Genesis: creation out of Chaos, and a notoriously negative description of the first woman, Pandora (*Theogony* 507-616), compared to Eve by the church fathers and by Milton.

The prologue of the *Theogony* includes an account of how the poet was inspired by the Muses to compose the poem while pasturing sheep on Mount Helicon in Boeotia (22-34). This passage became an exemplar for many later poets who boasted of similar encounters with the Muses or with Apollo. They were using a convention, self-consciously and sometimes playfully. Hesiod may already be employing a customary form of expression, or this may be the record of a genuine religious vision. The distinction should not be pressed: in a broad sense he is operating within a tradition, and must have listened to other poets reciting, but he may also have come to recognise something about his own talent when alone on the mountain. His language resembles that of the Old Testament prophets. This is the story of a call or commissioning: we may think of the voice of God heard by Isaiah ('Whom shall I send, and who will go for me?': Isa. 6:8), but a closer parallel is Amos, called from his job as a herdsman and dresser of sycamore trees to prophesy to Israel (Amos 7:14-15).[87] Wordsworth will use similar language, Romanticism typically appropriating the categories of theology (as we shall see in Chapter 5), but the ideas of religious and of literary inspiration are inextricably linked from the outset.

When we turn to *Works and Days* we can identify further similarities to the prophets and to the wisdom books of the Old Testament. The poem describes the proper conduct of a farm, but also the proper conduct of society (a model for Virgil in the *Georgics*, and more distantly an object of bitter parody for George Orwell). The poet, presenting himself as a curmudgeonly small farmer, admonishes both his wastrel brother Perses and the local ruling élite who selfishly scorn social justice. This is again very close to Amos, fired by his divine calling to oppose oppression and injustice (Amos 8:4-14). Hesiod's brother may be a real person or a literary fiction (the poet and he have some resemblance to Prometheus and Epimetheus in myth), but the stance taken in advising him is clear: prudent planning and industry issue in prosperity, carelessness and sloth lead inexorably to ruin. A similar worldly wisdom marks the book of Proverbs. The Hesiodic picture of justice rewarded by acorns, honey and fleeces (*Works and Days* 232-4) mirrors the Old Testament image of the contented patriarch surrounded by his flocks and herds. The gospels will repudiate the idea of divine favour shown by material rewards, but the contrast of wisdom and folly remains central: the houses built on rock and on sand, the virgins with and without oil in their lamps (Matt. 7:24-7 and 25:1-13).

The widespread theme of a choice between contrasted ways of life is seen most famously in classical literature in the fable of the Choice of Heracles, used by the Sophist Prodicus and recorded by Xenophon (*Memorabilia* 2.1.21-34): virtue and vice are personified as two women, the modest (personally unassertive, realistic about how the gods give nothing without toil) and the superficially more winning wanton. Hesiod seems to say something similar:

> Worthlessness can be got in droves, easily; the way to it is smooth and it lives very near us; but in front of Excellence the immortal gods have stationed sweat: long and steep is the road to her, and rough at first. (*Works and Days* 287-92)

The obvious parallel here is in Matthew:

Enter by the narrow gate; for the gate is wide and the way is easy, that leads to destruction, and those who enter by it are many. For the gate is narrow and the way is hard, that leads to life, and those who find it are few. (Matt. 7:13-14)

At the beginning of *Works and Days* Hesiod talks about Zeus:

easily he makes strong, and easily he crushes the strong, easily he diminishes the conspicuous and magnifies the inconspicuous, and easily he makes the crooked straight and withers the proud. (5-7)

This seems reminiscent of the Magnificat:

He has shown strength with his arm, he has scattered the proud in the imagination of their hearts, he has put down the mighty from their thrones, and exalted those of low degree. (Luke 1:51-2)

In both cases the resemblances of expression are compelling, but are the thoughts the same? In the first example much depends on the sense of *aretê*, translated 'excellence'. In Greek usage generally it moves on a scale between 'success' and 'virtue', but the primary reference in this passage seems to be to a man's standing in society.[88] The second quotation is closer to its biblical equivalent: the idea might indeed seem at first to be simply one of divine caprice, but the last clause clearly implies that it is specifically the unjust who are brought low. Hesiod has a pervasive concern for justice in society, and his poems (like the *Odyssey*) reflect the later stages of the epic tradition where Zeus is firmly identified as its guarantor.[89]

The so-called *Homeric Hymns* (of unknown authorship and various dates) appear to have originated as overtures to bardic performances, but the longer ones in the collection have outgrown this role and are important poems in their own right. Several of them involve stories of disguised gods engaging with mortals.[90] Dionysus is kidnapped by pirates who realise their captive is divine when bonds cannot hold him, and their ship begins to sprout vine and ivy (*Hymn to Dionysus* 6-15 and 38-41); Aphrodite initially denies her divinity but after gently seducing Anchises appears before him as a goddess to foretell the birth of Aeneas (*Hymn to Aphrodite* 108-10 and 191-9). These encounters, and in particular the characteristic moment of epiphany, perhaps reflect (at a later date, but in more original form) the traditional narrative pattern which lies behind the human recognitions and self-revelations in the *Odyssey*. Richest of all these texts is the *Hymn to Demeter*, written probably in the sixth century. It has received particular attention in recent years, for a variety of reasons.[91] It explains how an aspect of the world came to be as it is, and how the deities involved acquired their familiar powers:[92] in this respect it is akin to the *Theogony*. In particular it has important links to the Eleusinian Mysteries, the secret religious cult for which it provides an aetiological charter.

Demeter (like Dionysus) had only a peripheral role in grand epic; here she is central, and the hymn is unusual in Greek literature for its sustained focus on female experience. With its extended and attractive narrative element, it is an episodic but self-contained short epic.[93] We shall see in Chapter 3 that Hellenistic and Roman poets were importantly influenced by features both of the *Hymn to Demeter* and of the Hesiodic poems.

Persephone, daughter of the goddess of corn and agriculture, is carried off by Hades, god of the Underworld (and her uncle). Demeter in mourning travels through the cities of men, disguised as an old woman. At Eleusis near Athens she is met at a well (that significant place of encounter in so many classical and biblical stories) by the daughters of the local ruler Celeus and his wife Metanira. Though the emphasis is not here explicitly on the testing of those who receive the goddess,[94] she is welcomed hospitably into their house and entrusted with the care of their infant son Demophon: it is psychologically realistic that she finds thereby some comfort for her own loss. But she is caught by Metanira holding the boy in the fire to make him immortal: the mother's alarmed interference angers the goddess and denies him eternal life (*Hymn to Demeter* 91-291). Human dullness has failed to recognise Demeter, and human folly forfeits the intended reward. This may seem therefore a failed theoxeny. But from a longer perspective an offer of immortality is made nonetheless, in a different sense and on a larger scale. For it is because of this visit that the Eleusinians build a temple to Demeter, whose cult will hold out to initiates the promise of blessedness after death. The story and the subsequent rite here stand in unusually close relation to each other, and the events described in the hymn were some of the most significant ever to take place on Attic soil.[95] Persephone is released to spend part of each year with her mother, this narrative of absence and return providing additionally an allegorical explanation for the origin of the seasons.

Much here resonates with texts we have considered already and with others we shall look at in later chapters. This theoxeny story is highly Odyssean in character.[96] The goddess disguised as a helpless old woman resembles Odysseus masquerading as a beggar. The welcome by the girls echoes the scene where Odysseus meets Nausicaa and her attendants (*Odyssey* 6.135-210). The old woman tells them a false story of being brought against her will from Crete (*Hymn to Demeter* 123-34), prompting the reader to recall the several Cretan stories told by the disguised Odysseus (for example *Od.* 13.256-86). The experience of Demeter resembles that of the divine visitors Jupiter and Mercury in Ovid's account of Baucis and Philemon, who likewise find only one house to receive them: that story too ends with the aetiological account of a shrine. The language and iconography of the Eleusinian cult prominently involved the corn of which Demeter was patron goddess. The details of the mysteries remain obscure, for their secret was well kept, and it is a matter of controversy

34

how far this and similar cults had any direct influence on Christianity. But the underlying idea, the claim of analogy rather than contrast between the cycle of nature and the doom of humankind, echoes in the words of St Paul: 'that which thou sowest is not quickened, except it die' (1 Cor. 15:36).[97]

History, Tragedy and Philosophy

Nineteenth-century German scholars envisaged a sequence of lyric and rationalist ages in biblical history to follow its epic period, all modelled overtly on Greek literary development.[1] That is too schematic, but the literature of classical Athens does have striking parallels in the historical and poetic books of the Old Testament. In this chapter I consider first Herodotus in relation to the Old Testament (particularly the Deutero-nomic history), then three Greek examples of tragedy interspersed with two biblical ones. The final section takes a different direction, looking at similarities between the figures of Socrates and Jesus, and at Plato in relation to New Testament texts.

Homer underlies all subsequent Greek literature, but in fifth-century Athens the legacy of epic is seen particularly in tragic drama and in historical writing. The Iliadic vision of man's place in the world is the starting-point of tragedy. Odyssean recognition scenes are used on stage in increasingly varied forms from Aeschylus onwards. The ostensibly contrasted genres of verse drama and prose history have many intercon-nections. Herodotus and Thucydides show the Persian and Peloponnesian wars as rivalling the Trojan conflict in grandeur, even as re-playing it, and thereby cast themselves as latter-day equivalents of the poet of the *Iliad*. They tell stories of imperialist ambition, and see in them a tragic pattern of hubristic pride and its inevitable consequences.

Individual characters and themes in tragedy have compelling biblical analogues: in addition to those considered in this chapter, we could cite Prometheus in the play traditionally attributed to Aeschylus (bound and suffering for his love of humanity), Alcestis in Euripides (offering herself as a voluntary and vicarious sacrifice), Heracles both in the same play (motivated by compassion to fight and conquer death) and in the later one named after him (posing the problem of undeserved suffering), or Philoc-tetes in Sophocles (a pariah saviour). More generally it is because they make us confront fundamental questions that the tragedians challenge comparison with biblical authors. What we now categorise as theology (as well as philosophy and literary criticism) was in Greece traditionally considered the province of the poets: the theatre was the most important arena for debate about the gods, and recent critics have stressed its role in shaping as well as reflecting religious experience.[2]

Drama in the sense of plays written for entertainment is the major classical genre most obviously absent from the Bible.[3] Theatre was viewed with disapproval in ancient Israel, as it was in early Rome. Current archaeology suggests that Nazareth in the time of Jesus was a satellite village to the nearby town of Sepphoris, rebuilt in Greek style by Herod Antipas.[4] But the possibility that Jesus could have seen (say) a play of Euripides in its theatre, or even have found work as a carpenter there during the building boom, is no more than intriguing speculation. Sepphoris is not mentioned in the gospels, and although Jesus is recorded as travelling through the hellenised cities of the Decapolis (Mark 7:31), he seems in general to have avoided them, though it is now commonly assumed that he will have known at least some Greek.

In a broader sense stories throughout the Bible have dramatic qualities: narratives progress through successive scenes to denouement, and characters pass from ignorance to knowledge. The book of Job comes closest in formal shape to a play, but Old Testament stories typically concentrate on a few people, as Greek tragedy does: often two are in conversation, though a third may be listening, as Rebecca listens to the conversation between Isaac and Esau (Gen. 27:5).[5] Passages of high poetry punctuate Old Testament narrative, and like choral odes in tragedy they generalise or recapitulate in more formal style events that have preceded: the song of Deborah (Judg. 5:2-31) is a celebrated example. The Psalms too resemble choral lyric, and because more than half of them deal with misfortune the parallel extends from form to content. 'O that I had wings like a dove!' (Ps. 55:6), uttered amid encompassing troubles, expresses the escapist aspiration characteristic of a Euripidean chorus beginning *eithe genoimên*: 'would that I were (somewhere other than here)', for example *Hippolytus* 732-51. Laments over Jerusalem in the Old Testament correspond to laments over Troy on the tragic stage. Those laments in Euripides' *Trojan Women* are taken by many critics as coded censure of Athenian foreign policy (the suffering of Troy echoing that of Melos, crushed by Athens a year before the production), and more generally all three tragedians are now widely seen as holding up the values of their city to critical scrutiny, so that the content of a play is in tension with the institutional context of its performance. This view assigns to the dramatists a role analogous to that of the Hebrew prophets, reproaching the kings and people of Israel. Jeremiah (castigating his countrymen though satire) and Ezekiel (making metaphors literal in his acted parables) both also have something in common with Aristophanes. Jonah, Esther, Ruth and Susanna feature in texts formally akin to novels, yet they feel like characters for the stage.

The question whether tragedy is possible in the Judaeo-Christian tradition is too unwieldy to be useful: George Steiner denied that Jewish tragedy could exist; others point to the tragic character of Jewish collective history.[6] The distinction from Greek literature cannot however rest on a contrast between community and individual. A main theme of the *Iliad* is the tragedy of Troy, and both Herodotus and Thucydides cast Athens as a tragic hero, whilst conversely the Old Testament has many individual tragic figures: Adam, Moses, Saul, David and Job. Jephthah in responding to one crisis brings on another, just as Oedipus does. Jeremiah by interweaving his own sufferings and those of his community resembles Oedipus in a different way. Samson (often compared to Heracles) qualifies in suffering but falls short of tragic stature by lacking the reflectiveness Milton gives him in *Samson Agonistes*. Sometimes particular incidents suggest a parallel: Tobit in burying the body of a murdered Jew in defiance of regulations becomes momentarily an Antigone (Tobit 2:3-7). Many Old Testament stories are thematically akin to Greek tragedy: the account of the Tower of Babel (Gen. 11:1-9) reads like a textbook account of hubris. The recurrent biblical call to turn and repent makes internalised recognition into a major theological theme.

Christian tragedy is sometimes considered a contradiction in terms because of an ultimate happy ending. Yet the gospels have much in common with tragic drama, whilst many tragedies end happily: not just the late plays of Euripides which are closer to romance or comedy, but works like the *Oresteia, Philoctetes,* or *Oedipus at Colonus*, whose status as tragedy is beyond question. Some plays of Sophocles leave it unclear whether the ending is happy or not, depending on whether we read in our knowledge of what happens next in the story, which might mitigate an apparently gloomy ending (in *Women of Trachis,* if apotheosis awaits Heracles) or disturb an ostensibly optimistic one (in *Electra,* if the Furies lie in wait for Orestes). This question of how far our reading is affected by awareness of later events is controversial in the criticism of classical authors, not least because there were alternative versions of many myths. But in practice we inevitably reflect on the larger story of which an individual text handles part. This provides an important further similarity to the Bible. Gabriel Josipovici stresses how as we read on we constantly find that people prove different from what we first thought, or less important than they seemed:[7] descent is not through the obvious line, divine favour rests on the unpromising, and the race is not to the swift (Eccles. 9:11). The message seems close to the Greek proverbial wisdom of looking to the end and not judging too soon.

Herodotus and the Old Testament

The Greeks and the Israelites pioneered the writing of history: Roman historiography is a late development, dependent on Greek. The Trojan War and the Exodus have a central and exemplary place in their respective traditions. Writers in many genres and over many centuries come back again and again to these two formative stories. Second only to these events are another pair: the Persian Wars (crucial to Greek self-definition) and the Babylonian Exile (the shocked response to which determined the final form of many Old Testament books). These are accounts respectively of victory and defeat for the two history-writing communities, but both involve Persia (Greece and Israel sharing the experience of dealing with this imperial power), and both offer ominous as well as optimistic lessons. Flemming Nielsen in *The Tragedy in History* explores the far-reaching similarities between the historical writings to which they respectively gave rise.[8]

The *Histories* of Herodotus have the wars between Greece and Persia as their climax. The first campaign, culminating in the battle of Marathon in 490 BC, coincided approximately with the historian's birth, and was followed by the major invasion led by Xerxes ten years later. Because Herodotus sees this conflict as the expression of a fundamental cultural divide between east and west, more than half his work (forming a vast introduction) explores the world of the Mediterranean and the Near East in the century or so before his time. The account is loosely organised around the theme of the increase of Persian power, but Herodotus has great interest in foreign countries and customs for their own sake. He grew up in Halicarnassus, a Greek city on the margin of Persian territory, where he will have acquired an early awareness of cultural difference. The *Histories* are the first substantial work of Greek prose, and in effect a prose epic. Herodotus implicitly rivals but significantly varies his Homeric models: versions of both poems are incorporated, but Odyssean travels here precede Iliadic warfare (distantly foreshadowing the shape of the *Aeneid*). Grand narrative requires a grand subject: by setting up his war to rival Homer's war, his book to rival Homer's book, Herodotus implicitly claims that recent events can properly be compared with the heroic stories of the past. In this he had been anticipated by the lyric poet Simonides, whose elegy on the campaign at Plataea in 479 BC seems from surviving fragments to have begun with a hymn to Achilles and to have juxtaposed Homeric heroes with their successors in his own day.[9] Aeschylus likewise in *Persians* (472 BC) had boldly made tragic drama from contemporary history, again emphasising a parallel with the Trojan War.[10] This assertion of the stature of modernity is an important theme that we shall meet again.

The great sweep of Old Testament narrative now usually called the Deuteronomic history (the books from Deuteronomy to 2 Kings) takes us from the plains of Moab where the Israelites receive a final charge from Moses before entering the land of Canaan, through their gradual conquest of the land, the establishment of the monarchy and building of the Temple, to the division of the kingdom, the conquest of the northern kingdom by the Assyrians in the late eighth century and finally in 586 BC the fall of Jerusalem to the Babylonians: from the end of the Exodus to the beginning of the Exile. This history resembles the work of Herodotus in its ambitious scale and narrative power, and like his writing it is often close in atmosphere to tragic drama.

Although the first five books of the Bible form a traditional unity, Deuteronomy occupies an ambiguous position. It differs importantly from the first four books of the Pentateuch but shares with Joshua, Judges, and the books of Samuel and Kings a distinct theological perspective, the idea of a covenant (expressed in terms which can be paralleled in contemporary political treaties) between God and his chosen people.[11] If the people (like vassals of an earthly ruler) are unfaithful and disobedient, the covenant promises will be abrogated and possession of the land will be forfeit. In the final form in which the texts come down to us, that loss is an accomplished fact. But (as in other literature of the Exile) the hope of return is held out: the story of the entry into the land under Joshua has a message for those who will in due course re-enter it. For Herodotus and likewise for the anonymous writer who gave final shape to the Deuteronomic history, exile is an important stimulus to writing about the past, and in each case the past described has a lesson for the present.

Cyrus the Great, founder of the Persian empire, defeated the Babylonians in 539 and allowed the exiled Jews to return to Jerusalem. Because of his interest in their cause, Isaiah calls him 'shepherd of the Lord' and 'anointed': the only gentile given these titles in the Bible (Isa. 44:28 and 45:1). Cyrus is familiar also from Herodotus, biblical prophet and classical historian each describing him in their own characteristic terms: he is the most obvious example of an important historical figure portrayed by both traditions. Herodotus describes his march on Babylon: as he draws near, the Babylonians engage him, but on losing this encounter retire into the city with equanimity, food stockpiled for a long siege. An impasse follows, until Cyrus has the idea of diverting the course of the Euphrates so that his troops can march into the city along its tunnelled bed. This they do, the Babylonians blithely unaware because 'at the time of the city's fall they were dancing and enjoying themselves, as it happened to be a feast-day – until indeed they found out what was going on' (Hdt. 1.191). How and Wells in their standard commentary laconically observe that the detail of the feast 'agrees with the well-known story in Dan. V'. More dramatically, Dorothy L. Sayers in a 1946 essay described reading in childhood the account of Cyrus: 'I realised with a shock ... that on that famous expedition he had marched clean out of Herodotus and slap into the Bible', just at the point where 'Belshazzar's feast had broken up in disorder under the stern and warning eye of the prophet Daniel'.[12]

It is now generally agreed that the Book of Daniel was written some 400 years after the events it purports to describe, making of them a homiletic parable for Jews suffering persecution under the Hellenistic Syrian king Antiochus IV Epiphanes (thus resembling Greek tragedy, and the *Aeneid*, by using a story set in one period to comment on another). It is therefore unsurprising that many details have become distorted: the conqueror of Babylon is named as 'Darius the Mede' (this designation conflating a post-Cyrus king and a pre-Cyrus power), and Nabonidus rather than his son Belshazzar was the last king of Babylon. But the author of Daniel agrees with Herodotus (and Xenophon: *Cyropaedia* 7.5.15) on the crucial point that a feast was being held on the night the city fell: these are versions of the same story, attesting the impression made by the fall of Babylon on popular imagination and oral tradition.

The account of the feast is for the writer of Daniel a story of hubris, because of the profane use of gold and silver vessels seized from Solomon's Temple during the sack of Jerusalem by the previous king Nebuchadnezzar. In earlier chapters we have learned how, prior to this, Daniel and other noble Jewish youths have been brought to Babylon to serve as scribes. They progress in Chaldaean learning but maintain their Jewish faith. Daniel interprets the king's ominous dreams where his own wise men have failed, and rises to high position (Dan. 2:48). Nebuchadnezzar veers between despotic arrogance and self-knowledge: he is duly impressed when Daniel's three companions emerge miraculously unscathed from the ordeal of the fiery furnace (3:28-30), but ignores his call to repent of his sinfully oppressive ways, learning wisdom only when visited with madness (4:27-37). All this sets the scene for the great feast held by Belshazzar. After the company have drunk wine from the sacred vessels, a mysterious hand appears and writes a message on the wall (5:5). Daniel is summoned and recapitulates the story of Nebuchadnezzar's chastisement, showing that its lesson has not been learned: the message reveals that Belshazzar has been weighed in the balance and found wanting, and in the same night he is killed and his kingdom seized (5:13-30). As in the *Odyssey*, arrogant feasting is the prelude to conflict. In this story of corrupt hospitality and the recognition of ineluctable destiny (memorably captured by Rembrandt), the biblical account of the Persian expedition against Babylon acquires the character of Greek tragedy.

Herodotus in recounting the early life of Cyrus uses motifs recognisably borrowed from myth (Hdt. 1.108-19). Astyages king of the Medes receives a prophecy that a son of his daughter will rule in his place, as Acrisius in the story of Perseus learns he will be killed by his grandson. When a child is born Astyages resolves to be rid of it (again like Acrisius, or like Laius in the story of Oedipus). The courtier Harpagus shirks the job, so the infant is passed to a herdsman: he substitutes and provides for burial a stillborn baby delivered to his wife, and the royal child is brought up as theirs. At the age of ten the natural kingliness of Cyrus is revealed in a children's game; he is brought before the old king, and a classic recognition scene follows. Harpagus is punished by being served his own son at a banquet (a scene of perverted hospitality echoing the myth of Thyestes). Cyrus is an enemy to the Greeks and a friend to the Jews, but this makes less difference to their respective portrayals of him than might be imagined: Herodotus inherits from Homer a remarkable degree of sympathy and relative impartiality in depicting the opponents of his own people.

Both Herodotus and the Deuteronomic history set out to explain surprising events: in one case how a small and divided people could withstand the hosts of Asia, and in the other why the chosen people lost their land.[13]

Both have a tragic dimension, though Herodotus describes the tragedy of others whilst the Deuteronomic history concerns the tragedy of the Israelites themselves. Herodotus wrote single-handed (using oral tradition, some documents, and his own experience), whereas the Deuteronomic historian was working with texts which themselves already had a significant history. Herodotus nonetheless resembles that anonymous editor by operating on a large scale and by incorporating complex material from various genres (including popular story-telling), yet with relatively simple recurrent themes. His leading ideas (equivalent to the covenant theology of the Deuteronomist) are that people reap the consequences of their actions, and that human prosperity never abides long in one place (Hdt. 1.5): the two come together in the recurrent demonstration that when proper bounds are hubristically breached, equilibrium in the natural order will somehow be restored sooner or later.[14]

Both Greek and Jewish historiography reflect the experience of a small nation on the edge of an eastern empire.[15] Herodotus and the Old Testament are full of stories depicting an individual Greek or Jew at an oriental court. The Greek doctor Democedes who heals Darius after a hunting accident (Hdt. 3.129-30) can be compared to Daniel in the palace of Nebuchadnezzar, and the story of Daniel itself echoes that of Joseph in Egypt. The books of Judith and Esther show Jewish heroines asserting their identity, and vindicated. The Israelites are about to surrender to their Assyrian enemies when Judith enters the Assyrian camp in the guise of an informer and charms the general Holofernes. She takes advantage of his drunken sleep at a banquet to seize a sword and decapitate him, escaping with his head and without detection (Judith 10:9-13:15). Esther and her cousin Mordecai are descendants of the Jewish captives taken to Babylon by Nebuchadnezzar. She marries the Persian king Ahasuerus (usually identified with Xerxes) who is unaware of her race. Mordecai, an official in the palace at Susa, alienates the king's chief minister Haman by refusing to bow down to him. In retaliation Haman persuades the king to persecute the Jews. Again resolution comes at a banquet: Esther denounces Haman to the king, who receives poetic justice of Odyssean neatness by being hanged on the gallows he had erected for Mordecai (Esther 2:5-7:10). Like many stories in Herodotus, the book of Esther moves in a world of palace intrigue fascinating because unfamiliar: kingship belonged for most Greeks to the distant past, and for the Jews formed no part of the post-Exilic restoration community.

'The notion that too much success incurs a supernatural danger, especially if one brags about it, has appeared independently in many different cultures and has deep roots in human nature', wrote E.R. Dodds.[16] For Herodotus this is exemplified by the proverbially wealthy Lydian king Croesus. The historian describes how the Athenian statesman Solon comes to the royal court at Sardis and is shown its treasures (Hdt. 1.29-87), receiving in Homeric fashion hospitality in return for information. When asked by the king if there is any man he considers the most fortunate, Solon cites an Athenian called Tellus, a good all-rounder: of only local distinction and moderate resources, but (because he lives to see his grandchildren yet dies heroically in battle) resolving the stark Iliadic choice between short glorious and long inglorious life. Croesus takes the point with reasonable grace, but is angered when Solon's second choice falls on the two Argive brothers Cleobis and Biton who stood in for absent oxen to take their priestess mother by cart to a festival, and on arriving fell asleep and died in their glory: more straightforwardly Iliadic than Tellus, if less obviously enviable to modern readers. Croesus loses patience with this guest who is also admonisher and judge, but after Solon leaves is quickly overtaken by retribution: his son is killed, and the Lydians are defeated by Cyrus. Put alive on a pyre by his conqueror, Croesus experiences a painful moment of internalised recognition, invoking the name of Solon whose wisdom he now perceives (1.86). The powerful effect of this scene on the Greek imagination is confirmed by the famous red-figure amphora by Myson, dating from about 500 BC: the first known use of an historical rather than mythological subject,[17] and a foretaste of Herodotus' demonstration of heroic grandeur in recent events.

Tellus may not be fictional, but his name puns on *telos* ('end'). The Herodotean Solon insists on looking to the end of everything, not judging a life or event before its course is complete. The sage speaks for the historian (a new version of the Homeric equation of hero and bard), and we are invited to apply this advice to the story Herodotus himself is telling: of Croesus, of the wars between east and west, and (implicitly, beyond his text) of continuing imperial ambition in his own day, with Athens now switched into the role of hubristic quasi-Persian aggressor. Solon and Croesus foreshadow Artabanus and Xerxes much later in the narrative. The Persian king debating whether to invade Greece is warned by his uncle 'the god blasts living things that are prominent and prevents displays of superiority ..... it is always the biggest buildings and the tallest trees on which he hurls his thunderbolts' (7.10). Again we think of the story of Babel: Herodotus and the Old Testament alike stress that man should keep his place. And although Greek religion generally sees prosperity as a sign of divine favour, wealth can be a source of danger, a temptation to forget human limitations. When Herodotus begins his story of the Egyptian king Rhampsinitus by saying that he had a greater fortune than any of his predecessors and so commissioned an especially secure building in which to keep it (2.121), we sense immediately that something will go wrong. Long before the New Testament, storing up treasure on earth is a dicey business.

Croesus is an ambiguous figure: benefactor of Greek shrines but oppressor of Greek cities, symbolic precursor of Xerxes as an oriental despot yet himself the victim of Persian aggression. Yet even Xerxes can be portrayed in a sympathetic light, when on surveying his great army he weeps at the realisation that all will soon die, and is for a moment a representative man (7.45-6). This largeness of vision constantly characterises the theological passages in Herodotus. Polycrates the sixth-century tyrant of Samos, enjoying an alarming degree of good fortune, is advised by the Egyptian king Amasis to throw away a valued possession lest he incur divine jealousy (3.40-3). He throws a gold ring into the sea, but when a few days later a fisherman presents him with a fine fish and it is cooked and cut open, he finds the ring in its belly and at that moment of recognition accepts (like Belshazzar seeing the writing on the wall) the inevitability of his doom. Amasis in the story breaks off their alliance on concluding that his friend is condemned. In reality Polycrates may have severed it to ingratiate himself with the Persians who were attacking Egypt.

We should not however assume (as critics have often done) that the first task in reading Herodotus is to strip away a veneer of folktale moralising: Thomas Harrison in *Divinity and History* shows that the whole organising principle of his book is religious.[18] A progressive distancing of deity has traditionally been traced from Homer (who shows anthropomorphic gods routinely intervening), through Herodotus (who speaks more vaguely of 'the divine'), to Thucydides (who at least on the surface excludes divine action). In broad terms this is persuasive, and the contrast between Homer and Herodotus again here corresponds to a difference between the Pentateuch and the Deuteronomic history, with God taking a less direct role from the book of Joshua onwards: both in Herodotus and in the historical books of the Old Testament, divine activity is often hard to discern, and deceptive in operation. Nevertheless theophanies are not for Herodotus in principle excluded: Pan appearing in the mountains of Arcadia to Pheidippides is the classic example (6.105). As in the *Odyssey*, recognition scenes involving human beings can be assimilated by vocabulary and atmosphere to the appearances of gods: thus the bard Arion after his rescue by the dolphin discomfits by a seemingly miraculous epiphany the criminal Corinthian sailors who had robbed and tried to kill him (1.23-4). An incidental detail is eloquent: Euphorion, the father of one of the suitors competing for the hand of the daughter of Cleisthenes of Sicyon (a story Homeric in atmosphere but involving real people only about a century before the historian's time) had according to Arcadian tradition once received the heavenly twins Castor and Polydeuces in his house, and after that theoxeny never turned away any guest (6.127).[19]

Aeschylus: *Oresteia*

Agamemnon returns victorious to Argos from Troy. He is insincerely welcomed by his wife Clytemnestra, then killed by her because he had sacrificed their daughter Iphigenia to enable the Greek fleet to sail, because she has taken as her lover his cousin Aegisthus, and because he comes provocatively accompanied by his Trojan concubine Cassandra.

Their son Orestes returns from exile, is recognised by his sister Electra, enters the palace in disguise, and kills Clytemnestra and Aegisthus. Pursued by avenging Furies for his matricide, Orestes seeks refuge first in Delphi and then in Athens. The court of the Areopagus is set up to try him, but he is acquitted through the intervention of Athene. This is the story of the *Oresteia*, produced at Athens in 458 BC: the only surviving trilogy, and a powerful influence on all later tragedy.

At the beginning of the first play, *Agamemnon*, a watchman on the palace roof at Argos awaits a beacon fire signalling the fall of Troy. The expectant mood resembles that of 'Wachet Auf' ('Wake, awake, for night is flying'), Philip Nicolai's sixteenth-century hymn combining watchmen on the walls of Jerusalem from Isaiah and Ezekiel with lighted torches from the story of the bridegroom and the wise virgins (Matt. 25:1-13). We may think too of the Psalmist ('Except the Lord keep the city the watchman waketh but in vain': Ps. 127:1): *Agamemnon* raises similar anxiety about the spiritual condition of the community. The watchman compares himself to a dog (*Ag.* 3), recalling the patient Argus awaiting the return of his master Odysseus, though (as we shall see again with *Oedipus Tyrannus*) tragedy typically rewrites the optimistic epic in an ominous minor key. Homer already contrasted the homecoming of its hero with that of Agamemnon: a long but finally happy return to a loyal wife set against a quick but tragic return to a treacherous one. Aeschylus tackles the comparison from the other side, with the *Odyssey* itself as a template.

The beacon appears just after the watchman's complaint of its delay (*Ag.* 20-2). His feelings reflect those of the audience: they have waited in the theatre of Dionysus for the play to start, and they have waited months for the festival. Each long day of performances started at dawn, so the beacon light may even (with luck) have coincided with the rising sun. The story starts in Argos and ends in Athens, but in a metatheatrical sense has also started in Athens, and so circles round to where it began. Light is an obvious symbol of rescue and hope, an overarching image in the trilogy as it also is in the Bible, from Genesis through Isaiah to John and Revelation. The watchman begs the gods for deliverance from toils: his own vigil is soon ended, but deliverance in the fullest sense will come only at the end of the trilogy. Meanwhile there is foreboding in his speech, as he alludes obliquely to the uneasy regime in the palace (both like and unlike Ithaca in the absence of its king) whilst studiously avoiding words of ill omen. The potency of words and their portending of good or ill is a pervasive Aeschylean theme, like the recurrent motif in Genesis of the blessing that cannot be retracted.

We sense that long-awaited events are finally getting under way. This is an uneasy reverse of the atmosphere created at the beginning of Luke's gospel; and the sense of liturgical expectancy in the audience has a parallel in the Christian annual drama as it moves towards Advent but also as it moves towards the Passion. The play has the same basic shape as the gospels: an eagerly expected person arrives, makes a triumphal entry, and is killed. Agamemnon's entry is ominously qualified and uncomfortable: he walks his appointed way in a paradoxical combination of royal splendour and aching vulnerability. Jesus in similar ambiguity and lowly pomp rides into Jerusalem (Matt. 21:1-11): the Messianic king enters David's capital city in an atmosphere of celebration but also of ominous inevitability, because we know that Jerusalem is where prophets perish. Cassandra, silent as yet, will resemble those prophets in her frenzy and her utterance of unheeded truths. Clytemnestra spreads red tapestries for Agamemnon to walk on, and he reluctantly complies. They assume when the palace doors are closed the ominous appearance of streams of blood. As in the *Iliad* and in the gospels, the coming death is forcefully foreshadowed.

The imagery of the *Oresteia* emphasises how Agamemnon as a sacrificing priest killed Iphigenia only to become himself in turn a victim. The story pattern of the priest who is also victim is another version of the Odyssean boomerang quest, and an example of the paradoxical merging of roles which we see repeatedly in tragedy. Agamemnon's transition from one to the other is a matter of poetic justice, illustrating the recurrent theme of the trilogy that the doer suffers (for example *Ag.* 1564). The Bible merges priest and victim in a different way. The Old Testament can be read as a long search both for an adequate priest and for an adequate victim to offer to God. The New Testament shows that quest fulfilled, but in a characteristically unexpected sense. This is emphasised in the fourth gospel by creative reordering of the chronology of the final days of Jesus. John forfeits the symbolism used by the other evangelists (for whom the Last Supper is a Passover meal) and puts the Passover a day later, in order to have Jesus killed at the time of preparation for the feast, as the supreme paschal lamb (John 19:31). The Epistle to the Hebrews explicitly presents Jesus as performing the two roles simultaneously: 'Thou on earth both Priest and Victim' (William Chatterton Dix paraphrasing Heb. 7:27).

Through the choral songs of the Argive elders in *Agamemnon*, the trilogy opens up perspectives of time in the more distant past, the dark history of the house of Atreus: the effects of an inherited curse over successive generations are especially suited to expression in a connected set of plays. Here again is the theme of perverted hospitality (in a story already alluded to for its Herodotean parallel), for when Thyestes seduced the wife and attempted to seize the kingdom of his brother Atreus, the father of Agamemnon, he was punished by having the flesh of his own children served up to him at a banquet; and that story itself re-enacted a still earlier episode where Tantalus served up his son Pelops to the gods to test their powers of discrimination. Clytemnestra's hypocritical reception of Agamemnon is in the same tradition, though Aeschylus changed the Homeric version, where Agamemnon is killed at a banquet by Aegisthus (*Od.* 4.535), to have him killed in his bath by Clytemnestra.

The sacrifice of Iphigenia has compelling Old Testament parallels.

46

Jephthah in Judges 11 vows that if he defeats the Ammonites he will sacrifice whatever creature comes first from his house when he returns victorious. We read on dreading the recognition scene, for it will be his daughter and only child, coming to greet him (Judg. 11:34):[20] this has an even closer classical analogy in the story told by the fourth-century Virgilian commentator Servius of the Cretan king Idomeneus, who vows in a storm at sea to sacrifice what he first sees on landing, which proves to be his son.[21] Jephthah's daughter accepts that her father's oath cannot be broken, but is granted a respite during which she 'bewailed her virginity upon the mountains' (Judg. 11:38). Greek tragedy often similarly dwells on the pathos of an unfulfilled life cut off, and on events which grimly parody those that should properly be taking place: an altar replaces a marriage bed, and a girl's life is ended by her father instead of being renewed by a husband. This passage in Judges resembles the handling of the Agamemnon story by Euripides in *Iphigenia at Aulis*, where the victim (after some prevarication) in a last powerful speech accepts that she must be killed (*IA* 1368-1401). When Jephthah's daughter returns from the mountains the sacrifice is carried out (Judg. 11:39), with the poignant final comment, 'She had never known a man.' The passage is again reminiscent of Euripides when it ends with the aetiological explanation of a later ritual: in *Hippolytus* (1422-30) it is prophesied that girls of Troezen will commemorate the virginal hero, as the daughters of Israel annually lament the daughter of Jephthah (Judg. 11:40). In the text she is poignantly never named, but George Buchanan's Renaissance drama *Jephthes* (followed by Handel in his oratorio) invites us to compare the Hebrew and Greek stories by calling her Iphis.[22]

The account of Jephthah and his daughter already carries an implicit comparison with the more famous story of Abraham and Isaac (Gen. 22:1-14). That is a narrative of averted sacrifice: at the climax an angel intervenes and a ram is substituted. In Aeschylus Iphigenia has indeed been killed, but Greek tradition also knew a version where her sacrifice too was averted. That was famously used later by Euripides in *Iphigenia among the Taurians*, but it was probably the canonical account: the lost early epic *Cypria* seems to have recounted the last-minute substitution of a deer by Artemis.[23] Aeschylus will thus have innovated boldly with his more shocking version: stories of animal substitution may in origin have been designed to justify the abandonment of human sacrifice when society no longer found it acceptable, but dramatic potential in tragedy depends upon both killing and rescue being real possibilities.

The second play in the Aeschylus trilogy takes its title *Choephori* ('Libation Bearers') from its chorus of mourners for the dead Agamemnon. Orestes is like his father long awaited, by Electra (who prays for his return as a 'light to the house': *Cho.* 131) and by all those loyal to Agamemnon's memory. It is Orestes who is now identified as the awaited deliverer, like the idealised Messianic figure repeatedly envisaged in Old Testament prophecy. The *Oresteia* like the Bible constantly shifts its typology, keeping us guessing about who will occupy an anticipated role or correspond to a figure from an earlier story. Orestes was in Homer the model for Telemachus (*Od.* 1.298-300), but in Aeschylus Orestes resembles Odysseus as the deliverer whose arrival promises to right the wrongs of the house, succeeding where Agamemnon had failed (though true deliverance will be postponed yet again). The opening monologue of Orestes in which he greets his native land is partly lost in the manuscript tradition, but some gaps can be filled from quotations in Aristophanes' *Frogs*. During the literary contest in the Underworld, Euripides ridicules for its apparent tautology the line in which Orestes says 'I come and I return' (*Cho.* 3/*Frogs* 1128). In fact it is a powerful expression of the significance of his intervention in the story; and the sense of an arrival which is also a return adumbrates an important theme which we shall meet again in *Oedipus Tyrannus*, in *Bacchae*, and in the *Aeneid*.

The recognition scene between Orestes and Electra (*Cho.* 166-263) is the first in extant tragedy, and a specific model for several later ones. It is categorised by Aristotle (*Poetics* 1455a) as recognition by reasoning: Electra infers that a lock of hair and footprints resembling her own must be those of her long-lost brother. Euripides anticipated his Aristophanic role by subjecting this scene to gentle mockery in his rewriting of the story (*Electra* 524-37): how could Electra know the shoe size of her long-lost brother? The criterion of realism he applied is perhaps inappropriate, but the process traced by Terence Cave in *Recognitions* can be seen beginning here: recognition by tokens moves down-market as a literary device, to the trinkets which in late Greek and in Roman comedy identify slave girls as well born, and eventually to handbags left in terminal railway stations.[24] We shall see however in later chapters that *anagnôrisis* can itself be restored to high position, not least in the New Testament. At the stage of literary evolution represented by *Choephori*, however, the recognition scene (like the contrast between loyal and disloyal members of the household, the use of disguise, and the revenge killings in the palace) is chiefly important as an element from the *Odyssey* re-used in a new setting.

The third play is *Eumenides* ('Kindly Ones'), its title both an apotropaically euphemistic name for the Furies avenging the killing of Clytemnestra and a description of the new character they finally assume. Unusually for Greek tragic drama, it brings two changes of scene. Delphi is the shrine of Apollo and thus supposedly an abode of light, but the problem of the Fury-hounded Orestes who seeks refuge there proves beyond its powers. The true light of deliverance comes only in a proto-democratic Athens. By a deliberate anachronism Aeschylus describes the establishment of the first lawcourt (in fact a much later development), providing a charter myth for the Areopagus council whose functions had been redefined a few years before the trilogy was performed, and stressing its original function of dealing with homicide (*Eum*. 681-710).[25] Arguments about which parent is the more important (and thus whether Orestes was right to kill his mother in order to avenge his father) are likewise anachronistically derived from scientific speculation in the playwright's own day (657-61). The intervention of Athene (female, but a virgin warrior born fully-armed from the head of Zeus) decides in favour of the father. The Furies are indignant at their defeat but pacified by Athene's promise of a new role as guardians of the city, ready to defend it as necessary by resuming their traditional powers.

Ancient literature set in a heroic past depends upon complex interplay between the time the story is set and the time the work was written.[26] The bold technique of *Eumenides* sets the agenda for much that is to follow. According to a traditional reading still in many ways persuasive, the play puts the justice of city and lawcourt in place of revenge and family vendetta: as domestic conflict moves onto a national and public plane and the cycle of retribution is ended, we are offered a parable about the evolution of civilisation. The change of scene to Athens is also a change of atmosphere, to a world more familiar to the audience (a sense reinforced on a formal level by markedly simpler language than in *Agamemnon*, and a reduction in the amount of choral lyric). Events in the story have gone forward only by weeks or months, yet we are given the sense that they have moved through centuries. The creation of this feeling by a manipulation of time is an important legacy of the *Oresteia* to the *Aeneid*. In both works too the chronological span is mirrored by a great geographical arc, taking us away from a place representing the past to a city of present centrality. Aeschylus rewrites Homeric epic for fifth-century Athens as Virgil will re-write it for first-century Rome.

The *Oresteia* and the *Aeneid* also however have it in common that many modern critics are reluctant to see in them unambiguously optimistic stories of progress, preferring in each case a darker reading and an emphasis on unresolved problems: ostensible eulogy is seen as a vehicle for subtle criticism.[27] The social settlement achieved in *Eumenides* may indeed be marked by tension (and certainly exacts a price in vigilance), but we must allow too for anachronistic embarrassment over its patriarchal nature, and a fashionable predilection for gloom. The traditional reading of the trilogy has also been challenged in another way. Hugh Lloyd-Jones in *The Justice of Zeus* influentially argued against the linear development often assumed to have taken place in Greek values: blood feud was already from early times regulated by a notion of divine justice, and conversely it is stressed in *Eumenides* that the Furies who preside over it retain a necessary role in the new world.[28] He showed that the idea of a moral development in the character of Zeus posited as central to the thought of Aeschylus is largely a modern invention. Here it is tempting to suspect an unacknowledged biblical analogy: critics who traced a dramatic evolution in the nature of Zeus and the standard of his administration of justice were perhaps unconsciously swayed by the idea (itself a simplistic half-truth) of a vengeful deity in the Old Testament succeeded by a benevolent one in the New.[29]

Debate about the specifics of theology or politics cannot however obscure the central point that the trilogy explores justice both in the community and in the cosmos. It is a further important legacy of the *Oresteia* to the *Aeneid* to show that the governance of one reflects that of the other.[30] The Old Testament likewise presents God as sovereign simultaneously of the universe and of his own people Israel, and the New Testament constantly puts localised events in a cosmic perspective. Both the Bible and the *Oresteia* begin and end with light. The darkness of primeval chaos is dispelled (Gen. 1:3), and no humanly created light is needed in the New Jerusalem (Rev. 22:5). The beacon light seen by the Watchman at the beginning of *Agamemnon* is echoed by the torchlight procession which ends *Eumenides*. We sense in each case that a vast journey has been accomplished. The end of the *Oresteia* like its opening mirrors the experience of the audience. Through the sustained intensity of the trilogy we feel ourselves to have crossed an abyss of time. Even before the final play ends we have in effect returned from the heroic past to the fifth century, and in the closing prayer for the welfare of Athens it is as if 'drama has dissolved into worship'.[31]

Saul

Tragedy flourishes in times of transition, when an old world-view is being replaced by a new, as in fifth-century Athens or Elizabethan England.[32] That observation refers usually to the time when tragedy is written, but with Saul in the books of Samuel it applies rather to the time when the story is set. The first king of Israel is the most obviously tragic figure of the Old Testament, his career a terrifying transition from fame and royal prosperity to desperate isolation. Cheryl Exum in *Tragedy and Biblical Narrative* shows how Saul qualifies as a tragic hero because of his stature both as a king and as a man.[33] Yet his tragedy is specifically that he is overshadowed: first by Samuel, the last of the judges; and then by David, the preferred and greater king.[34] He becomes a figure of pathos because history leaves him behind.

As in a typical Greek play, all starts off well: Saul when we first meet him as a young man in his father's service is an appealing character (1 Sam. 9:1-2). The previous chapter has described the demand of Israel for a king as the community develops from tribal federation into nationhood, and we sense at once that the choice will fall on him. He is recognised by Samuel under divine prompting, received as an honoured guest, and anointed as king. His potential seems realised when this private designation receives public acknowledgement after his defeat of the Ammonites at Jabesh-gilead (1 Sam. 11:11-15). Yet we read of his early successes with

50

unease, realising gradually that Saul is a doomed figure, trapped between two eras and two styles of leadership.[35]

There is a parallel here with the themes handled by Sophocles in *Ajax*. Deluded by Athene into butchering captive livestock when he intends to attack Agamemnon and Menelaus for awarding the arms of the dead Achilles to Odysseus rather than to him, and killing himself after he has thus lost face, Ajax is shown as the last of the unreconstructed Homeric heroes. The survivors who argue over his right to burial are revealed as lesser men (though Odysseus is a more reasonable one), and in effect people of a later age, with the mundanely practical concerns of fifth-century Athenian politicians. As in the *Oresteia*, we feel to have moved on in centuries, though here the action nominally spans only hours. The story of Saul gives an unrelieved portrait of a man confronted by forces beyond his control and comprehension, and like Ajax he is driven into jealousy and madness. Saul seeks to destroy David after Samuel secretly anoints him in his place, but David twice spares his life, albeit with a theatricality that underlines his superior power (1 Sam. 24:1-15 and 26:1-22).[36] So too Ajax is defended and has his right to burial asserted by his hated enemy Odysseus (*Ajax* 1332-73). In each case the tragic figure resents the man who has won what he considers rightly his.

Lee Humphreys in *The Tragic Vision and the Hebrew Tradition* shows that Saul also resembles another Sophoclean hero. He turns on David as Oedipus does on Creon, with an accusation of plotting to unseat him (*Oedipus Tyrannus* 532-42). Like Oedipus he is deaf to the moderate advice of a cooler mind.[37] Both confrontations contain the irony that the accused person will indeed subsequently occupy the throne. The hubris of Saul's ill-timed oath after his first victory over the Philistines (1 Sam. 14:39) parallels the bold but ominous vow of Oedipus to avenge the murder of the former king and to play the role of son to him (*OT* 258-68). Yet Saul like Oedipus attains nobility by the powers he summons up in himself even as his tragic end seems fixed. Saul knows that God has chosen another, but struggles to retain his kingdom. His actions and decisions in the last days of his life confirm it as tragic. He resembles Achilles in the *Iliad* by accepting his destiny even as he wrestles against it, and so making it his own.

Similarities to the *Iliad* also mark the most dramatic and atmospheric part of the story of Saul, his encounter with the Witch of Endor. Byron called this the finest ghost story ever written.[38] Its atmosphere is reminiscent of *Macbeth*, which indeed it importantly influenced: Macbeth like Saul is filled with fear about the future, and learns that after his coming defeat and death he will be succeeded by his virtuous rival.[39] The narrator sets the scene by telling us that Samuel has died, and has been mourned and buried; Saul (perhaps presented here by the Deuteronomic historian as a forerunner of the later reforming king Josiah) has banished mediums and wizards from the land. As the Israelites are encamped at Gilboa, the

Philistine enemy gather in formidable number. Saul's heart trembles and he enquires of the Lord, but no response is granted.

> Then Saul said to his servants, 'Seek out for me a woman who is a medium, that I may go and inquire of her.' And his servants said to him, 'Behold, there is a medium at Endor.' So Saul disguised himself and put on other garments, and went, he and two men with him; and they came to the woman by night. And he said, 'Divine for me by a spirit, and bring up for me whomever I shall name to you.' The woman said to him, 'Surely you know what Saul has done, how he has cut off the mediums and the wizards from the land. Why then are you laying a snare for my life to bring about my death?' But Saul swore to her by the Lord, 'As the Lord lives, no punishment shall come upon you for this thing.' Then the woman said, 'Whom shall I bring up for you?' He said, 'Bring up Samuel for me.' (1 Sam. 28:7-11)

Consulting the witch is an act of desperation when legitimate means of communication with the divine are silent: Saul himself has specifically forbidden resort to necromancy. Why does he seek out the dead Samuel who in life has already rejected him? Because he can stand no more ambiguity: like Oedipus, Saul must know the truth.[40] He goes to the cave at Endor in disguise, in part because he has to go through the Philistine camp to get there: his journey resembles the one Priam makes by night across the battlefield to the tent of Achilles in *Iliad* 24. When he arrives, the witch cites the royal prohibition but is persuaded by an assurance of impunity to call up the spirit of Samuel. Martin West in *The East Face of Helicon* points to the similarities between this scene and the raising of the ghost of Darius in Aeschylus' *Persians* (607-848).[41] Queen Atossa, alarmed by news of the disastrous defeat of her son Xerxes at Salamis, resorts like Saul to desperate measures and instigates evocation of the ghost of her husband, who foretells a yet greater defeat at Plataea. Saul similarly hears from the previous ruler a prophecy of military disaster. The recognition scene at Endor has a special character and complexity: at the moment Samuel appears, the witch recognises Saul (1 Sam. 28:12). A parallel in Greek tragedy for this double and transferred recognition is the scene in Sophocles' *Electra* (1475-80) where Aegisthus uncovers and recognises the corpse of Clytemnestra, having thought it to be that of Orestes (falsely reported a chariot-racing fatality), and thereby immediately recognises instead the stranger standing beside him as the Orestes who has returned in disguise and killed her.

Samuel thunders a doom on the now terrified Saul, telling him unambiguously that the Lord has turned from him and that the Israelite army will fall into the hands of the Philistines the next day. Saul realises (as simultaneously we do) that his doom is sealed. The witch, seeing Saul's distress, has compassion for her ominous guest and prepares food for him and his servants. This is a moving moment: once more the themes of recognition and hospitality are linked, and we think again of *Iliad* 24, with its scene of Priam and Achilles eating together. In both passages the need to eat amid trauma offers what Josipovici calls 'a muted celebration of the basic elements of life'.[42] Plain practicalities point up by contrast the numinous quality of the encounter we have just witnessed. Saul then leaves, going in haste to a murderous dawn. The whole story, terse and understated, occupies only nineteen verses. If *anagnôrisis* came at Endor, the Aristotelian corollary *peripeteia* ('reversal') follows on the heights of Gilboa.[43] Saul finally takes his own life rather than becoming an object of scorn and mockery to the Philistines. Again we think of Ajax, falling on his sword as Saul does: the fear of being mocked is a recurrent characteristic of the Sophoclean hero. Oedipus blinds himself as an act of his own will, as Saul by his suicide makes a last desperate attempt to wrest meaning from his destiny. The lament of David for Saul and his son Jonathan calls to mind the bald summarising words of Sophocles' chorus in their final speech: 'This was Oedipus' (*OT* 1524).

Kingship is deeply ambiguous in the story of Saul. This too mirrors Greek tragedy: we have seen already in Herodotus a reflection of the paradox that the theatre of democratic Athens was so concerned with the fortunes of royal houses outside the direct experience of the audience. God initially opposes the demand for a king, yet grants it, only to select one who fails to live up to his calling.[44] A longer perspective may indeed temper the individual tragedy of Saul: great days for Israel under David and Solomon lie ahead. Yet David too will be a tragic figure, punished for his selfish passion and violence. Solomon in all his glory has marked touches of hubris: it is ominous that his palace exceeds the Temple in size and splendour (1 Kgs. 6:1-18 and 7:1-12), and after him the monarchy will split apart. The Old Testament like Greek tragedy discourages men from thinking too highly of themselves.

Handel's dramatic oratorio *Saul* (1739) richly attests perception of this similarity in an earlier age: 'its story may be from the Bible, but it is conceived in the epic and tragic terms of classical antiquity'.[45] The librettist Charles Jennens was an accomplished classical scholar, and the story is given the shape and atmosphere of a Greek play. An opening *epinikion* (a song of victory reminiscent of Pindar) ushers in the young David, triumphant over the Philistines, bearing the head of Goliath. Saul falls gradually prey to the Aristotelian *hamartia* of 'Envy, eldest born of hell' (as the Chorus describe it at the beginning of Act II). Failed attempts to kill David are followed by a highly dramatic scene with the Witch and the apparition of Samuel. The Amalekite (who in the version followed here finished off Saul's suicide attempt) in conversation with David gives us a brief messenger speech, in which we learn of the disaster at Gilboa. The famous Dead March in lamentation for Saul and Jonathan corresponds to the recurrent scene at the end of a Greek play where the dead are brought on stage in solemn procession.

Sophocles: *Oedipus Tyrannus*

Like the *Oresteia*, this play (of perhaps about 425 BC) stands in a complex
relation to the *Odyssey*, not least by starting near the end of the story.
Admired especially by Aristotle in the *Poetics*, it is often seen as the
archetypal Greek tragedy. Oedipus, king of Thebes and husband of Jocasta, discovers during its course that he is the son of the same Jocasta
and of the previous king Laius whom he has unwittingly killed (his
parents sent him as a baby to be exposed on Mount Cithaeron because of
a prophecy of these events, but he was rescued, and brought up by the king
and queen of Corinth); he blinds himself, and Jocasta commits suicide.
Again the story is a boomerang quest, a story of an arrival that is also a
return: Oedipus was born at Thebes, and comes back there as king.

Odyssean themes are intensified and given a grim twist. In myth the
hero commonly wins his bride by passing a test. Homer already offers a
sophisticated variant: Odysseus by shooting the arrow through the axes
wins back the woman to whom he is married already, the poem re-enacts
their union, and an interrupted happiness is resumed. Oedipus by answer-
ing the riddle of the Sphinx wins the hand of Jocasta, but the Odyssean
story pattern of restoration to a woman already familiar is dreadfully
perverted: he wins a wife who is also his mother. The true identity of the
returned Odysseus is unknown to those around him, but the true identity
of Oedipus is unknown also to himself. Odysseus initially fails to recognise
Ithaca as his home, as Oedipus fails to recognise Thebes. But whereas
Odysseus realises his error quickly and with relief, for Oedipus the recognition is long postponed and devastating when it happens. Odysseus
returns to his origins, to his place of birth, by coming back to Ithaca.
Oedipus too comes back to his place of birth, but in an extreme and
terrifying sense, returning by the act of incest even to the bed and body of
his mother. Odysseus seeks his home, Oedipus (unknowingly at home
already) is in quest of himself. Both heroes undergo some loss of identity
on their travels, but to differing degrees. When Odysseus names himself
to the Cyclops as 'Noman' (*Od.* 9.366) we reflect that he might indeed
become a cipher without Ithaca (and in a different sense without the
Odyssey), but his false identity is no more than a temporary and voluntary
ploy. Oedipus in contrast has involuntarily grown up with a false identity
as the son of Polybus and Merope. Odysseus on returning home recovers
his own true identity by learning anew his role as husband, father and
king. Oedipus also discovers himself in those guises, but in a hideously
distorted way. In the *Odyssey* we infer that Telemachus will in due time
successfully take over his father's role: he will be able to wield the bow,
and to rule Ithaca, according to the proper succession of generations.
Oedipus by marrying Jocasta also takes over his father's role, but unwittingly, and with a grotesque wrenching of nature and chronology.

In Jewish legend amplifying the biblical account of Solomon and the

Queen of Sheba (1 Kgs. 10:1-3), the answer to one of the riddles she puts to him is the female body: the setter herself, cast as an archetypal but also an exceptional example of womanhood.[46] The riddle of the Sphinx in contrast has a special relevance to the solver. The question what has four legs in the morning, two at noon and three in the evening refers to Man: successively crawling baby, *homo erectus*, and an old man with a walking stick. By a common analogy, a human span is equated to a day ('life's little day'), and the play stresses how the one crucial day of its action will both demystify and ruin the life of its hero (*OT* 438). The riddle of the Sphinx is literally the riddle of life: the play emphasises that Oedipus can solve intellectually the enigma of man, but has more difficulty with the lived riddle of his own life. Like Joseph in Genesis, he is a knower with much to learn. John Drury has well said that 'riddle is the most aggressive kind of parable: little, hard and menacing'.[47] This is a parable like the one told by Nathan to David, but Oedipus takes longer to recognise that this is a story about himself. His life enacts the riddle but is also an intensified and exceptional version of it. He was a baby who could not even crawl, because a pin was put through his ankles when he was sent to be exposed on Mount Cithaeron, as an extra precaution against his survival. His noonday pride is that not only of an adult male but of a king and the famed saviour of his people from the plague brought by the Sphinx. At the end of the story he needs the old man's stick more urgently and ahead of the normal time because of his self-inflicted blindness.

Like many Old Testament stories, and like the gospels, the play leaves little doubt about what is going to happen: suspense applies to the process rather than the outcome. Most of the audience probably knew the story already, though they might notice differences from earlier treatments: Sophocles omits reference to an inherited curse, making the sufferings of Oedipus seem more arbitrary (like those of Job). But even spectators not aware already of what is to happen learn it from the prophet Teiresias who is provoked into revealing the essential facts, though Oedipus is too proud and angry to take in what is said (449-62). This knowledge is crucial for the audience to appreciate the dramatic irony which pervades the play. Events long before it starts form a quest story: the return of Oedipus to Thebes, and his winning of Jocasta. Within the play Oedipus by vowing to find the killer of Laius sets himself another quest: here (in the structural-ist terms we considered for the story of Jacob at the Jabbok) originator and hero are one. Ironically and unknowingly he sets himself to act like Orestes, fulfilling the duty to avenge a murdered father. But whereas Orestes is the deliverer awaited from outside, this avenger is already at hand. The language of Theoclymenus in the *Odyssey*, about the eagerly expected person being even now here, can thus be re-used to powerfully ominous effect.

In her 1935 essay 'Aristotle on Detective Fiction', Dorothy L. Sayers reads the *Poetics* as a treatise on the modern murder mystery,[48] wittily developing a common observation about *Oedipus Tyrannus* as the story of the reconstruction of a hidden other story.[49] Here the detective is also the murderer: a version of the genre analogous to the boomerang quest or the priest who is also victim. Agatha Christie used a device of this kind more than once. In the most famous example, *The Murder of Roger Ackroyd*, the 1926 novel that made her name, the culprit (doctor rather than detective, but the point remains) is fully aware of his guilt and his first-person narrative is simply an extended lie, albeit with studied ambiguities: the denouement is sensational, but we feel that the author is cheating.[50] Oedipus in contrast is unaware of his own guilt until the moment of recognition (*OT* 1182-5). Like Demodocus in the *Odyssey*, Teiresias is physically blind but has compensatory spiritual insight. It is when Oedipus attains similar inward vision that he makes himself physically blind. The powerful contrast between outward and inner forms of sight and blindness is variously used by later writers: in John 9 the man born blind recognises who Jesus is whilst both the disciples and the Pharisees are spiritually blind, and in *King Lear* the aged Gloucester attains spiritual insight only after blinding himself.

The recognition scene in *Oedipus Tyrannus* is internalised, but not simply reduced to a metaphor. Other Sophoclean heroes at similar moments see for the first time the true pattern of their lives. Oedipus certainly does this, but he also recognises the identity of a person, or rather recognises that several people (the killer of Laius, the baby once sent to the mountain, and himself) are one. The hero of the quest who was already also its originator now proves to be the opponent as well, the enemy within. The play both collapses and multiplies identities (as well as telescoping time). Simon Goldhill points out that Oedipus, who at the start addressed his people as children, loses the possibility of using the simplest vocabulary of human relationship without ambiguity.[51] After his discovery he gives a list of confused relationships: 'fathers who are brothers and sons, an incestuous kinship, and brides, already wives and mothers' (1406-7). His own name involves multiple wordplay: an implied derivation from *oidaô* ('I swell') and *pous* ('foot') suggests the effects of the pin once put through his ankles, whilst another from *oida* ('I know') and *pou* ('where') comments ironically on his initial ignorance and truthfully on his eventual knowledge of his origin. The word Latinised as *tyrannus* (probably post-Arisotelian as the title of the play, but prominently recurrent within the first half of it), is likewise ambiguous. Though in tragedy often simply a general term for a ruler, it refers properly to one who assumes monarchical power as an outsider, rather than being born to it. Oedipus is thus ostensibly *tyrannus*, whilst all the time *basileus*, a traditional hereditary king.

Like *Agamemnon*, the play draws on deep-seated ideas about kingship, particularly the sense of a connection between the physical and moral health of the ruler and that of his realm (the story of the Fisher King in

Arthurian legend offers a parallel): the plague blighting Thebes is explained by and also symbolises the concealed pollution of its ruler, and we remember too that in Hesiod (*Work and Days* 238-47) barrenness and plague afflict a city through the hubris of one man. Throughout the early scenes Oedipus is seen by the Theban people as the deliverer who came once to decisive effect and who can surely save them again. In time that saviour leaves the city, despised and rejected. The scapegoat in Leviticus (16:15-28), driven out into the wilderness to bear the sins of the community, has a parallel in Greek religion in the notion of a *pharmakos*, the human scapegoat who in the festival of the Thargelia in Athens and other Ionian cities was ritually expelled to cleanse the city. This idea has many echoes in tragedy: Pentheus will likewise be cast as a victim on behalf of Thebes (*Bacchae* 963). The *pharmakos* was a marginal person, typically a criminal, but pampered and privileged in the period before the rite. In earlier times he had perhaps actually been a human sacrifice: here in embryo is the story with which J.G. Frazer began *The Golden Bough*, of the priest of Diana at Nemi who won his year of office by killing his predecessor and would himself be killed. This seemed to Frazer a key to all religion and mythology in the way the original Golden Bough was for Aeneas a key to the Underworld (*Aen.* 6.140-8).[52] In many myths however the offering needed to save the city is not drawn from the dregs of society but is a royal figure (the effectiveness of the sacrifice here thought of as proportionate to the status of the victim), hence the major Frazerian theme of the king who must die.[53] Jean-Pierre Vernant points out that Oedipus is simultaneously *pharmakos* and king.[54] That there are biblical resonances in this paradox was shown by Tyrone Guthrie in his famous 1955 production, portraying Oedipus as at once Christ figure and sacrificial beast.[55]

Freud's theory of the Oedipus complex (claiming that the hero enacts the feelings of every male towards his parents) may be discredited, but he was right to give Oedipus a universal significance. In the *Odyssey* the idea of the hero as Everyman is only implicit. In this play the chorus twice draw general conclusions from the plight of Oedipus, an extraordinary man who is yet a figure for the ordinary. Hauntingly in the immediate aftermath of the recognition scene they sing:

Ah, generations of men, how close to nothing I reckon your life to be. For what man, what man wins more of happiness than the appearance, that after appearing sinks away? With your example before me, your fate, wretched Oedipus, I call no man happy. (1186-96)

Again at the end of the play he is explicitly a model for the understanding of man:

Inhabitants of our native land of Thebes, see: this was Oedipus, who knew the famous riddle, and was a most powerful man. Which of the citizens did not look on his fortunes with envy? But see now into what a stormy sea of trouble he has come! So, looking carefully to the final day, we must call no one among mortals happy, until he has passed the boundary of life without suffering grief. (1524-30)

Oedipus Tyrannus is designed to challenge the audience to self-reflection: the play is about the intelligibility of life itself,[56] and in this sense is a religious text. Goldhill shows that its import is broadly Freudian because it suggests we must look backwards in time and inwards for self-knowledge.[57] It claims disturbingly that it is exactly at the moment when we think we know fully who we are, when we find affirmation from status and from the admiration of others, that we are most at risk of self-deception.[58] Oedipus resembles the rich fool who resolved to tear down his barns and build bigger ones, unaware that his priorities offered no security and that his life would be required of him that very night (Luke 12:16-21). He is also, however (like Odysseus who must confront the Cyclops), the hero who will not be deterred by considerations of comfort from pursuit of the truth wherever it leads, and it is in this that his final nobility consists.

Job

Like a Greek tragedian, the anonymous author of the book of Job took an old story and made something new from it. Writing at about the same time as Sophocles, he likewise meditates on human suffering and raises disturbing questions about divine justice. Job himself is vaguely located in the patriarchal period and in the land of Uz, south of the Dead Sea. The original folktale seems to have portrayed him simply as a prosperous and righteous man who suffered afflictions to test his faith in God, and proved steadfast. In effect he is a fictional character, in a minimalist setting.[59] This emphasises the universal dimension which the book shares with *Oedipus Tyrannus*. The story is implied to be about any person anywhere, without ties to a specific religious and cultural tradition. The book of Job is a stylised philosophic fable, like the invented myths with which Plato ends many of his dialogues. By being portrayed as 'the greatest man in all the East' (Job 1:3), extremely rich as well as pious, Job has something in common with Croesus in Herodotus, and like Croesus he learns wisdom painfully.

A prose prologue and epilogue frame the most sustained poetic work in the Old Testament (for Edmund Burke a *locus classicus* of the sublime[60]): the book of Job is frequently described as a dramatic poem, though the speeches of the characters are reported (again in the manner of a Platonic dialogue) rather than set out like a script. Above all, it depends importantly on dramatic irony. Like a Greek theatre audience, we listen with knowledge the characters do not have. In the prologue's picture of the heavenly council, Satan reports that he has just returned from roving the earth: this suggests the activity of the gods in Homeric theoxeny stories, observing individuals and testing their behaviour. God asks if he has come across the pious Job. Satan scornfully replies that piety is easy for the rich, and God accepts the challenge that his favourite should be put to the test: all that Job has is put in the power of Satan, though his person is initially inviolable (1:6-12). This scene resembles debates among the gods on Olympus in Homer (for example the exchange between Zeus and Thetis in *Iliad* 1) where plans are made which we then see put into effect. In Job as in Homer, scenes in the divine world frame the action on earth: there are distinct divine and human layers of action. There is a more specific similarity to a characteristic technique of Euripides, who often uses the gods as a framing device: witness for example the discussion between Poseidon and Athene at the beginning of *Trojan Women* (1-97).

Messengers arrive with bad news. This happens frequently in tragedy: Creon in the second half of *Antigone* hears of one disaster after another, but in no Greek play do messengers arrive in such abrupt and concentrated succession as here. Job's abundant livestock falls prey to marauders and storms, and finally all his children perish when a roof collapses during a family celebration. Job rends his clothes and shaves his head in mourning, but remains philosophical: 'The Lord gave, and the Lord has taken away; blessed be the name of the Lord' (1:21). Satan reports back, and is next enabled to touch the bone and flesh of Job, sparing only his life. Job is afflicted by loathsome sores, and sits among the ashes scraping himself with a potsherd. His wife urges him to curse God; his three friends arriving to console him fail initially to recognise him. All that gives texture and meaning to life is taken from him (critics have compared Lear), and the opening section culminates in Job cursing the day he was born (3:16). Oedipus in a parallel way curses the man who rescued him as a baby (1349-55); and shortly afterwards, in defending his decision to blind himself rather than commit suicide, he rounds on the Chorus with the command to stop giving him advice. This is essentially the attitude of Job to his friends, whose debates occupy the central section of the book. They try to console him with traditional and pious views about his sufferings, variations on the theme that these must somehow be deserved. The friends are in effect fighting for their own religious lives and security, but the reader knows from the explicit statement of the prologue that Job is blameless.[61] He makes no attempt to conceal his exasperation. It is at this point that he famously reflects on the futility of life:

> Man that is born of woman is of a few days and full of trouble. He comes forth like a flower and withers, he flees like a shadow and continues not. (Job 14:1-2)

We may think here of the Iliadic simile of the leaves, or the passage in

Oedipus Tyrannus on the generations of men. Like the Sophoclean chorus, both Job and his friends pass back and forth between his particular case and the general conditions of humanity. In chapter 28 there is a remarkable hymn to the technological potential of mankind, with vivid descriptions of mining and civil engineering, but it ends in resignation: this control over nature cannot conceal the fact that one thing of overarching importance remains beyond man's power, namely the finding of true wisdom (28:1-23). The poem resembles a famous choral ode in Sophocles' *Antigone* (332-64): there too the achievements of human conquest of sea and earth are celebrated, only to contrast with one crucial failure, the defeating of death.

Job nonetheless remains spirited: he is ready to account for all his actions, and he defiantly calls on God to hand him a list of charges to wear as a badge of honour (Job 31:35-6). Job resembles Oedipus in having the truth of his integrity. He also has something of Prometheus, shouting defiance at Zeus. It is a distortion to read his story as a parable of patience. He strikes back at his fate and at his friends with words that are among the most boldly challenging in the Hebrew tradition.[62] It is a critical commonplace that Milton makes Satan the most interesting character in *Paradise Lost*, but it is already true in the Old Testament that the great heroes are often those who stand up against God, whether through disobedience (like Samson, Saul, and David) or in a direct clash of wills (like Abraham, Moses, and Job himself), and the great speeches addressed to God are often polemical in character.[63] This tradition lies behind the protest of Jesus on the cross: 'My God, my God, why hast thou forsaken me?' (Mark 15:34, quoting Ps. 22:1).

At this point a new character enters: Elihu is young and bombastic, and has little to add to the arguments of the three friends.[64] This section has often been seen as a clumsy later insertion, but it is perhaps a burlesque interlude before God's great reply from the whirlwind, a responding series of questions:

Where were you when I laid the foundation of the earth ...
When the morning stars sang together, and all the sons of God shouted for joy? (Job 38:4 and 7)

The tragic vision is affirmed but transcended: the gulf between human and divine is too wide to cross. Job is overwhelmed at the presence of God, and humbled at the majestic and mysterious working of the universe.

In an internalised recognition scene Job comes to himself:

I have uttered what I did not understand, things too wonderful for me, which I did not know ... I had heard of thee by the hearing of the ear, but now my eye sees thee; therefore I despise myself, and repent in dust and ashes. (Job 42:3 and 5-6)

60

He accepts that there are things beyond his comprehension, that human justice is too limited a construct to apply to the divine.[65] This echoes what many interpreters have found in Sophocles: E.R. Dodds wrote that the poet 'did not believe, or did not always believe, that the gods are in any human sense "just".'[66] God is not so much cleared of the charges as seen to belong to a realm where human justification is irrelevant.

Greek tragedies typically have their moments of highest drama some way short of the end, descending to a quieter close. Similarly in Job a short prose epilogue takes us back to the original story and gives it a happy ending. Job is restored to prosperity and public esteem, and (though nothing can replace those he lost) has a second quiverful of offspring (42:7-16). He must now pray for his friends, to deliver them from divine wrath. He who was the object of their patronising attention and scorn is now to be their saviour. Job here resembles the hero not of *Oedipus Tyrannus* but of the later *Oedipus at Colonus*, who has passed beyond his sufferings, and because of their redemptive quality has power to bless the community that receives him.

Euripides: *Bacchae*

With *Oedipus at Colonus* the aged Sophocles returned to a story of which he had tackled other parts in *Antigone* and *Oedipus Tyrannus*. Its setting is the playwright's native village outside Athens, and the central character has (like Prospero in *The Tempest*) predictably been scrutinised for an element of self-portraiture. Euripides in his late masterpiece *Bacchae* (produced posthumously, perhaps in 405 BC) also looked backwards: to the more formal style of an earlier era, and perhaps to the origins of tragedy itself. The subject is notoriously controversial, but it is a plausible speculation that the earliest plays in the theatre and festival of Dionysus dealt with the story of the god himself. Dionysus is the god of *ekstasis*, of standing outside your normal self. That happens through the wine of which he is patron, through the heightened consciousness created by trance or ecstatic prayer, and through putting on a mask and acting as another person. In *Bacchae* the god of the theatre appears as a character in a play performed there.

Dionysus has come to Thebes disguised as a priest of his own cult. He brings a new form of worship from the east, but his origins lie in Thebes. He is the son of Zeus and the Theban princess Semele, though his divinity has been denied even by her sister Agave, mother of the young king Pentheus. He has made the women of Thebes mad and sent them to celebrate his ecstatic rites on Mount Cithaeron. Cadmus, the aged and abdicated founding king, father of Agave and Semele, accepts the new religion, as does the seer Teiresias. But Pentheus is violently hostile: he has the disguised Dionysus imprisoned, though the miracle-working god shows this to be futile. Pentheus falls gradually under the power of his captive, who induces him to dress as a woman and spy on the mountain revellers. They detect and in deluded frenzy dismember him. Agave in triumph bears his head to Thebes believing that her prey is a lion. A recognition scene reveals the terrifying truth.

The play ostensibly dramatises an historical event, the coming of a new cult to a Greek city. The arrival of Dionysus was re-enacted each year in Athens at the start of the festival, his cult statue brought in procession from the border at Eleutherae as if being introduced for the first time.[67] The ritual thus mirrored one of the paradoxes explored in *Bacchae*: the sense of the cult as simultaneously old and new. Euripides at the end of his life lived at the royal court of Macedon, and perhaps through experience in the northern mountains of primitively vigorous Dionysiac worship gained a renewed sense of its original power. It has been suggested too that he intends an oblique comment on foreign cults coming into Athens in his own day, such as the worship of the Thracian goddess Bendis described by Plato at the beginning of the *Republic* (327a).[68]

The play is strongly intertextual with the *Odyssey* and with earlier tragedy. Like *Agamemnon* it is the story of the killing of a king, but it stands in an especially close relationship to *Oedipus Tyrannus* (written perhaps twenty years earlier, though set two or three generations later).[69] Dionysus like Oedipus originates from Thebes and comes back there as a stranger: another boomerang journey, another story of a visitor coming in disguise to his own place. *Bacchae* is a narrative of host and guest with ambiguities.[70] This is the account of an arriver: will he be received or rejected, bring havoc or blessing? It is a grim and failed theoxeny, but as in the *Homeric Hymn to Demeter* the gloom is mitigated by reflecting on what followed. Like many theoxeny stories, it provides an explanation of later ritual, and the final speech of Dionysus (surviving only in fragments) seems to have described the founding of the kind of cult from which tragic drama itself developed.[71]

Reading the play from within the Christian tradition is like seeing the tesserae of a familiar mosaic rearranged in a strange new pattern. Mark Stibbe in *John as Storyteller* demonstrates the especially close parallels between *Bacchae* and the fourth gospel.[72] Dionysus comes as a god in human form (and not just for a fleeting appearance as the Olympians in Homer typically do). He comes in disguise to his own domain. Unrecognised, he is rejected specifically by members of his own family ('his own received him not'). He faces hostility and unbelief from the ruling powers of the city, but is welcomed by the meek and lowly. He works miracles. Dionysus as a prisoner answers the questions of Pentheus in a studiedly enigmatic way, so that we sense it is the interrogator who is really on trial.

This seems remarkably similar to Jesus before Pilate, again particularly in John's version which gives us two notable dialogues not in the synoptic gospels (John 18:33-8 and 19:8-11). These exchanges are full of dramatic irony: they attest John's stature as a creative writer, but they may suggest also the direct influence of Euripides. Jesus like Dionysus uses language in a less literal way than his questioner ('my kingdom is not of this world'): he answers questions with questions, or with statements of a profundity and irony which Pilate is incapable of comprehending. Pilate's own 'What is truth?' might indeed seem to a modern reader also potentially profound, but in its context it simply signals loss of integrity and control. The interruption of the interrogation when Jesus is taken outside, flogged and mocked is not historically realistic: it is perhaps indebted to the punctuation provided in *Bacchae* by the imprisonment of Dionysus between his first and second encounters with Pentheus. Jesus when threatened with crucifixion calmly replies that the worldly power of Pilate is derivative from God: this echoes the claim of Dionysus that imprisonment and violence are useless, as the god will set him free whenever he wishes (*Ba.* 498 and 504). In each text the interview ends with the superior power of the prisoner clearly shown.

The analogy was noticed at an early date. About AD 175 the otherwise unknown Platonist philosopher Celsus wrote the first comprehensive attack on Christianity, a polemical tract modestly entitled *The True Logos*: a watershed in intellectual engagement with the new faith, and the earliest pagan text which shows clear first-hand knowledge of the gospels.[73] The work itself is lost, but large parts survive as embedded quotations in the reply *Contra Celsum* written about seventy years later by the church father Origen. Citing *Bacchae*, Celsus claimed that Jesus when bound and arrested failed to act like a real god in disguise (*Contra Celsum* 2.34). His cross and his claims to divinity were in the eyes of the philosopher incompatible: why did he not like Dionysus burst his bonds and scatter his enemies? Pentheus was punished for the presumption of his interrogation: how then were Pilate and the high priest Annas able to get away with their probings?

So far we have considered similarities of theme between Greek tragedy and biblical texts not themselves in dramatic form. Hellenised Judaism and Christianity did however in due course directly emulate the Greek theatrical tradition. The *Exagoge*, written in perhaps the second century BC by one Ezekiel, told the story of Moses and the Exodus in the form of a classical drama.[74] Surviving fragments do not suggest that a great work of literature has been lost: the conversation between Moses and the Burning Bush is faintly ludicrous,[75] and the play was perhaps little more than a cross-cultural oddity. The underlying impetus was however a serious and interesting one: to show an Alexandrian audience of cultivated Jews and pagans that Old Testament material could be accommodated to a venerable Greek literary form. A similar impulse in a later age made a tragic drama out of the Passion. The text of *Christus Patiens* bears the name of the fourth-century church father Gregory of Nazianzus, but should probably be attributed instead to a Byzantine writer of the eleventh or twelfth century AD. It borrows extensively from *Bacchae*, to the extent that a gap in the transmitted text of the Euripides play can be partially filled by lines quoted in it.[76] The main parallel exploited by *Christus Patiens* is between the suffering of Jesus and that of Pentheus, which is indeed compelling. Both victims are dressed in humiliating garb, and both led out of the city to an accursed hill, with the lament of Agave for her dead son providing a model for the lament of Mary at the foot of the cross. But there has been a crucial change: the typology has switched sides. Whereas for Celsus it was Dionysus near the start of *Bacchae* who resembled Jesus, for the Byzantine poet it is Pentheus near the end, although of course in each case the identified figure is the one who at the relevant point in the original play has the sympathy of the audience.

Bacchae was a popular play in antiquity, often alluded to by later authors: indeed it acquired something approaching the status of a sacred text.[77] For several passages in Acts a convincing case can be made for direct influence. The escape of Dionysus from prison in a miraculous earthquake (*Ba.* 580-603) is very similar to the experience of Paul and Silas at Philippi (Acts 16:25-30). Richard Seaford shows that this scene in *Bacchae* also resembles a more famous episode in Acts: the conversion of Saul on the road to Damascus (Acts 9:3-9).[78] The two biblical stories and the Euripides passage allow a fascinating triangulation of themes, again with shifting typology. Saul is initially (like Pentheus) the persecutor, the opponent of the new cult, but it is an indication of how dramatically the story has developed that within a few pages Paul has become the incarcerated victim like Dionysus. Both on the Damascus road and at Philippi the suddenness of the divine manifestation is explicitly stressed (Acts 9:3 and 16:26), as it also is in *Bacchae* (576). An invisible voice and lightning are common to *Bacchae* and the scene on the Damascus road; the jailer at Philippi rushes in with drawn sword and collapses, as Pentheus also does. The followers of Dionysus like Paul and Silas are singing a hymn to their god when the epiphany occurs. Dionysus once freed reassures Pentheus he will not run away, and Paul similarly confirms to the jailer that the prisoners have not fled. Saul and later the jailer accept and are converted by the successive epiphanies, and the followers of Dionysus are turned from desolation to joy by the miraculous appearance of their god.

Bacchae may also colour other accounts of miraculous escapes from prison in Acts: the apostles when imprisoned by the priestly party in Jerusalem (Acts 5:19) and Peter after his arrest by Herod Antipas (12:7-10) are released by angels. The description in the second messenger speech of how the voice of Dionysus was heard from above and 'a light of holy fire towered from heaven and earth' (*Ba.* 1078-83) is a further possible model for the scene in Acts 9. The question to Saul 'Why are you persecuting me?' (Acts 9:4) shares with the plan of Pentheus to attack the women (*Ba.* 781-5) the assumption that the god is persecuted if his followers are. When later Paul recounts that incident before Agrippa, he says of the divine voice 'it is hard to kick against the goads' (Acts 26:14): this expression, unique in the New Testament, echoes Dionysus urging Pentheus not to 'kick against the goads' (*Ba.* 795). Convention or coincidence might explain individual parallels, but these examples seem cumulatively persuasive evidence of direct debt.

Alongside this is the separate phenomenon of thematic similarity, extending beyond the broad equivalence of story pattern noted already. *Bacchae* shares with the Bible a basic religious grammar. Wine is central to Dionysiac as it is to Christian ritual. The discussion in *Bacchae* of Dionysus in relation to Demeter emphasises the elements of bread and wine, the staples for which those deities respectively stand. The paradox that Dionysus is himself poured out as wine in worship (*Ba.* 284) has something in common with the words of Jesus at the Last Supper ('This is my blood of the new covenant': Mark 14:24). The importance of the vine in Dionysiac cult and iconography foreshadows its role in the imagery of John's gospel ('I am the true vine': John 15:1). The herdsman describes how the worshippers strike rock or earth to receive streams of water or wine, with milk and honey also miraculously produced (*Ba.* 704-11): we may think of Moses in the wilderness, and of the attributes of the land towards which he is travelling (Exod. 17:6 and 13:5), as well as the miracle at Cana (John 2:1-11). The idea of incorporation into Dionysus by his worshippers (for example *Ba.* 75) is similar to Paul's language about being 'in Christ' (Rom. 6:1-10 and 8:1-11).[79] The recurrent contrast in *Bacchae* (for example 395) of true and false forms of wisdom is paralleled by Paul's description of God making the wisdom of the world look foolish, and of the foolishness of God which is wiser than men (1 Cor. 1:20 and 25).

When Teiresias is trying to persuade Pentheus to accept the new cult, he says he need not believe the myth of the infant Dionysus sewn up by Zeus in his thigh (*mêros*): Zeus simply broke off a piece of ether and gave it as a hostage (*homêros*) to his wife Hera (*Ba.* 287-97). It is not immediately obvious that one story is more plausible than the other, and Euripides here perhaps pokes mild fun at a style of liberal rationalisation favoured by religious exegetes in his own day.[80] We seem close to the scene in *Monty Python's Life of Brian* where one of the Beatitudes (Matt. 5:9) is misheard by the crowd as 'Blessed are the cheesemakers': they are reassured by a helpful commentator that it is not to be taken literally but refers to any manufacturer of dairy products. Allegorical interpretation of Homer had long sought to evade the unacceptable surface sense of many accounts of the gods.[81] Pindar protested against divine cannibalism in treating the story of Tantalus and Pelops (*Olympian* 1.52-3). We can trace a rationalist, reductionist strand in explanations of religion: thus Herodotus (7.129) on the tradition about the Vale of Tempe being created by Poseidon (fine, if you take Poseidon to represent an earthquake), or Socrates in *Phaedrus* (229b-e) on the abduction of Oreithyia by Boreas (she was just swept off her feet by a violent north wind). Indeed the main modern secular theories of religion all have ancient analogues. The well-known fragment of the sixth-century philosopher Xenophanes (if horses and cows could draw, they would portray gods as horses and cows[82]) is in effect a Freudian theory of projection. The view of Durkheim that religion is essentially social cement and an assertion of group identity is implicit in much ancient discussion of civic religion, particularly in reactions when it is threatened. A fragment of a satyr play *Sisyphus* (often attributed to the Sophist Critias but conceivably by Euripides) has a character claim that the gods were invented by rulers to keep people in their place:[83] a theory we immediately recognise as Marxist.

Pentheus in a moment of insight as he is about to be killed acknowledges his errors (*Ba.* 1118-21), but the main recognition scene comes later. Agave enters wildly exultant with the head which to her is spoil of the hunt. Pentheus had spoken earlier of hunting down the women, and now the hunter has himself been hunted. The sadly patient prompting of Cadmus brings her to see that she holds the head not of a lion but of her son (*Ba.* 1284): her physical recognition of it is also a psychological reorientation, a return to reality. The head, described by Oliver Taplin as 'one of the most memorably significant stage properties in all Greek tragedy',[84] is probably also the mask which the actor now playing Agave wore in an earlier scene as Pentheus. *Bacchae* not only brings us chronologically full circle to the likely origins of Greek theatre but also circles upon itself by contemplating the nature of theatre. Pentheus had been costumed by Dionysus, groomed for a role like an actor; and he mistakenly thought he was going to the mountain like a spectator to the theatre.

The perception of theatrical self-reference is a modern critical orthodoxy, but in *Bacchae* more than in any other Greek play each generation sees different things, and perhaps sees itself. Victorian commentators debated whether Euripides was for or against religion: was the play a recantation of the poet's notorious atheism, evidence of a deathbed conversion (for it surely showed the hazard of resisting a god), or did it covertly press home the attack (for the cruelty of Dionysus surely at the end stood condemned)? Every term of that discussion would now be challenged. The idea of Euripides as a religious sceptic derives largely from the satire of Aristophanes in *Frogs*, influentially amplified by German Romantic critics. Some modern scholars even see him as the most religious of the three tragedians, not the least. The aphorisms of Euripidean characters seem often to foreshadow the religious revisionism of the gospels. Thus the insistence in *Orestes* (1604) that clean hands are not enough, because the heart must be clean also, can be compared with the emphasis in the Sermon on the Mount on purity of heart (Matt. 5:8) in contrast to the Levitical purity achieved by ritual ablutions. In *Hippolytus* (1379-84) we find a protest against the idea of inherited guilt analogous to the words of Jesus about the man born blind (John 9:3). It is sometimes denied that we can usefully discuss the personal views of ancient authors at all. We can surely grant however that Euripides intends Dionysus to stand for something beyond good and evil, or rather able to be either. Ordinary people in the play (the soldier and the herdsman), whose wisdom is taken more seriously than it usually is in pre-Christian sources, repeatedly attest his gentleness and beneficence (*Ba.* 436-40 and 771-2). Yet this 'grim predecessor of Christ'[85] is less a god who suffers than one who inflicts suffering, and relishes it.

The early twentieth century produced readings inspired by anthropology (the play dramatises a fertility ritual about the cycle of the year) and by Freudian psychology (Pentheus represses the Dionysiac in himself). The appeal of the play in the second half of the century depended in part on its appropriation by various liberation movements. But its lesson is, like Dionysus himself, deeply ambiguous. *Bacchae* invariably divides its readers, and of all Greek plays is the most sure-fire success in the classroom. I remember a usually reticent sixth-form class stung into passionate debate when asked whether they sided with the authoritarian Pentheus or the subversive Dionysus. When *Bacchae* was performed in Greek at Bradfield College in 1973, the boy due to play Dionysus was expelled just beforehand: a play on the subject by Terence Rattigan could perhaps be imagined. Donna Tartt's novel *The Secret History* (1992) shows us classical undergraduates acting out Dionysiac ritual in the New England countryside. The consequences are predictably unfortunate, and although the conventions of the detective story are inverted to the extent that their misdeeds escape discovery, we are left in no doubt of the permanent damage to their lives. The irrationalism represented by Dionysus is memorably described in *Bacchae* and its power is acknowledged, but it is not altogether admired.[86]

Dionysus existed always on the fringe of the Olympian pantheon. He receives only slight attention in Homer, perhaps because (in character, or because of a populist following) he falls somehow below the criterion of epic dignity. Until his name was found on a Mycenaean Linear B tablet, he was considered a latecomer on the religious scene.[87] Even after his pedigree was extended, many scholars continued to assume a basic historicity in the story of his arrival from abroad. But the ambiguity in the myth (describing the native of Thebes who is also a newcomer from the east) symbolises what is surely his real nature, as a construct of the Greek imagination: a symbol of disruptive difference, and a radical reconciler of opposites. The epiphanic aspect of Dionysus, stressed in particular by W.F. Otto,[88] is now seen as central to understanding his myth and cult. The account of his arrival in one city in the heroic past encapsulates his character, because it describes also the impact of 'the god who comes' on the individual heart and mind.

Historians of Greek religion here use (knowingly or not) the language of existentialist theology, according to which the true significance of the story of the Christ who came at one point in history, and promised to come again, is that he comes now to those who hear his message. The language of encounter is Pauline, but in other respects this existentialist perspective has its roots in the fourth gospel. It is significant that its most famous exponent Rudolf Bultmann explored his ideas in his exegesis of John: the commentary is perhaps more often the medium of creative thought in biblical than in classical studies (though Dodds on *Bacchae* is a distinguished exception).[89] John strives constantly to describe things beyond space and time, particularly in his concept of Christ as pre-existent ('Before Abraham was, I am': John 8:58), and in his distinctive idea of 'eternal life', describing simultaneously a future state and a quality of present experience.

The link between Dionysus and John has a curious coda. In the fifth century AD the Egyptian Greek poet Nonnus wrote a forty-eight-book epic on the adventures of Dionysus, aiming to rival Homer both in length and by incorporating a major military expedition, of the god and his followers against the Indians. The account of the god's eastern journey in Euripides (*Ba.* 13-22) gives us the embryo of this story. Its later development has a complicated relationship to the campaigns of Alexander the Great, who was perhaps already in his lifetime hailed as a 'new Dionysus'.[90] Nonnus also, and probably at an earlier date, wrote a hexameter paraphrase of John's gospel. If his Dionysus is intended as a *figura Christi*, this is left entirely implicit. Biographical speculation is unfashionable, and there are other examples from the period of Christians steeped in traditional pagan learning, but it would be interesting to know what Nonnus in the end made of it all.

Socrates and Jesus

Like the perception of biblical parallels in *Bacchae*, the comparison between Socrates and Jesus goes back a long way. Theirs are the two most famous and influential trials in history. In both cases the precise grounds for sentence have been endlessly debated, and the combination of religious and political factors variously estimated. Their deaths in Athens and Jerusalem have been emblematic of the two cities since the church fathers.[91] Neither Socrates nor Jesus wrote anything, or at least nothing survives: Socrates according to Plato stressed the limitations of written texts (*Phaedrus* 278a), and Jesus is recorded as writing only on the ground (John 8:6). Nothing comes unmediated from either.

Plato's *Apology of Socrates* presents itself as the speech of self-defence made by his teacher when on trial in Athens in 399 BC for introducing new gods, and for corrupting the youth of the city. Xenophon wrote a different account of what Socrates said, and a late tradition recorded by the orator Maximus of Tyre in the second century AD even claimed he said nothing at all.[92] It is likely that Plato gives the gist of the actual defence Socrates put to the large jury of Athenian citizens, but the *Apology* is designed also as a challenge to the reader, who is put in the position of a juror.[93] We do not have the speeches of his accusers, but the *Apology* itself is an implicit accusation of the authorities who put Socrates to death. Charged with disruptive religious innovation, Socrates on trial is reminiscent of Dionysus before Pentheus, and like him seems to foreshadow Jesus before Pilate. The *Apology* challenges us to pass judgement on Socrates as the gospels challenge us to form a verdict on Jesus.

Like the *Iliad*, like many tragedies, and like the gospels, the story of Socrates funnels inexorably towards the death of its hero. It is probable that the account of his last days early assumed a fairly fixed form, like the Passion story in the oral tradition underlying the gospels, and that the dialogues set in the prison (*Crito* and *Phaedo*) deal with events already familiar in outline to their original readers. Plato frequently invites us to read in the light of later events: as usual in ancient literature, the full effect depends on knowing the story already. The portrait of the young Alcibiades in the *Symposium* is coloured by our awareness of his chequered later career. The picture of the family of Cephalus in *Republic* 1 (328b-331d) is affected by our knowledge of how they were to suffer under the oligarchic regime at the end of the Peloponnesian War. Above all, the shadow of the death of Socrates is constantly cast forward.

The parable of the Cave in *Republic* 7 (514a-517a) is justly celebrated, and remarkable in a society with no cinema. The underground audience, chained to their seats, watch on a screen shadows created by the light of a fire and objects carried to and fro behind their backs: this virtual reality is for them the universe. One man breaks loose, sees how the images are created, then crawls from the cave and sees the real world in the much brighter light of the sun, whose control over everything he comes gradually to understand. Pitying his erstwhile colleagues, he returns to the cave and sees the petty audience rivalries over the interpretation of the shadows for what they are. But he is now incomprehensible to his fellows: indeed, if anyone tried to lead them out of the cave, they would kill him. This is a story about the ascent to philosophical understanding, a synecdoche for the whole *Republic*, expressing Plato's central and vastly influential idea that our true home is in eternity. It is also however a parable about Socrates: the man with a message from another realm is disbelieved, rejected as in a myth of failed theoxeny, and ultimately executed. Luke's story of Dives and Lazarus makes a similar point. The rich man who failed to feed the poor wishes to return and warn his family, but is sternly told by Abraham 'If they do not hear Moses and the prophets, neither will they be convinced if someone should rise from the dead' (Luke 16:31). Other parables likewise allude to the death of Jesus: the owner's son in the parable of the wicked tenants (Mark 12:1-8) must suffer the same fate as the man in Plato's story who tries to lead the others out of the cave.

Both Socrates and Jesus deal in homely metaphor and radical paradox. 'My yoke is easy, and my burden is light' (Matt. 11:30) was perhaps a publicity slogan over the door of the carpenter's shop at Nazareth. The occupation of the newly recruited disciples provides a vivid image for their future activity: 'I will make you fishers of men' (Mark 1:17). Socrates in *Theaetetus* (150b) uses his mother's job of midwife as a metaphor for his own activity in helping ideas to birth. He talks too about the moulding of souls, alluding to his father's trade of stonemason and sculptor (though the idea of the statue already present inside the block of stone, eminently Platonist in flavour, is not fully explored until the Renaissance). The paradoxes of Jesus and Socrates boldly challenge the assertion of self. 'Anyone who would be first must be last and the servant of all' (Mark 9:35) and 'he who loves his life loses it' (John 12:25) can be set alongside the repeated assertion of Socrates that it is better to suffer wrong than to do it (for example *Gorgias* 469c), and thus startlingly forego the important ancient pleasure of revenge and retribution:[94] it is no exaggeration to say that a fresh human type is depicted here. At the end of the same dialogue (527c) Callicles is told not to mind if someone insults and strikes him: this seems close to turning the other cheek (Matt. 5.39). Socrates is indifferent to the conventional rewards of success, and Jesus insists that the widow's mites are a more valuable offering than a rich man's gold (Mark 12:43-4). The parallel between Socrates and Jesus runs through the writings of the second-century apologist Justin (whom we shall consider in Chapter 5), but he claimed as one crucial difference that Socrates spoke only to the intelligent, whereas Jesus was a Socrates for all (*Second Apology* 10). It is true that the Socratic paradoxes have an intellectual cast:[95] it is because virtue is knowledge that no one errs willingly (for example *Gorgias* 509e and *Protagoras* 345d), for if people truly knew the nature and effect of wrong-doing they would necessarily eschew it; but the knowledge here described is perhaps a form of intuition or spiritual insight, rather than something inaccessibly cerebral.

How far does the comparison between Socrates and Jesus extend to the sources describing them? In both cases a new literary genre was created, Socratic dialogue and gospel. In both cases we ask which of several portraits is the most like. In both cases it has sometimes been concluded that the historical figure is irrecoverable, though Plato and Xenophon describe a known individual rather than an imaginary ideal philosopher, and we shall see in Chapter 4 that the formerly discredited idea of the gospels as biographies is once again taken seriously. It is tempting in both cases to contrast a straightforward account with a meditation tending towards mysticism, thus equating Xenophon to Mark and Plato to John. But although this model can claim the authority of Schleiermacher,[96] it quickly breaks down. Mark no less than John has a theological agenda, and traditional scholarship has rightly found in Plato the most reliable historical account of Socrates. Justin indeed calls the gospels in general the *Apomnêmoneumata* ('Memorabilia') of the apostles, an implicit pairing with Xenophon.[97] But it is Xenophon who most obviously depicts a Socrates like himself, and a strong argument against giving more weight to his account is that it is hard to see why this genial dispenser of practical advice would ever have been put to death. In some respects the most compelling parallel is between Plato and Paul, rather than any of the evangelists. Each decisively shaped the tradition he inherited. A recurrent question in the criticism of both is whether the legacy was fruitfully developed or excessively systematised: both are censured by some modern readers for authoritarianism. Their imagery and rhetorical techniques are often similar. Socrates in discussing the education of the Guardians (the élite of his ideal state) in *Republic* 3 describes them as spiritual athletes (403e). Paul frequently uses images from the stadium.[98] He writes to the church in Corinth about runners in a race and Christians in the race of life: 'They do it to obtain a corruptible crown, but we an incorruptible' (1 Cor. 9:25). Socrates also envisages life as a form of military service, and insists that we should stay at our post until dismissed by God (*Phaedo* 67a). Paul in turn exhorts his readers to 'put on the whole armour of God' (Eph. 6:11).

The accounts of the last days of Jesus and Socrates are remarkably alike. The Passion took place at the season of Passover, commemorating the Exodus, and the New Testament presents the Resurrection as a new Exodus, from the shackles of sinful mortality. Jesus is thus cast as a new Moses. The death of Socrates also took place at the time of an important religious event. Imprisonment was not itself his punishment: he was held because it was ill-omened to carry out the death penalty while the state galley was away on its annual sacred mission to Delos. This commemorated the deliverance of Athens from subjection to Crete, the king's son Theseus going himself among the human tribute and killing the Minotaur (*Phaedo* 58a-c). There is perhaps an implied suggestion that Socrates is a new Theseus, a deliverer from the shackles of ignorance.

The account of Socrates' time in prison and his calm acceptance of death were to have a powerful influence on Christian martyrology. Hemlock was humane in contrast to what many martyrs suffered, but death was not quite as painless as Plato suggests.[99] The jailer in *Phaedo* pays tribute to Socrates: 'the noblest and gentlest and best of all the men that have ever come here' (*Phaedo* 116c). For this theme of an outsider sensing greatness it is natural to compare the centurion at the Crucifixion: 'Certainly this was a righteous man' (Luke 23:47). Luke is close to Plato too in conveying a mood of calm acceptance (in Mark, Jesus goes much less gently). In Luke alone Jesus movingly reassures the penitent thief: 'Today you will be with me in Paradise' (23:43). Socrates throughout the final conversation shows concern for those around him, and he too speaks of a journey to the next world (*Phaedo* 115a). His final words are however at first sight surprising: 'Crito, we owe a cock to Asclepius: see to it and don't forget' (118a). Questions of historicity aside, there is more here than meets the eye. Plato wants to show Socrates as conventionally pious (thus defending him against the charge of not accepting the gods of the city), but with a significant twist. At the beginning of the *Republic* (327a) Socrates attends

71

the festival in the Piraeus of the Thracian goddess Bendis whose worship has recently been introduced (we saw that *Bacchae* may offer indirect comment on this and similar cults). Here too he is shown as interested in religious matters, but Plato also wants us to reflect on the irony that it is the city which introduces new gods, not Socrates. There may be a similar implication in the *Phaedo* passage, as the cult of Asclepius had been introduced to Athens only about twenty years earlier. More obviously, a sacrifice to Asclepius as god of healing would normally be in thanksgiving for recovery. Socrates turns this on its head, implying that death is the true cure for the ills of life.

The ambiguity here between tradition and innovation encapsulates a central controversy in the study of Socrates. Considerable freedom of interpretation was implicit in the emphasis of Greek religion on ortho-praxy rather than orthodoxy, and reform within any religious tradition typically presents itself as the legitimate development of what has gone before (Teiresias commends the new Dionysiac cult to Pentheus by assimilating it to 'ancestral customs': *Ba.* 201-2). In Rousseau's *Creed of a Priest of Savoy*, the priest challenges the comparison of Jesus and Socrates on the grounds that Socrates merely affirmed familiar Greek virtues.[100] This may be a reasonable comment on the figure portrayed by Xenophon, but it is not true of the Platonic Socrates: we have seen already that on important ethical questions he preaches radical change. Against the traditional definition of just conduct as helping friends and harming enemies, he argues in *Republic* 1 (335b) that it is never right to harm anyone. Except in his dying words, he rarely names the individual gods of traditional polytheism. He sees justice rather than sacrifice as the key to divine favour, and the gods as wholly beneficent to mankind. The description of his *daimonion*, the divine voice deterring him from wrongdoing (*Apology* 40a), is without obvious precedent as something close to what we should call conscience (and revolutionary simply by coming from within rather than grabbing him from outside, as gods and strong emotions in Greek literature usually do). Perhaps on the religious charge as understood by his prosecutors Socrates was indeed guilty.[101]

There is an important analogy here with debates about Jesus. Scholars argue about how much of his teaching can be paralleled in contemporary Judaism. The gospels have a deep-seated ambiguity about whether the new sweeps the old away, or blends with it and develops it. In the Sermon on the Mount the contrast 'You have heard ... but I say' occurs five times in succession (Matt. 5:21-44), yet this emphatic reiteration is preceded by the words 'Think not that I have come to abolish the law and the prophets; I have come not to abolish them but to fulfil them' (Matt. 5:17). There is the warning against putting new wine in old wineskins (Mark 2:22), the cursing of the barren fig-tree which represents the old dispensation (Mark 11:14), the recurrent contrast of ritual with righteousness: yet that contrast itself goes back to the Old Testament prophets (for example Micah

72

6:6-8). Debate is complicated by the fact that much that was written in the past about the failure or obsolescence of Judaism seems in an ecumenical age embarrassingly triumphalist, whilst traditional criticism of Pharisaic concern with ritual regulations often now reads as veiled Protestant polemic against the supposed preoccupations of Catholicism.[102]

All the Socratic literature and all the New Testament accounts of Jesus raise the question of where record ends and interpretation begins. The earliest Platonic dialogues have traditionally been seen as reflecting the historical Socrates. They are generally aporetic: the search for the definition of an abstract quality ends in Socrates not only exposing the ignorance of his interlocutor, but admitting his own. In subsequent dialogues he moves towards an answer through the Theory of Forms: a quality such as courage has an identity as a pure essence, at first imagined as existing in and through individual courageous acts ('immanent Forms'), but later located in eternity prior to and independent of actual examples ('transcendent Forms'). It is generally accepted that by this point Socrates is the mouthpiece of Plato. In the gospels, sayings of Jesus with good claim to be authentic sit alongside comments (for example on the mission of the church and its response to persecution) which it is natural to assume have been put into his mouth for the purposes of a later generation. Later still the church fathers formulated and enshrined in the creeds ideas not explicitly present in the New Testament (God as Trinity, Jesus as at once fully human and fully divine). There are proper questions here about the persuasiveness of the later developments, but the effect in practice for the reader, with knowledge of the subsequent superstructure, is highly Platonist: we have a sense of important but unspoken things somehow already there.

In a famous passage in *Meno*, Socrates prods an uneducated young slave into deducing the theorem of Pythagoras about the square on the hypotenuse simply by asking him questions (*Meno* 82b-85b). Our reaction might be that the slave is intelligent, the human mind can see patterns, and here is a skilled teacher at work. Socrates however concludes that the slave knew it already, from pre-natal experience of the Forms, which include mathematical as well as moral entities (86a). This is the idea of *anamnêsis* ('recollection'): understanding means being reminded of knowledge we once had. In the background here are Pythagorean doctrines about the transmigration of souls: at the time he wrote *Meno*, Plato was much influenced by the followers he had met in Sicily of the sixth-century mathematician and mystic. The Platonist theory of recollection is in *Phaedo* unhistorically described as a Socratic favourite, his friend Simmias wittily appropriating its theme by his claimed inability to recollect the arguments supporting it (*Phaedo* 72e-73a). When Wordsworth uses the idea ('our birth is but a sleeping and a forgetting') it is surely metaphor; whether the same can be said of Plato is an open question. But however literally or otherwise it was intended, cognition is figured as re-cognition:

73

anamnêsis is another version of *anagnôrisis*, and the notion of a decisive moment of insight experienced as recollection can best be understood within the tradition of recognition scenes in epic and tragedy.[103] Recognition itself implies the recovery of previous knowledge: we saw it internalised in Achilles, and in Oedipus who by recognising himself as another recognised also the truth about his own life. The moments of *anamnêsis* in Plato represent a more abstract version of internalised recognition. Knowledge is already present like the returned Odysseus in the prophecy of Theoclymenus, and the Platonist journey of the soul (pre-existent in eternity and at last returning there) gives us once more the story pattern of the epic.

Students coming to the dialogues for the first time often refer to them as plays: a revealing mistake, for they are plainly the product of a society where drama was central. They show the influence of the theatre in scene-setting, in the depiction of character through conversation, and in a forward thrust towards discovery and understanding. Gilbert Ryle in *Plato's Progress* saw them as transcripts of eristic moots conducted for tutorial purposes with Plato playing the part of Socrates.[104] That specific theory is less compelling than the demonstration it entails that Plato is a playwright *manqué*. He attests the dominance of drama, but aspires also to usurp it: the redefinition of recognition is part of a bigger project. Andrea Nightingale in *Genres in Dialogue* shows how Plato sets out systematically to define *philosophia* in opposition to more traditional sources of wisdom. He reworks the conventions of tragedy in order to supersede it as tragedy had itself superseded epic. The eschatological myth which ends many dialogues corresponds to the *deus ex machina* at the end of a play, and individual dialogues engage with the themes of particular plays: thus *Gorgias* discusses contemplative and active life-styles, as represented by Amphion and Zethus in Euripides' lost play *Antiope*.[105] Other literary genres (comedy, various forms of rhetoric, even epic itself) are appropriated to create a new discipline, specialised but with a claim to universality, as an overarching means of understanding human experience. The Platonic dialogue does not simply draw upon other genres, but puts those genres themselves (with their different visions of reality) into dialogue with each other, and the dialogues cumulatively amount almost to a one-man Bible.[106] Indeed the *Republic* alone seems all-embracing: its exploration of the nature of justice talks simultaneously about the individual and about society, intertwining those themes as tragedy often does: like the *Oresteia*, its perspective is at once human and cosmic. We shall see this incorporation of older literary forms to create an ambitious new interpretation of the world repeated in different ways in the *Aeneid* and in the New Testament.

According to a traditional account Transcendent Forms were attractive to Plato because they put moral absolutes beyond reach of the corrosive relativism of the Sophists, the professional providers of higher education in a newly meritocratic Athens. That reading is now treated with caution, as too obviously Plato's own: it caricatures important thinkers in order to exaggerate their difference from Socrates (the portrayal in the gospels of the Pharisees in relation to Jesus raises similar issues). Aristophanes in *Clouds* could satirise Socrates as a typical Sophist, and whilst an informed minority might see humour in a deliberate confusion, most of the audience were presumably content to bracket them together. Robert Parker has argued that the traditional idea of a moral and religious crisis in Athens is overstated,[107] scholars in the nineteenth and twentieth centuries projecting too readily onto the classical past the anxieties of their own society. Plato's lifetime did nonetheless encompass major social and political upheavals, and his career was importantly shaped by historical events, not least the death of Socrates. Defeat in the Peloponnesian War and the consequent loss of empire made Athens less confident and less tolerant of criticism, and men known as associates of Socrates engaged in violent right-wing revolution: if we ask not why he was prosecuted, but why he was not prosecuted sooner, the most convincing answer lies here.

The *Apology* ends with Socrates asserting the powerlessness of the court, since 'nothing can harm a good man either in life or after death, and his fortunes are not a matter of indifference to the gods' (40d). The thought seems close to Paul, who often uses imagery from the lawcourts: 'Who shall bring any charge against God's elect? It is God who justifies; who is to condemn?' (Rom. 8:33-4). We shall see in Chapter 5 that the sense of Socrates as a Christian before Christ forms part of the accommodating attitude of the Greek fathers of the early church towards much of classical culture. The theme of 'Socrates and Jesus Compared' (the title of an 1803 essay by the Unitarian Joseph Priestley) continued to occupy liberal religious thinkers: Matthew Arnold, echoing Schleiermacher, said that European Christianity had more in it of Plato and Socrates than of Joshua and David.[108] The end of the nineteenth century saw a reaction against Protestant liberalism of this kind, emphasising instead the radical otherness of the New Testament world-view, with its background in Jewish apocalyptic: the assimilation of Christianity to Platonism was now seen as a false familiarity, implicitly assimilating also the ancient world to the modern. The Cambridge classical scholar Jane Harrison described a parallel and contemporary reorientation when Hellenists saw the 'two great lights' of archaeology and anthropology, which informed her own studies of Greek religion.[109] Interpreters both of classical literature and of the Bible gained at the turn of the twentieth century a salutary new sense of the past as a place where things are done differently. Differently, but not beyond recognition.

3

Virgil Between Two Worlds

The title of this chapter alludes to Hermann Fränkel's *Ovid: A Poet Between Two Worlds* (1945), a neglected book which raises suggestive questions about classical literature at the turn of the era. Roman poets were not of course conscious of the transition from BC to AD, but Virgil and Ovid explore ideas with parallels in the New Testament, and events in Palestine have both direct and analogical links with contemporary Roman history. Virgil himself is a literary fulcrum: I begin with the Hellenistic background and Callimachus' poem *Hecale*, and end with Ovid and his story of Baucis and Philemon in *Metamorphoses*. These two rural theoxenies illuminate the grand epic deployment of the same theme in the *Aeneid*.

Alexander's legacy

The nineteenth-century German historian Gustav Droysen was inspired by Christian interests and conviction to write the first history of the Hellenistic world.[1] That period is now usually defined as beginning with the death of Alexander the Great in 323 BC and ending with the triumph at Actium in 31 BC of Octavian, who with the new name Augustus became the first Roman emperor. It is essential background for understanding the politics and literature of Augustan Rome, no less than for understanding the birth of Christianity. The shape of Hellenistic history was determined by the conquests of Alexander: his father Philip II of Macedon had gradually taken over the individual city-states of classical Greece, and Alexander himself established an empire extending from Greece to northern India. It incorporated the old dominions of Persia, through a lightning campaign begun at Granicus in 334 BC and completed at Gaugamela three years later: Alexander saw himself as avenging the invasions of Greece under Darius and Xerxes 150 years earlier.

A similarly large historical perspective is needed to appreciate the importance of Alexander himself. It is ultimately because of him that the Bible switches from Hebrew to Greek as it moves from the Old Testament to the New. His conquests are as important in the history of language as in the history of warfare.[2] The Macedonians were anxious to assert their Greekness: Philip's Athenian adversary Demosthenes (3.16) called them barbarians. Their own dialect, apparently unintelligible to other Greeks, lacked the prestige to match their imperial ambitions. The need was met by *Koinê* ('Common') Greek, a simplified version of the language of classical Athens, which in the aftermath of Alexander's campaigns became the vernacular of the eastern Mediterranean. In the fourth century AD the church historian Eusebius propounded the notion of *praeparatio evangelica* ('preparation for the gospel'): the rapid spread of Christianity had been made possible by a providential combination of circumstances, chief among them the peace of the Roman empire brought about by Augustus and the general currency of Greek brought about by Alexander.[3] Edward Gibbon in the eighteenth century called these factors 'secondary causes' of the rise of Christianity (*Decline and Fall* ch. 15), but with studied irony: readers in the Age of Enlightenment were implicitly asked to question whether, when full account was taken of these ancillary and human causes, a primary and divine one need any longer be posited.

Alexander founded seventy cities, but imperial control was thinly spread and inevitably precarious. After his early death his empire was split up among his generals, the *Diadochoi* ('Successors'). They founded and gave their names to the multiple Hellenistic monarchies: Antigonids in mainland Greece, Attalids in Pergamum, Ptolemies in Egypt, and Seleucids in much of Asia Minor. These dynasties are important for Roman history both because their territories became in due course Roman provinces (Egypt after Octavian's victory over Mark Antony and Cleopatra, last of the Ptolemies) and because their model of kingship with an aura of divinity importantly influenced the self-presentation of Augustus and later emperors. Behind the Hellenistic kings stands Alexander himself, but we can look back ultimately to Homeric heroes descended from gods, themselves aspiring to be godlike, and often also heroised in the technical religious sense when their supposed tombs were made the focus of cult. The odes of Pindar praise Olympic and other athletic victors in terms close to divinity. There are in the classical period occasional examples of individuals (such as the Spartan general Brasidas) whose tombs received yearly sacrifice like the heroes of old. At the end of the Peloponnesian War, Lysander, another Spartan general, was unprecedentedly worshipped as a god at Samos during his lifetime. Alexander's father Philip set up his own statue alongside those of the Olympian gods, as if he were the thirteenth of them.[4] Alexander himself after a formative visit to the Egyptian desert shrine of Ammon, where he was addressed as son of this god (equated to Zeus), seems to have formed a romantic but genuine conviction of his own divine nature, and at least some cities responded to his desire to receive worship.

This is the background to the cult of Hellenistic kings, and of the Roman emperor. It was always more at home in the eastern Mediterranean: Augustus and those later emperors whom the sources regard as virtuous trod carefully in Rome, only the wicked and insane insisting on being saluted as gods in their lifetime. Ruler cult is seen by modern historians as a response to power.[5] Ancient polytheism was capacious, and any patron or benefactor in the Hellenistic world could be praised in quasi-divine terms. Several kings took the title *Epiphanês*, a god made manifest and here present (the Latin *praesens deus*), in implicit contrast to the greater but remote gods visible only as inanimate representations. The title is closely linked to the concept of 'euergetism' or benefaction, the immediate and tangible blessings brought by such a god: this nexus of ideas is centrally important in Virgil. Modern scholars have rightly shown that questions about belief and sincerity framed with Christian assumptions do not provide appropriate categories for understanding ruler cult, but equally have insisted that it is a religious phenomenon rather than merely a political one.[6] We can speak of a religious as well as linguistic *Koinê*:[7] Adolf Deissmann in his classic *Light from the Ancient East* (1923) showed by a host of examples from papyri and inscriptions both that the language of the New Testament was the everyday Greek of its period (rather than a special variety used by Jews of the Near East, or by the Holy Ghost), and in particular that the titles and categories applied by the early Christians to Jesus are closed paralleled in the imperial cult: the words for *god, lord, son of god, saviour, gospel, advent,* and *epiphany* are all used in the eulogy of earthly rulers.[8] The Hellenistic world created a melting-pot of religions, and the idea of a *theios anêr* ('divine man') is found in many forms.

Alexander broke down national boundaries. Much that was written about him in the past expressed the perspective of the waning British Empire, and his supposed idea of the unity of mankind was often senti-mentalised: more realistic portrayals are now favoured. But Alexander seems genuinely to have wanted to export and to spread Hellenism. He compelled Jewish thinkers for the first time to see their national traditions in the context of world history: the Book of Daniel provides a good example, with its apocalyptic imagery about the beasts representing successive imperial powers (Dan. 7:15-27). Alexandria in Egypt, the first and greatest of his foundations, became the leading city of the Hellenistic world, a centre of learning as well as of commerce, and the first truly cosmopolitan place. It was in the Hellenised culture of the Jewish community there that the Hebrew scriptures were translated into Greek for Jews who could not read them in the original language, to create the Septuagint. That name derives from a legend preserved in the *Letter of Aristeas*, a Jewish Greek text probably of the second century BC. According to its account Ptolemy II Philadelphus, wanting a Greek version for the royal library, kept seventy (or seventy-two) translators in seclusion on the island of Pharos (where the great lighthouse, one of the Seven Wonders of the ancient world, also dates from his reign): their versions were then harmonised, or according to one tradition were miraculously identical. In reality the process was longer and more complicated, but it produced the version of the Old Testament used by the early church.[9] Hellenistic Judaism ac-cepted much of Greek culture (despite the reservations of the more orthodox), and Moses came to be portrayed as a Greek philosopher.

There is however another way in which Alexander may relate to the Bible, speculative and imponderable but potentially of great significance. He provided a model of a figure at once royal, divine, and universal. That is important for Virgil portraying Augustus, whether directly or indirectly through Aeneas: implicit reference to Alexander is perhaps more pervasive in the *Aeneid* than usually acknowledged. It also has a remarkable similarity to the image of Christ created by the early church. Royalty indeed is more obviously traceable to the Davidic kings of Israel, but although anointed and priestly they were not divine, nor was universal authority claimed for them. And we see once again in Alexander how the conquering hero who dies while still young haunts the imagination of the ancient world.

A key fact about Virgil is that he emulated Homer. But so had Alexander: the impetus exists in life as well as in literature. He took the *Iliad* with him wherever he went, and slept with it under his pillow. He believed himself descended from Achilles, and made a pilgrimage to his tomb at Troy. As a latter-day hero he re-played the wars both of Homer and of Herodotus.[10] Like Herodotus he showed that heroic deeds were still possible and did not belong only to a distant age, just as Virgil was to show that heroic epic could be written in the modern world. Alexander equated himself to a whole range of figures from the heroic tradition: Perseus (whose quest his journey to the shrine of Ammon echoed), Heracles (from whom he also claimed descent), and Dionysus (whose travels in the east were, or were made into, a pattern for his own). This self-modelling in real life anticipates the literary method of Virgil in comparing Aeneas (and thus indirectly Augustus) to a whole range of figures from myth and history. It is also analogous to the way in which New Testament authors compare Jesus to a whole range of figures from the Hebrew scriptures. In both traditions, the significance of a person now occupying centre stage is explored and expressed by comparison with great figures from earlier ages. In both traditions too, in the *Aeneid* and in the New Testament, the idea of a hero as a new version of a predecessor (or a superior combination of the merits of several predecessors) mirrors the way in which the text describing that hero locates itself in relation to earlier texts.

Callimachus: *Hecale*

The master text for Virgil is Homer, but Homer as mediated through practically all significant literature written in between: Greek history, tragedy and philosophy, earlier Latin epic, and not least the Hellenistic poets. All the important figures here (Callimachus, Apollonius Rhodius, and Theocritus) had connections with Alexandria and its great library. Their works are now rated highly for self-consciously playful ingenuity and high stylistic polish: it is no longer fashionable to say that Virgil in contemplating the peaks of early Greek literature overestimated the height of the Alexandrian foothills. But as scholar-poets they typically wrote for a coterie of learned readers, who were expected to recognise recondite allusions. Ancient authors routinely assume knowledge of earlier literature, but that expectation is here raised to a newly demanding level. Creative variation on a model is likewise entirely usual, but often here takes the form of deliberately defeating the reader's expectation: we sense an element of rebellion against the authority of the tradition upon which the poets depend.

The attitude of the Hellenistic poets to epic is particularly revealing. Greek literary history is an orderly succession of genres: Homeric epic, lyric, then history and drama in the fifth century, philosophy and oratory in the fourth (epic indeed continuing to be written occasionally, but without attracting authors of significant talent). The Hellenistic poets could survey and use this whole repertoire, but epic had to be re-invented. C.S. Lewis famously distinguished primary from secondary epic: not as a judgement of value, but to contrast the epic of early societies (when it was the natural or only thing to write) and the literary epic of later times, reanimating an earlier genre and incorporating into it elements from others of more recent origin.[11] Secondary epic began with the Hellenistic poets. The traditional account of a literary quarrel between Callimachus and Apollonius is now questioned, but it is at least true that they handled things differently. For although neither wrote at Homeric length, the *Argonautica* of Apollonius consists of four substantial books, whereas the *Hecale* of Callimachus (now surviving only in fragments) was more obviously a miniature epic. It deals with the adventures of the Athenian hero Theseus.[12] The fragments reveal that somewhere (perhaps as a flashback) we have the familiar account of the boy in Troezen lifting the stone to find the sword and sandals left by Aegeus, the father he has never met. Coming to Athens, he is recognised as the king's son only by Medea, to whom his father is now married. Perceiving a threat to the ascendancy of her own children, she persuades Aegeus to poison him, but the sword as token precipitates in the nick of time a second recognition. Theseus secretly leaves the palace to confront a bull which is ravaging the fields of Marathon (fragments 9-11, 4, 7-8, 17).[13] On his way he takes refuge from a storm in the hut of the old widow Hecale, and here the main part of the story begins.

Both *Hecale* and (even more strongly, as we shall see below) Ovid's story of Baucis and Philemon resemble the biblical account of Elijah and the Widow of Zarephath (1 Kgs 17:7-24), and it may be useful to have this in mind before we proceed. The prophet, on a collision course with the wicked king Ahab, has uttered a dire prediction of drought. He is miraculously fed in the wilderness by ravens, but when his water supply fails he goes under divine prompting to the Phoenician town of Zarephath where he meets a poor woman gathering sticks, and asks her for water and bread. She replies that she has only a handful of meal and a little oil, to form a final repast for her young son and herself. Elijah reassures her that these provisions will by a miracle feed all three of them until the drought ends. He is hospitably received in her humble home: the meal in the jar is not used up, nor does the cruse of oil run dry. When some time later the boy falls ill and dies, the widow (turning on her guest like Metanira in the *Homeric Hymn to Demeter*) accuses Elijah of having come expressly to remind her of her sin and to kill her son. Elijah without a word lies on the inert form with a prayer for his restoration to life. The boy revives and is presented to his mother, who recognises Elijah as a true prophet.

Hellenistic literature characteristically avoids the obvious narrative core of a story: *Hecale* is about rustic entertainment, not bull-fighting. One fragment evocatively describes the gathering storm before Theseus appears. Hecale observes her sputtering lamp: as in many theoxeny stories, the visitor arrives in the evening. While Theseus takes off his wet clothes, she fusses with logs for the fire, then with bread and olives (fragments 18, 25, 27-37). True to the rules of Homeric hospitality, questions follow food. Hecale talks about her own life: she movingly recalls meeting her future husband, perhaps reminded of him by the youthful visitor. She speaks of his death and of the two sons she brought up alone, then of their deaths, the younger one killed by the monstrous brigand Cercyon. Theseus reveals that he has killed Cercyon on his journey from Troezen: the service he has thereby done corresponds to the miracle in the Elijah story. Hecale says she could now die happy, an outcome soon realised. We last glimpse her saying goodbye to Theseus next morning (fragments 41-9, 161, 64-5). After subduing the bull he drives it triumphantly through Athens. At the end of the story he finds the neighbours of Hecale raising a tomb. He eulogises his late hostess, and describes the annual feast that will be held in her memory (fragments 67-9, 79-81, 83).

Although the impression may be heightened by the fragmentary nature of the text, the treatment was clearly episodic, a sequence of vignettes: in form and content alike, the poem seems both familiar and unexpected. We can identify in it many elements from the *Odyssey*: Hecale is a female Eumaeus, like him apostrophised by the narrator, and apparently like him of noble descent, though more impoverished. There is much too from Hesiod, who was greatly admired by the Hellenistic poets and seen by them as offering an alternative within the broad genre of epic to traditional grand themes, and a model for a sequence of descriptive passages rather than striding narrative. We can trace also the influence of Euripides. He relishes unpacking the myths he uses, treating them from an unfamiliar angle and putting ordinary recognisable people into extraordinary situations: he exploits to the full the limited freedom of the dramatist to change a traditional story. In his *Electra* the heroine is nominally married to a poor farmer, who yet has an innate nobility which puts most of the royal characters to shame. His reception of Orestes and Pylades in his cottage in the Argive hills (*Electra* 358-400) provides another model for the Hellenistic poets.[14]

81

They and their readers clearly enjoyed the theme of a hero entertained in simple surroundings, where the juxtaposition of grand and humble elements is savoured, and homely detail takes precedence over heroic action: two other examples may be briefly considered. Callimachus himself elsewhere told of Heracles entertained in the hut of the old man Molorchus before going out to kill the Nemean lion, and thus to found the Nemean Games: this narrative (again surviving only in fragments) seems to have begun the third book of his *Aitia* ('Causes'), a large collection of stories each explaining the origin of some ritual or institution.[15] In the Molorchus story we have again the account of a hero who before confronting a formidable beast is received in a humble country dwelling by an aged person in mourning: the son of Molorchus had been killed by the lion which Heracles is about to dispatch. The hospitality received by the hero is again commemorated by a continuing cult, and Molorchus gives his name to a place as Hecale also does.

Secondly, we can compare the work of a poet writing a generation after Callimachus. Eratosthenes, more famous as a scientist and polymath, in his *Erigone* (known from fragments and summaries) told how the poem's eponymous heroine and her aged father Icarius entertained Dionysus when he introduced to Attica the hitherto unknown cultivation of the vine.[16] Like *Bacchae*, this is a melancholy theoxeny. The old man's neighbours, believing themselves poisoned by the novel liquid, attack and kill the host of its provider: Erigone upon discovering her father's corpse hangs herself. The pair and their dog receive the compensation of catasterism, a transformation into stars or constellations: this characteristic Hellenistic interest is a version of the wider theme of metamorphosis which we shall consider below. Several different aetiological accounts seem to have been offered in *Erigone*: as well as the constellations, and an Attic deme named after Icarius, the suicide of the heroine was commemorated by Athenian women hanging small images on trees as part of the Anthesteria. This important spring festival honoured Dionysus as god of wine, but Eratosthenes seems also to have introduced a foundation myth for tragedy, commonly etymologised as 'goat-song'. For when Icarius found a goat gnawing his new vines, he tied it up and made his companions dance round it: such was the humble and unwitting origin of the choral dance later central to the prestigious genre. Nor would it have been lost on learned readers that Thespis, credited with the innovation of stepping forward from the chorus to become the first actor, came according to tradition from the deme of Icaria. What is happening here is of great interest for the later literary tradition. Callimachus and Apollonius are acknowledged as important influences on Virgil, who writes in a Hellenistic style but on a Homeric scale. Eratosthenes in *Erigone* seems still to have operated within a limited physical compass. But in his ambition for the aetiological story, its elevation to explaining something grander than a village or local rite, we seem already part way to the *Aeneid*, in which Virgil offers an *aition* for Rome itself.

3. Virgil Between Two Worlds

The Roman Revolution

Virgil started work on the *Aeneid* about two years after Actium: it occupied the remaining decade of his life. The themes handled in the epic suggest he was conscious of living at a decisive but uncharted period in the history of Rome. Octavian had ended decades of civil war, and his solution in the inauguration of the principate was to prove lasting. In 27 BC he took the name Augustus ('Revered'): carefully calculated to create an aura of quasi-religious authority whilst stopping short of a claim to divinity. He also set about consolidating and defining his position. Rome had not had a king since the expulsion in 510 BC of the discredited Tarquinius Superbus, and the still tainted title was avoided now. On the other hand Republican government, the tradition of the intervening centuries, was in reality already long dead. Designed for a city-state, it had fallen victim to the expansion of Rome, first within Italy and since the second century also overseas. The hundred years before Augustus had been marked by the rivalries of ambitious dynasts (some of whom saw themselves as Roman versions of Alexander, a claim implicit in the title 'the Great' assumed by Pompey), and by a series of increasingly bitter and bloody civil conflicts. Factional warfare turning a state on itself was viewed with particular horror in the Greek and Roman world. The literature of the late Republic is marked by a sense of gathering gloom, and of events hurtling towards an uncertain future. In very broad terms this is comparable to the atmosphere within Hellenistic Judaism which produced the apocalyptic visions exemplified by the books of Daniel in the Old Testament and Revelation in the New. Members of the desert community at Qumran whose life is revealed in the Dead Sea Scrolls felt themselves to be living in an end time, the prelude to some decisive intervention; and the gospels often give the sense that 'the denouement of the world-story is come'.[17]

The last and greatest of the Roman generals to break from the Republican framework was Julius Caesar. His assassination in 44 BC makes it impossible to know whether he aimed at a divine monarchy in the style of Alexander. But he was deified after death, which made his great-nephew and adopted heir Octavian *divi filius* ('son of a god'). Octavian was described in his rise to power as a 'chill and mature terrorist' by Ronald Syme,[18] who in *The Roman Revolution* (1939) influentially reasserted the negative view of Augustus held by Tacitus and by Gibbon, with an implicit sideways look at the totalitarian rulers dominant in Europe in the uneasy decade when his book was written. Since then more balanced assessments of Augustus have become current,[19] but Syme's legacy includes a central question in the study of Virgil: the attitude of the poet to the Augustan principate, and more generally to the Roman imperial enterprise. Is his apparent admiration real and unqualified?

The fact that expert Virgilian scholars take diametrically opposite views itself tells us something important about the *Aeneid* and the protean nature of Virgil's poetry. Some ambiguity about its central subject matter is not an unusual characteristic of serious literature: we saw this already with the attitude to war in the *Iliad*. It has often been observed in discussions of the British Empire that the greatest imperial literature is marked by an undercurrent of sadness (witness Rudyard Kipling, especially in his 1897 'Recessional'),[20] and it is a commonplace of Virgilian criticism that the poet has voices both of public support for the Roman enterprise and of private sympathy for losers and victims. But to speak of him as subversive or covertly anti-Augustan is crude and unconvincing. It is an idea derived from the Romantic picture of the artist as necessarily a rebel, and the American critics who have been its strongest advocates were perhaps influenced by their attitude to the quasi-imperialist involvement of their own government in south-east Asia and elsewhere. Questions about the optimism or pessimism of the *Aeneid* are important, but refer to much more than politics. It is probably right to see the poem as darker in overall tone than the *Iliad*, but that is a judgement about its view of human nature and man's place in the world rather than about forms of social organisation. Some pessimism at this grander level perhaps indeed goes more naturally with a positive than with a negative view of Augustus: recent history had shown that strong rule was necessary, and (to put it crudely) Augustus was the best that could be expected in a fallen world. It is important also to bear in mind that the regime was not a finished product held up for judgement: Augustus was feeling his way towards a new type of government even as Virgil was feeling his way towards a new type of epic poem. It is entirely plausible that the *Aeneid* contains warnings about roads that would be better not taken.

The analogy between what the emperor was doing and what the poet was doing is far-reaching: it is a new version of the Homeric idea of the comparable and mutually dependent activities of hero and bard. Religion is a central theme both in the *Aeneid* and in the culture of Augustan Rome. Augustus was concerned with the restoration of traditional values and built or rebuilt many temples. Virgil depicted a pious hero and sought to recover the grand seriousness of Homeric epic. There is a parallel here with what has been called the 'resacralisation' of Elizabethan England after the Reformation. The interest shown during that period in the role of figures such as Joseph of Arimathea or Merlin in the English past mirrors the preoccupation of the Augustan era with early Rome, seen above all in the early books of Livy. The idea of a special divine destiny ('Heaven's command') became prominent in the age of Elizabeth, and later underpinned the ideology of high empire. Stephen Prickett in *The Origins of Narrative* shows how the potent idea of fate applied to national history takes us from John of Gaunt's speech about 'This sceptred isle' in *Richard II* to William Blake's 'Jerusalem'.[21] Blake imagined Jesus coming to England as Geoffrey of Monmouth had long before through Brute the Trojan sought to connect English history to ancient epic. The impetus to establish links with a more venerable past seems fundamental to the creation of a national self-image: we see it in Latin literature almost from the beginning, the early epic poet Ennius already presenting himself as a Roman Homer. The theme in Elizabethan historical drama of unifying the nation and building the audience into the myth, against a contrasting background of civil strife, seems uncannily similar to the aims both of Augustus and of Virgil.[22] In Augustan Rome and again in Elizabethan England we see an ambitious new order defining itself by a particular reading of the past. The use of Jewish tradition in early Christianity is not altogether different.

The *Aeneid* and the New Testament

Virgil is to Homer broadly as the New Testament is to the Old. Authoritative texts from the past are reworked in a different language, and with a different message. These are our two supreme examples of intertextuality, the new texts empowered by their prolonged allusion to great predecessors. Grand narrative is rediscovered and a prophetic voice heard again. In Virgil the full might of heroic epic, which had long seemed obsolete, is achieved once more. John the Baptist by his voice crying in the wilderness, his camel's hair garment and his diet of locusts and wild honey is cast as a second Elijah (Matt. 3:3-4, echoing 2 Kgs. 1:8). John the Evangelist dares to rewrite the foundational text of Genesis: 'In the beginning was the Word' (John 1:1) echoes 'In the beginning God created the heavens and the earth' (Gen. 1:1). He simultaneously repeats its claim (for the Word summarises the ninefold 'God said' in the first chapter of Genesis) and moves radically beyond it (for that same Word has now been made flesh: John 1:14). Virgil dares to rewrite the foundational texts of the *Iliad* and *Odyssey*. The memorable first simile in the *Aeneid* (1.148-153) compares the calming of a storm at sea by Neptune to the calming of an unruly mob by a great statesman. Homer typically illustrates human activity with similes from wild nature. Virgil in reversing this, and in using a specifically Roman political image, indicates that the poem we have begun to read will both resemble Homeric epic and present something radically new.

The later texts in both traditions are extended meditations on the earlier ones. The sheer frequency of reference, the manifold examples combined and re-combined, would in themselves constitute significant similarity, but the analogies of method go much further than this. New Testament writers (especially Matthew and the author of the Epistle to the Hebrews) compare Jesus to a whole range of Old Testament characters, including Adam, Abraham, Moses, David and Elijah. For Matthew these multiple parallels are a means of creating a rich Christology, a many-faceted portrait of his central character. Virgil likewise compares Aeneas to Odysseus, Achilles, and Heracles from Greek myth, as well as

85

to Romulus from Roman tradition: a succession of founder heroes. Matthew's gospel has been seen as a new miniature version of the Pentateuch, and as a systematic commentary on the cycle of prescribed readings in the synagogue lectionary: radical in content, but in style recognisably within the Jewish tradition of Midrash (the creative exposition of scripture, in particular by crossing one passage with another).[23] The *Aeneid* is itself on a considerable scale, but likewise aspires (with a mixture of modesty and immodesty) to incorporate the forty-eight books of the *Iliad* and *Odyssey* within the smaller compass of twelve, and likewise forms a complex commentary not only on Homer but on a high proportion of intervening literature. But Virgil also compares Aeneas to Augustus from contemporary history, and here is an important difference. For whereas the New Testament writers compare a recent figure to people from the past, familiar to readers from texts themselves long revered, Virgil portrays his contemporary Augustus only indirectly, setting his new text in the heroic age. It is conceivable that he initially considered writing directly about recent events, but he must quickly have realised the problems inherent in juxtaposing the traditions of epic with the prosaic present, the risk of bathetic incongruity, and the desirability of distance.

History is re-cast as prognosis. Augustus and Rome are foreshadowed in the *Aeneid* through prophetic passages, written for the purpose and therefore necessarily fulfilled. W.H. Auden in his poem 'Secondary Epic' protested: 'No, Virgil, no: hindsight as foresight makes no sense.' In fact the sleight of hand is highly effective: the sense that we are witnessing events long awaited is one of the most powerful feelings that literature can create. It was important in the *Oresteia*, and is part of the complex legacy of that work to the *Aeneid*. The New Testament also constantly invites us to see prophecy fulfilled. The obvious difference that it deals in genuine prophecy delivered of old rather than in prophecy created for the occasion is less stark than it may seem. The perception of events as fore-ordained is intrinsically retrospective. The Old Testament passages traditionally cited as referring to Jesus are now generally acknowledged to have had a different meaning in their original context. This does not detract from the power of a passage such as Isaiah 9 ('unto us a child is born') chosen by E.W. Benson in the nineteenth century as third of the Christmas lessons. The gospel writers seem often to have accommodated the known facts about Jesus to Old Testament texts already familiar, for example in the prophecy about the king entering Jerusalem on 'a colt and the foal of an ass' (Zech. 9:9), the Hebrew parallel restatement notoriously misunderstood (or creatively re-interpreted) by Matthew as referring to two separate animals (Matt. 21:2). It is a commonplace of biblical criticism that to prophesy in the Old Testament is to forthtell rather than to foretell, and that the main concern of the great prophets was with their own society rather than with the future. Moreover the Bible itself frequently uses predictions and prescriptions written long after the events to which they ostensibly look forward. Daniel foretells the overthrow of a series of empires by *ex post facto* prophecy (Dan. 7-11). Deuteronomy lays down rules about temple offering which will apply when the Israelites have entered the Promised Land (Deut. 26:1-15), though they are in fact priestly regulations from a much later period. In his great speech at the end of that book Moses as he stands on the threshold of the Promised Land is made to take stock of the story so far, reminiscing about the past and envisaging what is to come, with warnings and promises drawing on the Deuteronomic historian's knowledge of later events (Deut. 32-3): this powerful passage is especially Virgilian in feeling. Knowledge of the fact they were written by the poet who also describes their fulfilment need not therefore compromise the great visions of Roman destiny in the *Aeneid*: the prophecy of Jupiter (1.257-96), the parade of future heroes described by Anchises in the Underworld (6.756-853), and the scenes on the shield given to Aeneas by his mother Venus (8.626-728).

New texts embody new values: both Virgil and the New Testament authors offer a world-view significantly unlike the works from which they partly derive. In each case a new human ideal is presented: Aeneas differs in important ways from a traditional Homeric hero as Jesus does from an Old Testament patriarch or warrior. Both the *Aeneid* and the gospels present a dedicated and in some sense godlike man who is lonely, suffering, and on occasions self-doubting and reluctant to undertake his appointed task: the evocatively unfinished line *Italiam non sponte sequor* ('I am not making for Italy of my own volition': *Aen.* 4.361) sits alongside 'let this cup pass from me' (Matt. 26:39). Yet we can turn anew from Virgil to the *Iliad* and more easily see some of those same traits already in Achilles, particularly in his great speech of self-questioning (*Il.* 9.308-429), just as we can turn anew from the gospels to the Old Testament and find similar characteristics in many of its leaders and prophets. In both cases too the new text helps us see how far a transvaluation of values has taken place already within the developing tradition: Greek tragedy and Plato had already explored new versions of heroism, and the second part of Isaiah had already given us the Suffering Servant (Isa. 52:13-53:12).

In both traditions too the typology, the method of comparison with earlier times, had already been explored. The prophet Ezra was seen as a second Moses before Jesus was (Neh. 8:2-18), and the Republican hero Camillus as a second Romulus before Augustus (Eutropius 1.19). The Exodus provided an explanatory model for the return from the Babylonian Exile before it did for the Resurrection or for Christian baptism. The idea of an earlier war re-played with the sides reversed had been used by Herodotus and Thucydides (the imperialist Athenians as the new Persians) before it was used by Virgil (the eventually triumphant Trojans as the new Greeks). The New Testament and the *Aeneid* are books about other books, themselves often books of which the same is already true. The typology of characters is also a typology of texts. If Jesus or Aeneas corresponds to a whole range of earlier characters, the texts describing them correspond to a whole range of earlier books.

There are nonetheless two important differences between Virgil's technique and biblical typology. In the New Testament the purpose of the comparison is normally to suggest that Jesus is a perfected version of the Old Testament figure, or a replacement where the original was faulty ('a second Adam to the fight and to the rescue came', as Newman paraphrased 1 Cor. 15:22). In Virgil the effect of assimilation to an earlier character is not always to present Aeneas as a superior substitute. On occasion he may be shown by implication as disturbingly similar to a character who cannot be admired. Thus for example because the poet's portrait of Dido in part evokes Medea in Euripides, Aeneas is potentially cast as the unlovely Jason. We should not indeed build too much on this: critics who use such cases to create a negative overall portrait of the hero (and thus by implication of Augustus) fail to see that the reader can be expected to draw contrasts as well as to observe similarities. But the fact that Virgil can use comparisons which are morally complex or ambiguous led Jasper Griffin to deny the analogy (drawn by the German scholar G.N. Knauer and others) with typology in the New Testament sense, whose exponents never do so.[24] It may nonetheless be felt that even when allowance has been made for this significant distinction, the overall similarity of approach remains striking.[25]

The second difference is connected to the treatment of time which we have considered already. When Jesus is compared to figures from Jewish tradition, he is presented as simultaneously a moral and a chronological culmination. In Virgil the situation is complicated by setting the story in the heroic past. Here it is useful to distinguish historical (or mythological) time from literary time. Aeneas is implicitly compared to characters familiar to the reader from earlier literature and tradition but who belong to a later period than the setting of the story: for example to Romulus, and to the Romans who fought the Carthaginians in the second century BC, as well as to Augustus who as Virgil's contemporary is being inscribed into literature before our eyes. If Virgil writes his own prophecies, he writes also his own equivalent of Exodus (a book which we shall see has strong similarities to the *Aeneid*). He himself presents the story of old in which the forerunner of a much later figure can be discerned: there is indeed a sense in which Virgil, like Plato, produced a whole Bible. The similarity of method between Virgil and the New Testament writers is thus clearer if we think of Augustus rather than Aeneas in a position analogous to that occupied by Jesus, as the contemporary or recent figure to whom the past is seen as inexorably leading.

Augustan ideology and New Testament theology faced comparable problems. In both cases a new central figure had to be incorporated into a tradition whose nature made that exercise difficult. In the vision of Roman heroes which Anchises describes to Aeneas in the Underworld, and likewise in the iconography of the new Forum of Augustus (with an equivalent set of heroes as statues in niches round the walls), the Republican past had to be presented, without too glaring an appearance of paradox, as leading to a quasi-monarchical present. Similarly when Paul was converted from Pharisaic to a newly radical version of Messianic Judaism, he had to work hard to show the significance of its central figure without too blatant a challenge to traditional Jewish monotheism. In both cases a solution was sought by a stress on historical models: on the individuals in Roman history who had single-handedly saved the state in times of crisis, and on the various Old Testament figures around whom Messianic hope crystal-lised. But in both cases too the sense of decisive culmination inevitably raised questions about what would happen next. Even to consider an heir or successor to Augustus involved the uncomfortable suggestion of heredi-tary monarchy, quite apart from the sequence of misfortunes which in practice dogged the emperor's attempt to find a suitable candidate. Much of the New Testament is concerned with the ways in which the very early church adjusted to the delay of the expected *parousia*, the second coming of Christ, and with the practical arrangements for the future put in place when the sense of its imminence receded.

Typology posits similarities (in character or narrative function) be-tween people of different eras who may otherwise be unconnected. But as well as this, both the New Testament and the *Aeneid* claim direct genea-logical continuity between the modern figure with whom they are concerned and his grand predecessors. Virgil uses a tradition already well established by his time that the Julian house, the family of Augustus, claimed descent from Aeneas. Similarly Matthew, again drawing on exist-ing tradition, on the hope for 'a branch from the stock of Jesse' (Isa. 11:1), begins with 'the genealogy of Jesus Christ, the son of David, the son of Abraham' (Matt. 1:1). In both cases the new central figure is shown to be the descendant of the founding fathers of the nation. Matthew imposes shape and arithmetical symmetry on the list that follows by identifying fourteen generations from Abraham to David, fourteen from David to the Exile, and fourteen from then to the Christ (Matt. 1:17). Virgil had the task of reconciling the Homeric tradition of Aeneas the survivor of Troy with the Italian story of the foundation of Rome. Earlier writers had made Romulus the grandson of Aeneas. Virgil uses a version which achieves more plausible dates and a geometric progression. Jupiter's great passage of history as prophecy (*Aen.* 1.257-96) foretells that Aeneas will found his city of Lavinium and live thereafter for three years. His son Ascanius (also known as Iulus, as forebear of the Julians) will transfer the city to Alba Longa and will reign for thirty years. The Alban kings will rule for 300 years. Romulus will then found Rome. To its dominion Jupiter explicitly sets no limit of time or space, but we are perhaps intended to hear a hint that it will endure for 3,000 years.

Cities as well as individuals are shown to exist in a line of descent, in

Jupiter's prophecy about future developments within Italy but also on a larger scale in the overall story of the *Aeneid*, summarised by Tennyson as 'Ilion falling, Rome arising'.[26] In narrating the fall of Troy, Virgil must avoid giving the impression that Aeneas is deserting a sinking ship. We must sense instead that the divine impetus has moved on, that the future lies elsewhere. It must be shown that Troy was doomed and belonged to the past. Augustan poetry often stresses its guilt (for example Horace *Odes* 3.3): there was ample mythological warrant for that, but the theme also has symbolic contemporary relevance. A positive reading of the character and achievement of Augustus must include the sense of necessarily putting the past behind us, to make a clean break and a new beginning. The guilty Troy from which Aeneas comes, but which he leaves, corresponds at some level to the years of faction fighting from which Augustus emerged.

The new includes important elements of the old, but we must be shown that it is misguided to try to restore too slavishly a previous order of things. Aeneas and his followers, looking for the place where their new city can be founded and having already made several false starts, come to Buthrotum on the coast of Epirus. Here Aeneas finds another group of Trojan survivors who have attempted to replicate the city they had left:

> As I walked along I recognised a little Troy, a citadel imitating great Pergamus and a dried-up stream they had given the name Xanthus. (*Aen.* 3.349-51)

This has a charming pathos (like Victorian attempts to recreate Tunbridge Wells in Simla or Darjeeling), but we are left in no doubt that it is the wrong response. Looking back is ill-omened, the action of an Orpheus. The imitation Troy in Buthrotum is small, and in effect a place of the dead: Andromache lives in the past, and takes Aeneas for a ghost.[27] The real new Troy will be something bigger, altogether different, and somewhere else. This is a comment on the city that will be founded in 753 BC by Romulus, but also on the Rome that Augustus will effectively found afresh. Octavian before settling on the name Augustus contemplated calling himself Romulus (Cassius Dio 53.16.7): here again life and literature are in step, and here again is a line of thought analogous to biblical typology, a second Romulus like a second Moses or a second David.

Buthrotum surely also has a metapoetic resonance. Types of city are like types of epic poem: in both cases there is an onward momentum. To write traditional epic when its day is past is like trying to recreate Troy on the coast of Epirus, or indeed like trying to resuscitate a defunct Republican form of government. The new Rome of Augustus must be celebrated by a new style of epic, distinctively original though with a strong traditional component, just as it must have a style of administration that answers the same description. Emperor and poet both embark on an enterprise with elements of experiment and risk, but both also have huge ambitions. The *Aeneid* aspires to be a national epic. Its content and its nature are analogous to each other: Rome derives from but supersedes Troy, just as Virgil derives from but aspires to supersede or at least equal Homer. The *Aeneid* is about relocation, of the Trojans and of literary authority.[28] It is an imperial epic not only by celebrating Roman dominion, but by its own nature. For just as Rome colonises and embraces other lands and cultures, so too the poem colonises and embraces other literary genres. The *Aeneid* is about history and empire, and itself embodies both.[29]

Much in all this has New Testament parallels. The idea of the new Augustan Rome, contrasting both with a guilty Troy and with a dark period in its own recent history, is broadly similar to the idea (prominent especially in Matthew) of the Christian church as a new Israel. The new draws on the old, and in some respects restores a former greatness, but also decisively replaces it. There is a necessary break with a flawed past: continuity indeed exists as well, but with new input and with a sense that a past process is now summed up and completed in definitive form. The old nation of Israel must (on this reading) give way to the new Christian community. The Epistle to the Hebrews opens with a statement about continuity and change, with a decisive culmination: 'In many and various ways God spoke of old to our fathers by the prophets; but in these last days he has spoken to us by a Son' (Heb. 1:1-2).

There is however an obvious difficulty here for the modern reader. The perspective of Matthew and Hebrews can appear uncomfortably triumphalist, and the literary imperialism of the *Aeneid* is a potentially disturbing analogy for the way in which the New Testament uses the Hebrew scriptures for its own purposes. Nonetheless in a pluralist age which emphasises that texts can be read in a variety of ways and are inseparable from their later reception, we may wish also to say that the traditional Christian conception of the Bible as a unity retains considerable power as means of interpretation: the New Testament is 'in essential literary continuity with the Hebrew Bible, without being its inevitable completion or sole interpretative key'.[30] The writers of the older scriptures naturally did not imagine that they were providing a prelude for another set of documents, to be written centuries later and in a different language, any more than Homer expected to be compared and contrasted with Virgil. But reading the earlier texts in the light of the later is not only inevitable: it is arguably also desirable and illuminating. This is intertextuality in a stronger sense than simply the study of influence. It is the point made by saying that we read *Bleak House* differently when we have read Kafka:[31] the story of the Byzantine workings of the Victorian Court of Chancery becomes an existential parable about the rootless and alienated individual at the mercy of arbitrary forces beyond his control. We do not so much read New Testament themes into the Old Testament as recognise them already there (again we meet that Platonist theme). Familiarity with the gospels assists rather than distracts our reading of Isaiah or the Psalms. If the greatest critic of Beethoven is Brahms, the greatest critic of Homer is Virgil, and familiarity with the *Aeneid* enables us to read the *Iliad* and *Odyssey* with heightened perception.

The shape imposed on its constituent texts by the Christian canon may not be the only context for reading them, but it is important in its own right in the history of ideas. It is the shape of an hour-glass. Gabriel Josipovici points out that the traditional Protestant ordering of the Bible gives the sense of an initial revelation, then a period when everything becomes murky and confused, before the second revelation brought and represented by Jesus:[32] the archetypal story of loss and restoration. This is also the shape which traditional handbooks impose on the history of classical literature: initial greatness in Homer and fifth-century Athens, Hellenistic loss of direction, and restored greatness in Augustan Rome. We are uneasy now with an hour-glass Bible for the reasons described. We are uneasy with an hour-glass literary history because it disparages authors now highly regarded. Yet in one sense, as a description rather than a judgement of value, there is undeniably a narrowing in the middle of this narrative. Early and classical Greek literature addressed grand issues for a large audience: it had a role in society which the Hellenistic poets lacked, despite their individual talent and charm and despite their important influence on what came later. That social centrality was won anew by Virgil and his contemporaries, and it is significant that the Augustan poets used the term *vates* ('prophet' or 'seer') for the inspired poet with the high seriousness of privileged insight.

The *'Messianic Eclogue'*

The perception of Virgil as *anima naturaliter Christiana* ('a naturally Christian soul') has a long history. An anonymous medieval poet records the legend that St Paul visited the poet's tomb in Naples and wept over the great convert he might, but for an accident of chronology, have made.[33] T.S. Eliot's two essays celebrating 'the classic of all Europe' influentially restated the perception of Virgil as a bridge between the pagan and Christian eras.[34] K.W. Gransden points to the enduringly powerful image of the poet 'poised uncertainly at the very end of the era of what Dante called the false and lying gods, unable to escape from the pagan world to whose values he seemed not wholly to assent'.[35] Kipling in his 'Last Ode' wrote of how 'Virgil died, aware of change at hand'. These are responses to themes running through all of Virgil's works, but in its traditional form the idea of the poet as a prophet of Christianity rests specifically on a reading of the fourth *Eclogue*.

The *Eclogues* are Virgil's earliest work: ten fairly short poems in the style of the *Idylls* of the Hellenistic poet Theocritus, and like their models usually described as pastorals. They describe the lives, loves, and not least the competitive singing of a group of rustic characters in an ethereal landscape which seems by turns Italian, Sicilian, and Arcadian. Like much of Latin poetry, they are about poetry itself, and as in his later works Virgil incorporates elements from other sources into the genre he inherits: the political reality of contemporary Rome breaks into this imagined world. Several of the *Eclogues* are modelled on individual poems of Theocritus, but the fourth has no single or obvious predecessor. It has over the centuries attracted more discussion than any other short poem in Latin.

It looks forward to the birth of a child who will inaugurate a new age. Written in 40 BC (the year of the consulship of its addressee, Virgil's first patron Asinius Pollio) it seems uncannily to foreshadow the turn of the era:

> The great line of centuries begins anew ... the reign of Saturn returns ... a new generation descends from heaven on high. (*Ecl.* 4.5-7)

It describes how the child will have the gift of divine life, and will rule the world to which his father's prowess has brought peace. In this new golden age, nature will be benignly co-operative:

> The goats will come home by themselves with milk-filled udders, and the cattle will not be in fear of great lions. The serpent too will perish, and perish will the plant which hides its poison. (21-5)

All this seems irresistibly reminiscent of Isaiah:

> The people who walked in darkness have seen a great light ... For unto us a child is born, unto us a son is given: and the government shall be upon his shoulder, and his name shall be called Wonderful, Counsellor, the Mighty God, the Everlasting Father, the Prince of Peace. (Isa. 9:2 and 6)

Isaiah likewise in his vision of future hope for Israel associates the birth of the child with a new order in the natural world, with the specific details of animals no longer fearing each other, and the sting of poison drawn:

> The wolf shall dwell with the lamb, and the leopard shall lie down with the kid, and the calf and the lion and the fatling together, and a little child shall lead them. ... The sucking child shall play over the hole of the asp, and the weaned child shall put his hand on the adder's den. (Isa. 11:6 and 8)

This compelling coincidence of language gave rise to the belief among early Christians that the poem was in some mysterious way a prophetic announcement of the coming of Jesus and of the new world-order he would inaugurate, leading to its description as the 'Messianic Eclogue'. This idea is found already in the church father Lactantius (writing about AD 300) and was developed later by St Augustine, but it received its most influential statement in a speech by the emperor Constantine, who thereby acknowledged the place of classical literature in his new Christian empire and claimed authority for its values in the most distinguished Latin author.[36]

Could Virgil have known Isaiah? It is possible that a *doctus poeta*, a learned Latin poet in the Hellenistic tradition, might have had access to the Septuagint version of the prophetic book, or that in some more general way (as Virgil's Victorian editor T.E. Page put it) 'vague rumours of Messianic hopes may have reached Rome from the East'.[37] On the whole, however, commentators have looked elsewhere for an explanation, observing that a parallel within classical literature can be cited for every significant element in the poem. The mixture is of typically Virgilian complexity. The idea of a succession of ages is from Hesiod (*Works and Days* 109-201), but his picture was one of decline (only the era of heroes, apparently inserted into an older scheme, interrupting the sequence from gold to iron): it is thus a surprise to find in Virgil the unprecedented prediction that a Golden Age traditionally located in the distant past is now to be restored. The poet could however draw on several different schemes involving eras invested with special significance. The theory of a *magnus annus* or 'great cycle' marked the successive occurrences of all heavenly bodies in the same position. A timetable in the Sibylline books (a collection of oracular sayings revered at Rome) had ten *saecula* of 110 years each culminating in a happy one under Apollo, who is referred to in the poem as now ruling (*Ecl.* 4.10). We shall see that the emphasis on Apollo felicitously foreshadows a central theme of Augustan ideology, and more generally it is plausible that Virgil exploits the emotive associations of these several apocalyptic images.

The identity of the child has predictably attracted inconclusive speculation. Pollio helped bring about the treaty of Brundisium between Mark Antony and Octavian, which seemed to promise an end to two decades of civil war. Hence a child of Pollio, a child of Antony and Octavia (this dynastic marriage to the sister of his rival being intended to cement the treaty), and a child of Octavian himself have all been sponsored as candidates. Others have detected in Virgil a prudent avoidance of specific statement, seeing the child rather as a symbolic figure. What can be said with confidence is that Virgil in this poem uses the images both of the Golden Age and of the wondrous birth to create a generalised atmosphere of hope for deliverance. It is in this broad sense both analogous to the vision of a better future once offered by Isaiah to Jerusalem, and also expressive (like the *Eclogues* generally) of the anxieties of late Republican Rome.

The *Aeneid* and the Old Testament

Virgil's epic and the Old Testament share the grand theme of national destiny linked to cosmic purposes. Both describe the formation of a people under the superintending hand of Providence. The theme is so familiar from the Bible that we may fail to appreciate how striking and unusual it is in classical literature. But it is striking too that the story of national origins, although central to the Old Testament, does not have the parallels in the literature of the ancient Near East which can be cited for almost any other biblical genre, perhaps because the cultures that produced it were autochthonous and had no clear sense of a beginning.[38] Virgil's epic and the Old Testament here seem closer in spirit to each other than either does to its nearer neighbours.

The *Aeneid* is framed not only by the action of the reigning Olympians but implicitly by the even larger perspective of clashing gods and Giants. Philip Hardie in *Cosmos and Imperium* shows how the poet draws a far-reaching parallel between the functioning of the Roman empire and the organisation of the universe, in both cases with a sense not only of their current operation but also of the struggles through which this precious and precarious ordering was achieved.[39] Likewise the vast cosmic perspective of heaven and earth in the first eleven chapters of Genesis provides the context for the national and quotidian theme which occupies the rest of the Pentateuch.

The *Aeneid* resembles the stories both of Abraham and of the Exodus. Moshe Weinfeld in *The Promise of the Land* shows the many parallels between Abraham and Aeneas, each story using the powerful theme of a man in the distant past with a glimmering of future glory.[40] Aeneas gains successive clues about his destination and destiny, and similarly the promise to Abraham is gradually fulfilled. From the viewpoint of a later age we look back in each case to an account of ancestors setting out to travel to a land divinely promised. For both of these chosen peoples, wanderings are followed by war, and dangers in a new homeland have to be met and overcome in Canaan and Italy alike. But in both cases the ultimate achievement is of more than national importance. The mission of Aeneas is to found (not in person but proleptically) a city that will rule the world. In Genesis it is already made clear that the seed of Abraham will become a great nation with a universal mission, and by the time we reach Isaiah it can be foretold of the city of Jerusalem (in the words of the Authorised Version which Kipling imagined Shakespeare to have had a hand in framing):[41] 'the Gentiles shall come to thy light, and kings to the brightness of thy rising' (Isa. 60:3).

Abraham (at first called Abram) sets out initially from Ur of the Chaldaeans (Gen. 11:31). Those rulers belong to a later period than his notional date, but the Sumerian city (if correctly identified as the site on the Euphrates excavated by Sir Leonard Woolley in the 1920s) was old and distinguished: like Aeneas, the patriarch leaves a rich and venerable civilisation. Abraham begins the first part of his journey from Ur with his father Terah who dies when they settle temporarily in Haran (Gen. 11:32), as Aeneas takes with him his father Anchises who dies during a sojourn in Sicily (*Aen.* 3.710). Haran will later be enemy territory, and Abraham has to be moved on by divine prompting:

95

Now the Lord said to Abram, 'Go from your country and your kindred and your father's house to the land that I will show you. And I will make of you a great nation, and I will bless you, and make your name great ... and in you all the families of the earth shall be blessed.' So Abram went, as the Lord had told him. (Gen. 12:1-4)

Likewise Aeneas settles temporarily in Carthage which will one day be enemy territory for Rome, and he too has to be reminded of his destiny by the intervention of heaven (*Aen.* 4.265-76).

Josipovici also juxtaposes the two stories, but contrasts Abraham with Aeneas whose 'ultimate success is as it were guaranteed by the poem'.[42] He sees Abraham as going more genuinely into the unknown: the story might drop him, or like other Old Testament characters he might prove less important than he initially seemed. That possibility however could exist only on a first reading and in a cultural vacuum. Genesis may be closer in date to the events it describes than the *Aeneid* is, but it was still written several centuries after them. In both texts it is simultaneously true that we know the successful outcome and that we nonetheless enter imaginatively into the adventures of the hero as if a different and darker plot were possible.

Abraham in the extant text of Genesis (the end product of a long tradition) is often seen as in part a retrojection of David: this provides a further similarity between the biblical author and Virgil, for whom Aeneas is partly a retrojection of Augustus. In each case an ethnic legend has later been developed into an imperial ideology. Ancient traditions relating originally simply to settlement in Canaan were during the period of David applied to the rule of an empire stretching from the Nile to the Euphrates (Gen. 15:18). Similarly traditions about the settlement in Latium (long predating Virgil) were reinterpreted to produce the prediction that the house of Aeneas would rule over all lands (*Aen.* 3.97-8). Both in Aeneas and in Abraham we have the figure of an ancestor who is specifically characterised as father of his people. Virgil refers frequently to his hero as *pater Aeneas* (for example 1.580). Abraham's name means 'exalted father': the familiar expanded form of it ritually given to Abram at the point when he is promised a multitude of descendants (Gen. 17:5) is in fact just a dialect variant, but was traditionally etymologised as 'father of a multitude'. The continuing story of Genesis is all about fathers and sons, and the Bible refers frequently to the God of Abraham, Isaac and Jacob (for example Exod. 3:15). The *Aeneid* is likewise the story of three male generations (Anchises, Aeneas, Ascanius), though here with the main hero in the middle. Aeneas is given the quasi-Homeric formulaic epithet *pius* ('dutiful', for example *Aen.* 1.305), and Abraham was throughout Jewish tradition seen as an exemplar of piety and faith. His story is recalled in the Epistle to the Hebrews:

By faith Abraham obeyed when he was called to go out into a place which he
was to receive as an inheritance; and he went out, not knowing where he was
to go ... For he looked forward to the city which has foundations, whose
builder and maker is God. (Heb. 11:8 and 10)

The object of his journey has become another country: we shall see in the
next section that a spiritual reading of this kind is itself highly Virgilian.
Direct influence of Genesis on the story of Aeneas is unlikely, but it
remains true that the figure of a man called to serve the high purpose of
history at the behest of heaven is without obvious precedent in the
classical tradition.

We have seen that the typological pattern which sees Augustus as a
second Aeneas is parallel to that which sees Jesus as a second Moses. We
have seen too that the stories of the Trojan War and of the Exodus have a
central place in their respective traditions: they raise broadly similar
questions of historicity, and (insofar as they record real events) belong to
roughly the same period, perhaps the thirteenth century BC. The account
of the fall of Troy told from the Trojan side in Virgil is, like the account of
the Exodus, a story of departure: to a glorious future indeed, but in an
atmosphere of anxiety and haste. Both stories focus on the dramatic
events of the last night before leaving (*Aen.* 2.250-795 and Exod. 12:1-42).
The Trojans are losers in the war, and the Hebrews are oppressed slaves:
Aeneas and Moses both have the responsibility of leading a sizeable and
initially discouraged community to a new home. From Exodus 13 onwards
the story not just of that book but of the rest of the Pentateuch is organised
as a great journey, using the evocative theme of a whole community on the
march. Here a different classical parallel suggests itself: Xenophon in the
Anabasis depicts his army of 10,000 Greek mercenary soldiers making
their way home from their ill-fated expedition into Persia as analogous to
a travelling city. More generally Xenophon shares with Virgil a concern
with ideal leadership: his *Cyropaedia*, the semi-fictional biography of
Cyrus the Great, stresses that this model prince rules by clemency, a
virtue claimed also for Augustus.

The message to Moses in the Burning Bush that is not consumed (Exod.
3:1-6) has a parallel in the sign shown to Aeneas by the flames that play
harmlessly around the head of the young Ascanius (*Aen.* 2.681-6). When
the journey is under way and becoming difficult, the followers of Moses
wish they had stayed and died in Egypt (Num. 14:2), as Aeneas wishes he
had stayed and died in Troy (*Aen.* 1.94-101). In both stories the travellers
carry with them important religious items, described in overtly anachronistic terms. The household gods taken from Troy are the Penates
(protectors of the state, as well as the household) familiar from later
Roman religion (*Aen.* 2.293 and 717), and the ark made by the Israelites
in the wilderness and carried with them thereafter is described in terms
which evoke the fittings of the Temple that would later stand in Jerusalem

97

(Exod. 25-7). In both stories these precious things will be established one day in a new home: the wandering communities take a divine presence with them. But in both stories too this is combined with the different idea of following a divine lead: hence the many signs and pieces of oracular advice Aeneas receives, from Hector's ghost (*Aen.* 2.293-5), from Apollo at Delos (3.94-8), from the Penates themselves (3.154-71) and from the prophet Helenus (3.374-462); hence likewise the pillars of fire and cloud in the wilderness (Exod. 13:21-2). In both stories the divine impetus goes on before, and the travellers must discern and pursue it.

Exodus does not glorify Moses, and Virgil presents Aeneas as a flawed and often uncertain hero. The divine promises are only partly fulfilled in the lifetime of Moses, who glimpses but does not enter the Promised Land (Deut. 34:1-5). Aeneas arrives in Italy, yet founds there not Rome but only a city which is the forerunner of a forerunner of Rome. In both stories many things go wrong after the initial arrival. In Homeric terms the wanderings which make up the Odyssean half of the *Aeneid* are followed by the warfare of the Iliadic half. If we apply the Old Testament template, we have seen already that the *Aeneid* has characteristics both of Genesis and of Exodus, with Aeneas comparable to Abraham as well as to Moses. Both of these models however apply mainly to the first half of the *Aeneid*. Virgil's equivalent of Exodus is followed by the part of his story that corresponds to the books of Joshua and Judges. In both narratives the newcomers have to fight or reach an accommodation with the existing inhabitants. Aeneas therefore also takes on a role similar to that of Joshua. Biblical critics have seen in those books an emergence from the heroic past into the cold light of day, with Joshua cast as the first modern man, living at a tragic moment when myth disintegrates.[43] That is an important characteristic also of Aeneas, for Virgil uses the Euripidean technique of putting into a grand mythological setting a man of ordinary vulnerability who seems our contemporary and equal.

Above all the Exodus story gives us once again the theme of the boomerang quest. The Promised Land to which Moses leads the Israelites is the place where Abraham found a home much earlier. Aeneas appears to be travelling into the unknown, but he too is in a sense returning to an older home. Virgil follows an antiquarian tradition that Dardanus, the ancestor of the kings of Troy, came originally from Italy (*Aen.* 3.167), but we shall see in the next section that this idea has further and richer resonances in the *Aeneid*.

Aeneas at the site of Rome

In Book 8 Aeneas arrives at the site where Rome will one day stand. This is the heart of the *Aeneid*, the place where all its themes meet, its most characteristically Virgilian book. A passage of great poetic power (and beautiful Latin) describes the Trojans rowing up the Tiber for the first time (*Aen.* 8.79-101). The pastoral setting contrasts with the busy, noisy, commercialised river familiar to Roman readers.[44] The kindly river god Tiberinus stays his stream to make their task easier: Warde Fowler compared the crossing of the Jordan, stopped from flowing so that it may be crossed by the Israelites (Josh. 3:14-17).[45] We read about both Tiber and Jordan with knowledge of their later associations. One of Virgil's typical techniques is to play tricks with time. The description of the journey up the Tiber moves us because we feel that this is a *nostos*, that Aeneas is coming home. The story about the Italian ancestry of the kings of Troy gives this an element of formal truth (Tiberinus says that Aeneas is 'bringing back' the continuing tradition of Troy: *Aen.* 8.37), but more importantly we have this sense because emotions which belong logically to the reader are projected onto the hero. The Tiber is new to Aeneas, but familiar (if with changed aspect) to Roman readers.

Another strong impetus to read the *Aeneid* as the story of a return to a known place is the fact that it rewrites the *Odyssey*. The feeling of familiarity derives from our knowledge of that text, combined with our awareness of how the Greek tragedians had in various ways developed the idea of an arrival which is also a return: some of those associations foreshadow coming conflict, but Book 8 provides a sunnily Odyssean interlude before the concentratedly Iliadic part of the *Aeneid*. Virgil describes how the Trojans rowed for many hours up the Tiber, then:

> They saw in the distance walls and a citadel and the roofs of scattered houses. What Roman power has now raised to the heights of the heaven was in those days occupied by Evander as his poor domain. (*Aen.* 8.98-100)

The Arcadian Evander has established the small settlement of Pallanteum. Aeneas when he disembarks naturally does not recognise it (he has never seen it before), but the reader does (for this is the site of Rome). Virgil evokes implicitly the scene in the *Odyssey* (13.187-96) where Odysseus fails to identify Ithaca. That association implies that the stranger Aeneas is the rightful possessor of the land to which he comes, which will indeed belong to his Roman descendants. Aeneas is hospitably received by Evander's son Pallas (we may think of Athene welcomed by Telemachus). The Arcadians are in the middle of a religious ritual. This is a good sign, and we recast Aeneas rather than Pallas as Telemachus, arriving in pious and hospitable Pylos (*Od.* 3.3-6): Virgilian typology like its biblical equivalent constantly changes, collapses and multiplies identities.

The assimilation of Aeneas to the young and uncertain Telemachus stresses his vulnerability but also his impressionable quality, his openness to wonder. This is a major theme of Book 8. Already in the voyage up the river a sense of wonder seemed to possess both travellers and landscape.[46] Making the familiar seem unfamiliar by giving us childlike eyes is a characteristic achievement of Virgil (and exemplifies a quality also commended by the gospels). It heightens the sense of dramatic irony. We have the advantage over Aeneas of knowing not merely the rest of his individual story, but the whole sweep of Roman history. Aeneas has brought the Penates with him, but he finds in Italy people who are pious already: what is brought is in a sense already present. The Arcadians are making their yearly sacrifice to Hercules. This is described in terms which evoke the Roman ritual familiar in Virgil's time at the Ara Maxima ('Greatest Altar'): the fullest of the many accounts of religious ceremonies in the epic (*Aen.* 8.102-305).

Aeneas and Evander exchange stories which establish both their shared descent from Atlas, and their common enmity to the Italian tribe of the Rutulians against whom Aeneas pledges alliance. In this very Odyssean book we have the Iliadic theme of comparing genealogies (like Diomedes and Glaucus), ahead of the battles to come. Evander describes meeting Anchises long ago (Aeneas is recognised from his resemblance to his father, like Telemachus in Sparta), invites the Trojans to join in the ritual, and tells the story of its origin. He offers a Callimachean *aition*: nominally he describes the relatively recent past, something that happened in his own time, but a Roman reader could supply his own longer perspective for the cult (though in reality it still post-dated the dramatic date of the poem). When returning from one of his Labours, Hercules (long established in tradition as a Stoic hero and a benefactor of humanity, as well as a superman figure[47]) passed through the area and delivered it from the ravages of the local monster Cacus (we may compare Theseus in *Hecale*). Hercules came once as a deliverer: time brought in response to their prayers *auxilium adventumque dei* ('the help and arrival of a god': 8.201). The evocative phrase emphasises that this story of a saviour hero long awaited is told to someone who in the guise of a hesitant stranger is himself such a deliverer. As the ritual is re-enacted, its hero in effect stands among us, like a conjured spirit: time is dissolved, and the anticipated deliverer already here unrecognised. That theme is of course Odyssean, and Aeneas has indeed in a sense come home. Evander tells him a story which is metaphorically about himself, and so we think of another Homeric scene: Aeneas is like Odysseus among the Phaeacians, hearing the songs of Demodocus (an even closer echo of that passage came when Aeneas wept at seeing scenes from the sack of Troy depicted on the doors of a newly-built temple in Dido's Carthage: 1.453-93). We are also implicitly invited to project the pattern of deliverance forward, to a time when Augustus in turn will come in another time of need, though Virgil never allows us to forget that real life (both for Aeneas in his coming wars in Italy, and for his own contemporaries) is more complex and morally demanding than a pious story.

After the ceremony, Aeneas walks with Evander and Pallas from the grove where it has taken place into the small city. Aeneas asks about monuments they see, and Evander begins by describing earlier inhabitants of the site. But imperceptibly Virgil takes over as guide, and the landmarks become those not of an era before Evander but of a period which is an unknown future to the characters but a familiar present to the Roman reader:

> From here he led the way to the house of Tarpeia and the Capitol, golden now, but in other days bristling with woodland thickets. Even then an awesome sense of a divine presence in the place caused fear among the country people, even then they trembled at the wood and the rock ... Talking in this way they were coming to the humble home of Evander, and they saw cattle everywhere, lowing in the Roman Forum and the now smart district of the Carinae. (*Aen.* 8.347-50 and 359-61)

Major themes come together here. The first sentence of this passage encapsulates Book 8. Virgil here draws on an old and important Roman religious idea in emphasising that the numinous presence of an unknown god marked out the site from earliest times: appropriately so, the reader is invited to reflect, for this is the site of the temple of Jupiter Optimus Maximus, 'the sacred heart of the world's central city'.[48] Evander invites Aeneas into his house by pointing out that Hercules did not despise it: Aeneas should mould himself worthy of godhead (364-5: the phrase implies assimilating himself to Hercules, with surely a sideways glance at Augustus). Receiving humble hospitality, Aeneas here joins the many heroes of theoxeny stories, but above all he resembles Odysseus in the hut of Eumaeus: the scene thus builds on the earlier equation between the arrival of Aeneas in Italy and the arrival of Odysseus in Ithaca. We remember too that Augustus lived on the Palatine in modest austerity and conspicuous reserve.

The lowing cattle are of a piece with the pastoral Tiber flowing between fields and woods. Does Virgil hint that cows may at some distant time graze in the Forum once again? The word *olim* ('in other days') can be used of the future as well as its more common reference to the past. The works of Piranesi and other artists remind us that by the eighteenth century this had indeed come about, and it was with tacit allusion to Virgil that Gibbon wrote the most famous passage of his *Autobiography*:

> It was at Rome, on the 15th of October, 1764, as I sat musing amidst the ruins of the Capitol, while the barefooted friars were singing vespers in the Temple of Jupiter, that the idea of writing the decline and fall of the city first started to my mind.[49]

The idea of reversal, the Herodotean theme of great cities becoming small and small ones great (Hdt. 1.5), had been used many times both ways round. The implication that even Rome will not last for ever would be entirely in the spirit of Virgil: again we note that the sombre side of the *Aeneid* is not subversive cynicism, but a 'noble and resigned melancholy'.[50]

In the final part of Book 8 new armour is made for Aeneas by Vulcan at the request of his mother Venus. The Cyclopes in their forge are usually occupied in making thunderbolts for Jupiter: now they are to put that work aside and engage in the more urgent task of making arms for a man (8.424-43). We think back to the opening phrase of the epic, *arma virumque* ('arms and the man'), representing its conjoined Iliadic and Odyssean themes, but also to the Homeric recognition scene between Telemachus and Odysseus (not a god but, more remarkably, the man who is his father). The shield depicts scenes from Roman history (once again history is presented as prophecy), in particular examples of deliverance from danger, the recurrent theme of Book 8: Horatius Cocles holding the Etruscans at bay, the Capitol saved from the invading Gauls by its resident geese raising the alarm, and as a climactic centrepiece the victory at Actium (8.626-728).

The account of this battle provides an illustration of how uncannily well the material he drew from diverse sources answered Virgil's purposes. Apollo was established in Homer as a prominent divine supporter of the Trojans, a tradition which Virgil naturally follows. By fortunate coincidence a famous temple of Apollo overlooked Actium. Suetonius (*Augustus* 18) records how Octavian commemorated his victory by restoring it, and by founding nearby the city of Nicopolis and its quinquennial games. Apollo in his Actian guise was thenceforth his patron. But already before this, Octavian had begun to develop the cult of Palatine Apollo as a parallel to Capitoline Jupiter, as part of his reinterpretation of the old messages of Roman religious and civic ritual. Apollo, who as a Greek healing god had once been worshipped only outside the *pomerium* (the sacred boundary of central Rome), was elevated to a central role as the emperor's own role-model and neighbour (the god's new temple on the Palatine was next to his house, with the preserved hut of Romulus on the other side).[51] Apollo became a symbol of the new age, the iconography of his portrayal frequently converging with that of its ruler. Augustus refashioned traditional religious and other institutions as Virgil refashioned traditional epic, and visual art (above all the great sculptures of the Ara Pacis of 13-9 BC) later followed the poet's lead in suggesting an analogy between the running of the Roman empire and the divine governance of the universe. Apollo had the advantage of being not only both Greek and Roman, but both a martial god and a patron of the arts: we may think back to a climactic moment of the *Odyssey* (21.404-11), where Apollo was the patron simultaneously of bow and lyre, of hero and bard. It is also very noticeable that the typology of Book 8 makes repeated play with proper names beginning with 'A'. The very drawback that the name 'Hercules' could not be accommodated in dactylic hexameter verse is turned to advantage: he is *Amphitryoniades* ('son of Amphitryon') or *Alcides* ('grandson of Alceus'), thus joining Aeneas, Anchises, Ascanius, Atlas, Apollo, Augustus (and perhaps an implicitly compared Alexander) in this story whose hinge is Actium. Might this

102

somehow suggest recruitment to a shared purpose, and symbolise a new beginning?

In the scenes on the shield (a visual miniature version of the *Aeneid* itself) the whole of Roman history down to the poet's own day is in effect already present: we might compare how the Archangel Michael in the final book of *Paradise Lost* (12.13-551) tells Adam what lies ahead, all the way to the Crucifixion. Yet to Aeneas himself the pictures are wonderful but unrecognised, and Virgil movingly describes how he lifts uncomprehendingly onto his shoulders the 'fame and fate' of his descendants (8.730-1). He is here momentarily like his ancestor Atlas, depicted in Hellenistic and Roman art as supporting not the sky but the globe, and thus also like Augustus sustaining the burden of world empire. The loneliness of their several tasks, and the dramatic irony made possible by the contrast between the ignorance of Aeneas and the reader's fuller knowledge, make him here also like a Sophoclean hero.

We have seen that the subject of the *Aeneid* reflects its own character. Book 8 describes small-scale beginnings in which the rise to glorious future achievement is somehow already implicit. This theme has an analogy in the poet's own career. Renaissance critics saw in the works of Virgil a triumphant ascent though a hierarchy of genres, conceived like architectural orders. Teleological narratives are less favoured now, and critics rightly insist that we should interpret his earlier works primarily on their own terms. But the inevitability of our reading any text in the light of what we know came later applies to the works of an individual poet as well as to literary history on a larger scale. Virgil's career does have a compelling pattern, looking to models of increasing scale, antiquity and prestige (and ostensibly contrasted, though all using epic hexameters): the Alexandrian pastoral of Theocritus, the didactic poems of Hesiod seen through Hellenistic intermediaries, and ultimately Homer. Some texts of the *Aeneid* are prefaced by an additional four lines: *ille ego qui quondam* ('I am he who once ...'), introducing allusive summaries of his earlier works. It is highly unlikely that these lines are original: they were perhaps provided for a luxury edition in later antiquity, to sit beneath a portrait of the poet as a frontispiece.[52] And yet in a curious way they are highly Virgilian in sentiment: his creative life has brought him on this apparently winding yet foreordained journey, analogous to the sense given by the *Aeneid* itself (the ultimate teleological narrative) of the course of Roman history from pastoral village to world empire.

When we read the *Eclogues* and *Georgics* we have an inescapable sense of the *Aeneid* somehow already there, like the religious presence which already marks the site of Rome when Aeneas arrives. The first *Eclogue* immediately gives us the godlike benefactor: *deus nobis haec otia fecit* ('it was a god who gave us this peace': *Ecl.* 1.6). Pastoral tradition and contemporary political reality are already blended, in a spiritual landscape seen characteristically in evening light (1.83-4, 6.85-6, 10.77). It is no longer fashionable to comb the poems for biographical information, for instance in confirmation of the ancient tradition about the confiscation and restoration of the poet's family property, but the theme of longing for a settled dwelling-place combined with questions about its possibility or permanence is already marked in the *Eclogues*, runs through the later works, and (like much in Virgil) seems constantly to point beyond its immediate context. The Victorian critic F.W.H. Myers detected in Virgil an 'obscure homesickness',[53] and the language of impossibility is marked throughout (witness those distinctive adjectives anglicised as irrevocable, irremediable, irreparable): the opening description of Aeneas as 'fated to be an exile' (*Aen.* 1.2) seems somehow to apply also to the poet. The souls in the Underworld in *Aeneid* 6 waiting to be ferried across the Styx are moved by 'longing for the farther shore' (6.314): that yearning has seemed to many readers a recurrent and characteristic note in Virgil, instinct with larger meaning. The fourth *Eclogue* is not the only reason for the traditional idea of the poet as somehow anticipating Christianity. In reading him we seem often close to the feeling of 'here have we no continuing city' (Heb. 13:14).

The four books of the *Georgics* offer instruction ostensibly in how to run a farm but really in how to conduct individual life and society. The poem is marked by a profound spiritual sympathy for all living things, and it presents man and the natural world as mysteriously joined. It is in part a challenge to the Epicurean materialism of Lucretius in *De rerum natura*, the remarkable didactic poem of the previous generation which had asserted that the gods did not intervene in the world. Virgil need not be envisaged as a doctrinaire adherent of Stoicism (the rival school, more attuned to traditional Roman attitudes), but we have noted that Hercules was established as a Stoic hero, and Aeneas resembles him in important respects. Consistently with Stoic views, Virgil reasserts divine providence: Lucretius had appropriated fervent religious language for an anti-religious purpose, and Virgil in turn reclaims it.[54] His stance is in broad terms comparable to that of Plato in relation to sophistic relativism, or the Romantics to eighteenth-century rationalism, and his rediscovery of religious tradition again unites him with Augustus. In a famous passage he pays tribute to Lucretius, but also implicitly defends his own enterprise and outlook:

> Happy is the man who could find out the causes of things ... But happy too is he who has got to know the countryside gods. (*Geo.* 2.490 and 493)

The great peroration of the first *Georgic* protests at the unhappy state of Italian farmland because of the ruinous civil wars following the death of Julius Caesar (1.493-514). Its spirit is that of Henry Scott Holland's hymn: 'and the homesteads and the woodlands plead in silence for their peace'.[55] Virgil envisages a farmer in days to come striking rusty javelins with his plough, or empty helmets with his harrow: the unearthed bones of civil war soldiers will look to him like those of giants. Here again is the complex layering of time. Virgil draws on Herodotean stories about people digging up bones from the heroic past (Hdt. 1.68), but it is the guilty and inglorious record of the poet's own day that will constitute the past for this farmer. His incomprehension about battles long ago (though a matter of recent experience for the reader) is a mirror image of the incomprehension of Aeneas contemplating on the shield battles of an unknown future (though part of a familiar past to the reader). The gleaming weapons that will one day be rusting in the ground are the obverse of the golden buildings that may one day again give place to a field of cattle. Aeneas encouraging his comrades in a storm at sea says *forsan et haec olim meminisse iuvabit* ('perhaps one day it will be a pleasure to remember even these things': *Aen.* 1.203). At one level that refers to our reading about them in the *Aeneid*. But it also makes the same point about time and mutability. Both present woes and present pride will be put in perspective by a longer view.

The scene where Aeneas is received by Evander and takes part in a religious ceremony at the site of the future city of Rome has several Old Testament parallels. Abraham on his return journey after rescuing his nephew Lot from the four kings who had taken him prisoner is hospitably received by Melchizedek king of Salem. This mysterious figure brings out bread and wine, and gives his guest a blessing (Gen. 14:17-20). Salem is usually identified as the later Jerusalem: Melchizedek, who like Abraham himself came to be seen as an exemplar of hospitality,[56] thus offered these proleptically rich symbols in a still insignificant settlement that would one day be David's capital city. Melchizedek exercises a sacral kingship and in later tradition is the archetype of a priest (Ps. 110:4, Heb. 5:6), yet his story is set in a period when no priesthood yet existed: as in Virgil, religious anachronism creates a powerful effect. Likewise the place where Jacob had his dream of the ladder to heaven (Gen. 28:10-19) came to be identified as Mount Moriah, the site once of the attempted sacrifice of Isaac (Gen. 22:2), and that in turn was believed to be the rock where later the Temple was built (2 Chron. 3:1). The phrase 'house of God' first occurred in Jacob's tribute to this place, and it seemed to early commentators natural to conclude that like the earliest settlers at the site of Rome he had perceived in it an intrinsically numinous quality.

The paradox of a journey to a new place which has the feeling of a familiar home is important in the story of Ruth. Her mother-in-law Naomi came originally from Bethlehem, but during a famine moved into the land of Moab with her husband and sons, both of whom married Moabite girls. When all three males die, Naomi resolves to return to Bethlehem, urging her widowed daughters-in-law to stay with their people. It is at this point that Ruth famously and touchingly cleaves to Naomi: 'your people shall be my people, and your God my God' (Ruth 1:16). After the two women return destitute, Ruth meets the kindly and prosperous farmer Boaz. He praises her for her care of Naomi, and her courage in leaving her birthplace for an unknown land (2:11). Robert Alter points out the unmistakable echo of God's instruction to Abraham (Gen. 12:1).[57] Ruth like Abraham travels westward from a foreign country to settle in the Promised Land. She has never seen it before, yet because it is her choice, and is already established in the story as the homeland familiar to the reader, she seems paradoxically to be returning there. Ruth is equated to Abraham because he is the founding father and she a founding mother: she marries Boaz, and becomes the great-grandmother of David, Israel's greatest king, and thus also an ancestor of Jesus. Like the *Aeneid*, this is a story of significant forebears.

In parts of the Old Testament dating from after the Babylonian Exile, Jerusalem is frequently envisaged as the centre of the world,[58] a role similar to that of Rome in Virgil and in Augustan ideology. The centre of the earthly realm is made also the centre of the universe: Jerusalem becomes a heavenly city, and we have seen that the governance of Rome is made to seem analogous to the ordering of the cosmos. Conversely transience can be stressed: the theme of the rise and fall of cities pervades the Old Testament, as it also shapes the *Aeneid*. The prophecy of Micah that 'Zion will one day be ploughed; Jerusalem shall become a heap of ruins' (Mic. 3:12) puts more directly what Virgil perhaps gently hints may be the ultimate fate of Rome. The theme of a long-awaited deliverer, which in classical literary tradition implicitly equates Aeneas to Odysseus and Orestes and Hercules, has a compelling similarity to the Messianic expectation which runs through much of the Old Testament and on into the New. We have seen that human and divine saviour figures are part of the cultural vocabulary of the turn of the era. But it is not in the end any single theme nor any use of a common idiom that constitutes the most haunting similarity between the *Aeneid* and the Bible, but the less tangible evocation of a distinctive feeling. C.S. Lewis characteristically captures it very well, in the Platonist and Johannine language of pre-existence: it was the achievement of Virgil, he writes, 'to take one single national legend and treat it in such a way that we feel the vaster theme to be somehow implicit in it ... we are never allowed to forget that Latium has been waiting for the Trojans from the beginning of the world ... we realise that we have just turned some great corner.'[59]

Ovid: *Baucis and Philemon*

Ovid comes after Virgil, but critics no longer see the influence as oppressive. Debate about whether the *Metamorphoses* should be regarded as an epic illustrates the complex ambiguity of the poem.[60] It lacks a single hero (indeed it sets out to overwhelm us with a welter of characters and stories) and its authorial voice is frequently mischievous, but it has a subject of undeniable grandeur. It is a universal history, from creation to the poet's own time, though it is history of a paradoxical kind, and the period from Aeneas to Julius Caesar is dealt with very quickly. The theme of transformation is a loose connecting thread enabling most of Romanised Greek myth to be incorporated. Many of the familiar stories have their decisive telling here, and the influence of the *Metamorphoses* on later European literature and art is very considerable. With its accounts of creation (vying with Plato's *Timaeus* as an equivalent to Genesis) and flood (considered below) it was for centuries seen as a pagan counterpart to the Bible.[61] This book full of stories provided Rubens and others with the subjects for mythological paintings which are also Christian allegories. An anonymous medieval author produced *Ovide Moralisé*, but arguably the poem did not need that treatment. For it resembles the plays of Oscar Wilde: the epigrams may be cynical, but the stories (even where they disturb a modern reader) typically have the morality of poetic justice.

The tone seems light, but Pythagoras in the final book describes metamorphosis as an all-pervading feature of the universe (*Meta.* 15.75-478), and critics have persistently sought a serious and historically specific dimension to the theme of transformation. Could the emphasis on change somehow reflect the transition of Rome from Republic to Principate? Andrew Wallace-Hadrill persuasively suggests that the transformational skill with which Augustus constructed his new order out of elements of the old is 'conceptually parallel' to the way in which Ovid characteristically describes a physical metamorphosis as a gradual, organic process, aptly using individual elements of the old body to create the new one.[62] The city of Rome itself had within Ovid's lifetime undergone a metamorphosis from its old ramshackle form to the gleaming marble and grand public spaces of a self-conscious imperial capital. Even more tantalisingly, the writing of the poem spanned what is by later calculation the change from BC to AD. Hermann Fränkel in *Ovid: A Poet Between Two Worlds* sought to link metamorphosis and the New Testament theme of *metanoia* ('repentance').[63] The idea of a fundamental change in personality is alien to the usual ancient theory of human character, so that apparent change has to be explained as the stripping away of a deceptive veneer: thus (to take a familiar example) Tacitus on the deteriorating character of the emperor Tiberius (*Annals* 6.51). The New Testament challenges that idea, but it is less clear that Ovid does: his people undergo dramatic physical transformation indeed, but the element of fit apportioning in many stories (the hard-hearted turned to stone) means that the characteristic in question is often not changed but advertised and intensified by being given physical form.

Preoccupation with metamorphosis at the turn of the era is uncanny but imponderable. More rewarding perhaps is the search for a self-referential significance: the themes of elegiac love poetry are turned into hexameter epic (notably in the programmatic story of Apollo and Daphne), and epic into something unlike any of its former selves. Ovid's poem indeed changes our perception of the *Aeneid* (again a later text affects the reading of an earlier one) by alerting us to the theme of metamorphosis within it, for example when Turnus tries to set fire to the Trojan ships and Neptune turns them into nymphs (*Aen.* 9.77-122). Stephen Hinds observes in *Allusion and Intertext* that we begin to see not Ovid as a derivative reader of Virgil, but Virgil as in some respects a hesitant precursor of Ovid.[64] We are prompted to look in the *Aeneid* too for the theme of change at a deeper level, for example in the way the defeated Trojans are turned into triumphant Romans.

Ovid's famous story of Baucis and Philemon comes almost at the centre of the vast poem, in the eighth of its fifteen books. It is told at leisurely length, and (though it does not lack humour) seems more earnest in tone than much of the rest. It is a story of rustic hospitality and the recognition of divine visitors. It echoes several passages in the *Odyssey* (most obviously the scenes with Eumaeus), and has clear resemblances to the *Homeric Hymn to Demeter*. In particular it has much in common with *Hecale* and the other Hellenistic theoxeny stories we have considered, though it is less self-conscious and angular than they are, and more genial, indeed almost sentimental in its celebration of conjugal fidelity in old age. Unlike most episodes in the *Metamorphoses* it has decent and psychologically normal people as its protagonists.[65] Like practically everything in the poem it refers implicitly to the *Aeneid*, especially to the scene where Aeneas is entertained by Evander. Although the general theme was popular, the story itself is not found before Ovid. Like many others in the poem, it is told within another story. Theseus and his companions on their return journey from the Calydonian boar-hunt are being entertained by the river god Achelous until his own waters subside (*Meta.* 8.547-623): Alessandro Barchiesi in *Speaking Volumes* points to the neatly Ovidian touch whereby a story about the entertainment of divine visitors by mortals is framed by one in which mortals are hosted by a god.[66] Achelous tells his guests that some neighbouring islands were formerly nymphs. Peirithous is blasphemously scornful of the possibility of metamorphosis, in effect challenging the poem itself, and taking us back to its opening announcement of its own subject.[67] In response the hero Lelex (another companion, described as ripe in years and wisdom) seeks to reaffirm the power of the gods, and to persuade the sceptic that he is mistaken, by telling the story behind two trees in a sacred enclosure in the Phrygian hills.

Jupiter and Mercury once came to this place, disguised in mortal form and seeking hospitality. A thousand homes were approached in vain, but the aged Baucis and her husband Philemon received them in the humble cottage where they had lived for the whole of their married life. Many of the details are familiar from earlier literature: the gods stoop to enter the low door, a comfortable seat is improvised, the fire is rekindled, preparations for a meal are put in train, and feet are washed (8.624-55): the flurry of activity is reminiscent of Abraham and Sarah at Mamre, and the establishment evidently a survival from the Golden Age. The gods recline at table. Several courses of simple but appetising food are described (the menu Italian rather than Phrygian, and recognisably indebted to idealised descriptions of country life in Virgil and Horace). Humour is provided by the wobbly table, and the vain attempts of the old couple to catch and kill their goose, the sole guardian of their house which they are nonetheless prepared to sacrifice: we think of Virgil's account of the geese who guarded the Capitol, and thus also of his juxtaposition of humility and grandeur. Meanwhile the old couple notice that the wine-bowl is miraculously replenished. Declining the offered sacrifice, the visitors confirm that they are gods: the neighbourhood will be punished for its impiety, but their hosts are to survive. As Baucis and Philemon follow their divine visitors into the mountains, they turn to see their cottage transformed into a temple (like *Aeneid* 8 fast-forwarded) whilst the surrounding area is flooded. Granted a wish, they choose to be guardians of the new shrine before simultaneous death. This is replaced by metamorphosis respectively into a linden tree and an oak (8.656-724). The story therefore ends in Callimachean style with the *aition* of a cult: although the specific location cannot be determined, a rural shrine surrounded by trees is a type familiar both to literature and to archaeology.[68]

Ovid's story has a remarkable New Testament parallel. In Acts 14, Paul and Barnabas come to the Lycaonian city of Lystra. When Paul heals a cripple, the crowd hail the two missionaries as gods: Barnabas as Zeus, and the more loquacious Paul as Hermes. Their delay in realising what is happening (because the people speak a local language) enables the priest of Zeus to fetch garlanded oxen, which he has to be restrained from sacrificing to them (Acts 14:8-13). The joint worship of Zeus and Hermes is attested in the area,[69] and their appearance in human form does not seem to cause surprise. It seems likely that this passage draws upon the same body of tradition that has produced the story of Baucis and Philemon: Ovid appears indeed to be thinking of northern or Hellespontine Phrygia (*Meta.* 8.719) rather than the area close to Lystra, but his geographical definition should not be pressed: we are in broadly the same part of the world, and it is plausible to assume that in Acts a local legend has been presented anew in Christian dress.[70] The passage also provides a rare example of Luke making a direct comparison between the preached gospel and the pagan religion it seeks to supplant. Paul is traditionally known as the Apostle to the Gentiles, yet only here and in Athens does he directly address a gentile audience. Indeed his brief impromptu homily to the people of Lystra is a skeletal version of the more ambitious sermon he will deliver on the Areopagus (as we shall see in Chapter 4). Paul assures his hearers:

We also are men, of like nature with you, and bring you good news, that you should turn from these vain things to a living God who made the heaven and the earth and all that is in them. In past generations he allowed all nations to walk in their own ways; yet he did not leave himself without witness, for he did good and gave you from heaven rains and fruitful seasons, satisfying your hearts with food and gladness. (Acts 14:15-17)

As in Athens, the impact of Paul's message is not obvious or immediate: the people are aggrieved at the aborted sacrifice (and the opportunity for feasting thereby lost), and he is driven from the city. The first readers of Acts however already had the benefit of hindsight: the text describes only painful inches gained, but greater success lay ahead. As the *Aeneid* elevated the Callimachean theme of aetiological explanation into an account of the rise of Rome to world empire, so this story in Acts ambitiously replaces the traditional theme of the founding of a new local shrine with the revelation of a new religion.

Ovid's story suggests many other biblical parallels. The hero of Eliza Lynn Linton's novel *The Autobiography of Christopher Kirkland* (1885) considered its simplicity and realism 'almost Scriptural', but sensed a challenge to his faith if he should 'bracket it with the visit of those three divine beings to Abraham and Sarah'.[71] The contrast between the many bolted houses and the humbly hospitable one has elements of 'no room for them in the inn' (Luke 2:7) set against 'as many as did receive him' (John 1:12). Ovid's account of generous though impoverished rural hospitality has several similarities to the story of Elijah at Zarephath: in particular, the miraculous replenishment of the wine is reminiscent of the widow's cruse of oil (1 Kgs 17:16). The moment of recognition which the miracle precipitates is analogous to the opened eyes of Cleopas and his companion at Emmaus (Luke 24:31). The flood story has obvious parallels with the account of Noah (Gen. 6-9), as well as with Deucalion in Greek myth. In 1872 George Smith while working in the British Museum on cuneiform tablets excavated twenty years earlier from the royal libraries at Nineveh famously discovered another flood story.[72] Thus began reconstruction of the Gilgamesh epic, quasi-Iliadic in its portrayal of warrior comradeship and the acceptance of mortality, and quasi-biblical in its description of the gigantic boat of Utnapishtim.[73] J.G. Frazer in *Folklore in the Old Testament* took such accounts of a great deluge as a classic illustration of the various ways in which similar stories might be explained, by diffusion from a common original or by coincidental independent occurrence, and of how it is usually impossible to decide.[74] A complicating factor may be that an originally separate local story tends to become assimilated to a more famous one. Something like that may have happened with the material used by Ovid here: a tradition of flood stories seems to have grown up around the rivers and lakes close to the Phrygian city of Apamea, causing the Jewish community there to identify a local hill as Mount Ararat where the ark had come to rest.[75]

110

The idea of a flood as a punishment for human wickedness is found already in Homer, in a simile in the *Iliad* (16.384-92). The theme of a few favoured survivors of a catastrophe serves already in Genesis to link the stories of Noah and of Lot, and the Flood story may have influenced the account of the destruction of Sodom (where Lot's wife suffers the only physical metamorphosis in the Old Testament). It seems likely that readers were expected to observe the parallel: the story about the perversion of hospitality in Genesis 19 echoes the earlier one about the punishment of human wickedness in Genesis 6. The story of Baucis and Philemon in the middle of Ovid's poem similarly suggests a link with the account of Lycaon (the first and programmatic human transformation) at its beginning. Ovid is there giving his version of the Hesiodic myth of the succession of ages. In the degenerate iron age, guest was not safe from host. Jupiter tells the other gods how, anxious to disprove rumours of human wickedness, he came down from Olympus and travelled through the world in disguise. One evening he came to the home of the Arcadian king Lycaon. Local people responded to a hint of his true nature and began to worship him. But his host decided (like Tantalus) to put the god to the test by feeding him human flesh (as in many stories, the ultimate perversion of hospitality). Jupiter however was not deceived: Lycaon was turned into a wolf, and his crime precipitated the destruction of mankind in the more famous flood which provides the context for the story of Deucalion which follows (*Meta.* 1.260-415).

In reporting that the story of Baucis and Philemon moved its audience (the heroes entertained by Achelous in the framing narrative), Ovid adds 'Theseus especially' (8.726). E.J. Kenney pointed out that he thus makes a slyly metaliterary point, nudging the reader to recognise the allusion to *Hecale.*[76] The hero 'remembers' his own role in an earlier text, affected by the story Lelex tells as he was once moved by the kindness of the aged widow. Simultaneously (by that merging of the experience of character and reader which goes back to Odysseus in Scherie) we recognise also the Ovidian transformation of Callimachus. Achelous reinforces the message of Lelex with another Callimachean story: paradoxically so, for a great river in spate was the figure Callimachus had in a famous passage (*Hymn to Apollo* 108-9) used to represent the grand style he eschewed.[77] The story of Erysichthon, condemned to perpetual hunger for impiously cutting down a grove sacred to Demeter, had been told in an almost comic way by Callimachus (*Hymn to Demeter* 31-117), but is here made more sinister in grand epic style (though Ovidian wit still peeps through).[78] It forms a pair with Baucis and Philemon: the two stories with their frame are the centrepiece of the poem. They express its generic complexity, but also form a coherent block of material in which a story of exemplary hospitality to divine visitors is followed and reinforced by an account of divine punishment: this sequence strangely mirrors the transition in Genesis from Mamre to Sodom.

Rembrandt in 1658 depicted Baucis and Philemon in a style different from most of his pictures with classical themes, but like his religious ones. Here he portrays the characters in the peasant clothes of his own day, and the story is implicitly assimilated (as it also is by other artists) to the supper at Emmaus (Luke 24:13-35). The head of Mercury silhouetted against the light echoes the portrayal of Christ in the artist's *Pilgrims at Emmaus* painted thirty years earlier, but that picture in turn is demonstrably influenced by Adam Elsheimer's *Philemon and Baucis* of 1609, which has Jupiter in a similar (though reversed) pose. Malcolm Bull in *The Mirror of the Gods* shows how the hospitality of Baucis and Philemon provides one of the best examples in the history of art of borrowings back and forth between a classical story and its biblical parallels (Abraham entertaining the heavenly visitors, as well as the scene at Emmaus).[79] This association of ideas in art has echoes in literature. It is well known that Charles Wesley's hymn 'Love Divine, all loves excelling' rewrites Dryden's lyric 'Fairest Isle, all isles excelling', but it has been suggested that it also uses components from Ovid's story of rustic hospitality, piety and metamorphosis: 'To earth come down ... Fix in us thy humble dwelling ... Never more thy temples leave ... Changed from glory into glory ...'.[80] The nineteenth-century American writer Nathaniel Hawthorne in his *Wonder Book* of moral tales for children made the old couple into teetotal New England smallholders: their pitcher replenishes itself with milk, and they serve the gods honey for tea.[81] This transference replicates Ovid's own technique, for the old couple in his story from a distant land are recognisably drawn from the hardy and wholesome stock with which Augustan Rome populated its own idealised past. How a tale from the Phrygian hills reached Ovid cannot be known, but a Roman army was fighting in the region of Lystra about 4 BC: an ingenious theory has the poet hear the tale of Baucis and Philemon from a member of this expedition under P. Sulpicius Quirinius,[82] who as governor of Syria oversaw the census[83] which brought Mary and Joseph to Bethlehem (Luke 2:2).

4

Foolishness to Greeks

A change of key now, as we look at some of the same themes from the biblical side. Resemblance by analogy (such as the secrecy about the identity of the hero in Mark and the *Odyssey* which we saw in Chapter 1) exists alongside resemblance suggesting direct debt or shared background (for example the use of speeches to mark important events in Acts and Thucydides).

The character of the gospels

The New Testament is not traditionally regarded as part of Greek litera-ture, but it is illuminating to read the gospels, Acts, epistles and Revela-tion as if they were classical texts, in conscious resistance to the anaesthetic of familiarity. There are good reasons for removing the im-plicit barrier: the Greek literary canon has become more inclusive, and there is growing interest in the Roman empire seen from new and poten-tially subversive angles. Richard Burridge in *What are the Gospels?* shows how comparison with classical literature can help to answer the question his title poses.[1] He settles an old debate by demonstrating that the gospels fall comfortably within the parameters of Graeco-Roman biographical writing: they form part of a tradition which we can trace back to Plato and Xenophon on Socrates, or Xenophon again on the Spartan king Agesilaus. In the decades just after the gospels were composed Suetonius in his *Lives of the Caesars* wrote biographies which like them sit loose to chronological order, whilst some of Plutarch's *Parallel Lives* (for example the accounts of Eumenes and the Younger Cato) focus on the death of their subject and thus have the shape of a passion narrative with extended introduction.[2] The gospels more specifically resemble philosophical biography: the story of a teacher, with a collection of illustrative incidents and memorable examples for disciples to follow. Yet they are also a revolutionary develop-ment within ancient literature. They represent a mixture of genres: as Auerbach showed in the second chapter of *Mimesis* (less familiar than the one on Homer and Genesis), they innovate by their focus on people of humble background, who previously could be found only in comedy or as a foil to the noble characters in grand literature.[3] George Eliot and Arthur Miller, for example, echo the gospels by showing ordinary people capable of tragic sublimity.

The idea of a canon in classical or modern literature derives from the history of the Bible. It is now typically challenged: late and formerly neglected genres such as the Greek novel are given new attention by classicists, and in English literature the voices of previously marginalised groups are properly heard. For the Bible itself, the canon is a theological entity buttressed by institutional tradition as well as a literary one, though even here apocryphal and Gnostic texts are viewed by many with increasing respect. On the other hand the concept of canonicity can show its strength in new ways. 'Canon criticism' of the Old Testament claims (for example) that the pessimism of Job must be read in a wider setting, as one strand within Wisdom literature: this is a version of the idea that we necessarily read with awareness of other texts (and in the case of Job with awareness too of the sheer variety of earlier interpretations). Previously neglected authors of the Hellenistic period and of later antiquity are studied with new seriousness, but because they write in self-conscious relation to a classical past (and therefore naturally invite intertextual analysis) the overall effect may paradoxically be to strengthen our sense of the very canon whose boundaries were extended to admit them.

The inclusion in the New Testament of four separate versions of the gospel story is so centrally familiar that we may miss its oddity. Does classical literature offer any parallel? We have many examples of different texts handling the same material, and there would be more if more literature survived. Thucydides died with a great historical work unfinished: Xenophon's *Hellenica* is the successful survivor from several attempts to complete the story of the Peloponnesian War and to continue the narrative into the fourth century. Plato and Xenophon are the successful survivors from a host of writers on the life and teaching of Socrates, all aiming to establish one reading of his life as authoritative: there is a parallel here with Luke who in his prologue contrasts the 'many who have undertaken to compile a narrative' with his own 'orderly account', implied to be superior (Luke 1:1-4).

Greek tragedy provides a closer analogy. We have three versions of the Electra story, and we know of many similar examples among lost plays. This is a natural consequence of the convention dictating a mythological subject, and of concentration on stories with dramatic potential. But here too there was an agonistic element: a play not only competed for the prize in its own festival, but might implicitly challenge the treatment by a rival playwright in a previous year. The Electra plays of Sophocles and Euripides seem to have appeared in quick succession, probably stimulated by a revival of the *Oresteia*, though we do not know the order, and it is debatable which counts as the more radical reinterpretation. Here again is a broad parallel with the gospels: Mark almost certainly came first and inspired at least two of the others (Matthew and Luke), but beyond that there is much disagreement about their inter-relation (though all four are now normally assigned to the last third of the first century). Ancient literary scholars commonly practised *sunkrisis*, the comparative assessment of texts: the orator Dio Chrysostom in an essay of about AD 100 describes how during a period of convalescence he set out to assess, as if awarding a prize, the treatment of the Philoctetes story by the three tragedians (only the Sophoclean version survives).[4] Early Christian readers likewise set the four gospels alongside each other, but the aim here was typically to produce a composite version: the second-century text *Diatessaron* ('one through four') by the Syrian writer Tatian is a surviving attempt to retell the separate stories of Jesus as one continuous narrative.

None of these classical examples however quite corresponds to the deliberate inclusion of alternative versions in a planned canon. The Old Testament does this: Chronicles presents again much of the material from Samuel and Kings. But perhaps more illuminating is the existence of alternative versions of a story within a single text, such as the two accounts of Creation (Gen. 1:1-2:4a and 2:4b-3:24), or the two introductions of David (1 Sam. 16:11-23 and 17:12-40). Critics normally now see in such cases conscious design rather than imperfect editing: the author or final redactor allows both versions to stand because each was hallowed by tradition, says something important in itself, and contributes to a richly stereoscopic vision.[5] The inclusion of four gospels in the New Testament canon can perhaps best be explained as the application of these considerations on a bolder scale.

Why stop at four? The church father Irenaeus offered parallels from nature (the seasons, the points of the compass), and the four were early equated to the four winged creatures described by Ezekiel: Matthew the man, Mark the lion, Luke the ox and John the eagle (Ezek. 1:5-14). But there were other candidates for inclusion, and some survive. M.R. James in *The Apocryphal New Testament* (1924) made a classic collection of non-canonical writings, both gospels and other recognisable genres (epistles, acts and apocalypses). James took a generally negative view of the material he presented.[6] Since then many other texts have emerged, in particular the library of Gnostic documents found at Nag Hammadi in Egypt in 1945. Elaine Pagels in *The Gnostic Gospels* shows how the esoteric theology of Gnosticism appears here as both more serious and more attractive than it had previously been considered,[7] and it is possible that the *Gospel of Thomas* (already familiar in part before these discoveries) may preserve some genuine sayings of Jesus not otherwise known. Yet some claims made for the new material are exaggerated: Philip Jenkins in *Hidden Gospels* argues that historically uncritical admiration for non-canonical texts frequently subserves a modern ideological agenda, attempting to present an alternative version of early Christianity free from traditional patriarchal authority in organisation and doctrine.[8]

The main point made by M.R. James still stands: to read the apocryphal texts after the canonical ones is to enter a different world and to descend to a lower literary level. They quickly pall because their effects are too sensational: the laws of nature are suspended, miraculous events become arbitrary and repetitive, and the supernatural is cheapened by excessive use. Here speaks the voice of experience, for James is more famous as the author of ghost stories which likewise owe their power to a controlled reticence in handling paranormal phenomena. We have seen that the supernatural is also used sparingly in Homer: Jasper Griffin in a well-known essay draws a contrast between the Homeric poems and the other poems of the epic cycle (insofar as they can be reconstructed from fragmentary evidence) which is essentially the same as the distinction James made between the canonical and apocryphal gospels.[9] The authors of the lost cyclic epics have since been defended against too drastic a subordination to the master poet.[10] We may nonetheless remain persuaded both of the uniqueness of Homer and of the wisdom of the church fathers who admitted to the New Testament canon only the familiar four gospels.

Their traditional order acknowledges the authoritative fullness of Matthew. It has the unfortunate effect of separating the gospel of Luke from its unique continuation in Acts. This however is the price paid for putting John properly last, as a meditation on what has preceded; and we shall see that the end of Luke chimes fortuitously with the beginning of John. The placing of the gospels in the larger perspective of the whole Bible takes us back to the hourglass shape we considered in Chapter 3. The traditional Protestant order of the Old Testament books, putting the prophets last, may be historically misleading but in literary terms is highly effective. For it gives a clear unity and forward thrust: Malachi announces that 'the Lord whom ye seek shall suddenly come to his temple' (Mal. 3:1), and two pages later we are reading Matthew's account of the Incarnation.[11] The Old Testament has repeatedly asked if God can indeed dwell on earth: the gospels offer an answer, and events long expected begin finally to happen.

Through all the complexity of the four gospels with their different emphases, a few themes are heard insistently. The first is a sense of concentrated urgency. In Mark particularly, this is created by the breathless rush of events in quick succession, with the word *euthus* ('immediately') repeated insistently in the early chapters, and characters constantly on the move: not even Jacob in the Old Testament is as relentlessly active as Jesus.[12] The narrator rarely pauses to fill in background detail, for he is showing us a *kairos*, a crucial time. There is a parallel here with the concentrated quality of the *Iliad*: in both cases the focus of the text corresponds to the worldview it embodies. The *Iliad* concentrates on a few days of fighting, and Achilles has a short time on earth. Mark pares away all inessentials, taking us straight to the baptism and preaching: Jesus too has a short time on earth, and the sense of urgency spills over.

Moments of decisive choice for characters in the story are moments of challenge also for the reader. We have seen already that the gospels constantly admire impulsive generosity, for instance the action of the woman with the precious ointment (Mark 14:3-9). Staid respectability is

116

in contrast disparaged, not least because it seems often to be accompanied by resentment: we think of Martha with her excessively laborious hospitality (Luke 10:40-1), or the stay-at-home elder brother of the Prodigal (Luke 15:25-32). Jesus typically urges his followers to eschew storing up treasure on earth, and to take no thought for the morrow (Matt. 6:19 and 34). The outlook of the gospels therefore has a paradoxical similarity to an attitude often seen as archetypally pagan, summed up by Horace's *carpe diem* ('pluck the day': *Odes* 1.11.8). The motive for focusing on the present and quashing anxiety about the future is of course very different: Jesus commends self-emptying openness and the overcoming of a natural desire for security, rather than sensual savouring of the moment. Nonetheless the basic imperative is the same: to concentrate on essentials (however conceived), and in a brief and uncertain life to do things now. The classical attitude surfaces more directly in the Bible in Ecclesiastes (of Hellenistic date, and the earliest book to show direct Greek influence), in a light frame of piety:

> Remember now thy Creator in the days of thy youth, while the evil days come not, nor the years draw nigh, when thou shalt say, I have no pleasure in them. (Eccles. 12:1)

The second recurrent theme is unexpectedness, the sense (which also marks the *Odyssey*) of things not as they seem. Prophecy is fulfilled, but (like pronouncements of the Delphic oracle in Herodotus or Sophocles) in unforeseen and disruptive ways. Established or anticipated roles are reversed: the last are first, and those who humble themselves are exalted (Luke 13:30 and 14:11). Unlikely people understand the message of Jesus while those close to him do not. The apparent outsider is revealed as the true insider, and the stone the builders rejected becomes the head of the corner (Matt. 21:42, quoting Ps. 118:22). Hesiodic righting of social wrongs, Herodotean inversion of fortune, Aeschylean light out of darkness, and Socratic paradox seem to be combined and intensified. The man who tears down his barns to build bigger ones (Luke 12:18) resembles Rhampsinitus with his new treasury (Hdt. 2.121), or the Athenians invading Sicily (Thuc. 6.8-32): the New Testament shares with classical literature the narrative convention that the more elaborate and ambitious are the human plans described, the more assuredly we know that they will fail.[13]

The third theme is redefinition. We have seen that Jesus is a new Adam, a new Moses, a new David, but in another sense he is the new nation. We saw parallels in *Oedipus Tyrannus* and in the *Republic* for the intertwining of the story of an individual and the story of a community, and Israel in the Old Testament was already the name of both a man and a nation. The history of the people is re-read in the gospels as the life of their central character. The infant Jesus is called out of Egypt after his parents have taken refuge there from Herod, as Israel was called out of Egypt in the Exodus (Matt. 2:15, quoting Hos. 11:1). His twelve disciples recall the twelve tribes of the Israelites, and his forty days in the wilderness are a miniature of their forty years. Roles in the story are assigned and combined in new ways, identities (again as in *Oedipus Tyrannus*) collapsed and multiplied. Jesus preaches but also is the Word, so that the signifier and the signified are one, as Odysseus was already both the teller and the subject of stories. The Temple is redefined as his own body (John 2:19-21), a person replacing a building as the place of reconciliation with God. Israel had been cast as a faulty vine (Jer. 2:21), but now Jesus describes himself as the true vine (John 15:1). The purity which had been the desirable attribute of a sacrificial victim is now (picking up a theme from Isaiah and the Psalms) applied to the worshipper. The reign of God is neither a datable event nor a distant destination. Instead, 'the kingdom of God is within you' (Luke 17:21): the Pharisees and the disciples need to be told that this is a boomerang quest. Northrop Frye described the gospels as a sequence of epiphanies.[14] The sense of urgency, the unexpectedness of the events described, the constant challenge to redefinition as we work out the real significance of what has gone before and of what is happening before our eyes: all these things give to the reader of the texts the recurrent experience of *anagnôrisis*.

Hospitality and parables

Hospitality pervades the gospels. Much teaching takes place over the table. In John's account the first miracle of Jesus is an act of hospitality, when the wine runs out during the wedding feast at Cana (John 2:1-11). Jesus provocatively dines with publicans and sinners, which in the eyes of his critics is dangerous and inappropriate eating (Luke 5:29-32). Zacchaeus the despised outsider is admitted into the community by his offer of hospitality, accompanied by the extravagant gesture of giving half his goods to the poor and repaying extorted money fourfold (Luke 19:1-10). When Jesus is being entertained by Simon the Pharisee, the woman who washes his feet with her tears and hair shows that their host has been remiss in neglecting rules which seem Homeric in flavour but are the timeless convention of an eastern society with dusty roads (Luke 7:44). The Good Samaritan shows his charity by ensuring that the man who has been mugged is looked after at an inn (Luke 10:33-5). In John's version of the Last Supper Jesus washes the disciples' feet (John 13:4-14), with a reversal of the roles of master and servant reminiscent of the Roman Saturnalia. The kingdom of heaven is constantly likened to a banquet. The favourite Jewish image of a Messianic feast is re-used with new emphasis: the themes of reversal and unexpectedness are exemplified when the people invited do not come but are replaced by conscripts from the highways and byways (Luke 14:16-24). Especially in Luke, it is constantly the humble and those outside society who recognise and welcome Jesus, and are brought by him from the margins to a central and honoured place. The hospitality of God (a sort of reverse theoxeny, picking up a theme from Psalm 23) is shown as freely offered, with no expectation of Homeric reciprocity. In mediating it Jesus himself meets with inhospitality and rejection, from the time of his birth when there is no room in the inn (Luke 2:7) to his sufferings and death.[15] After the Resurrection the themes of hospitality and recognition coalesce fully at Emmaus (Luke 24:28-32).

Menus normally go unspecified in the Bible (in contrast to Homer), but John Drury points out that the parable section of Luke is as full of domestic detail as a Dutch painting: the lost coin, the lighted lamp, the rejoicing neighbours (Luke 15:8-9).[16] Parables draw us in, often to disturbing effect: the story of the Pharisee and the tax collector praying in the Temple is interactive in a particularly ingenious way. The Pharisee thanks God that he is 'not like other men, extortioners, unjust, adulterers, or even like this tax collector' but instead fulfils his religious duties scrupulously; the tax collector says simply 'God, be merciful to me a sinner' (Luke 18:11-13). Jesus comments that it was he, not the Pharisee, who went home justified. Again we see the themes of unexpectedness and reversal: 'for every one who exalts himself will be humbled, but he who humbles himself will be exalted' (18:14), and thus the story seems to achieve satisfactorily didactic closure. But there is a pungent after-taste: for who in reading did not feel self-congratulatory satisfaction at being unlike the Pharisee, and thus fall into the same trap as he?

Some of the parables are nominally expressed as similes ('The Kingdom of Heaven is like ...'), but it is rather as vividly evocative vignettes that they resemble the extended similes in Homer: not the great visions of wild nature, the mountain torrents and ravening lions, but the equally frequent descriptions of domestic life, of the farm with its dogs and donkeys, pails of milk and crying children.[17] Analysis of the language of the similes suggests that they are a late development within the epic tradition, and perhaps in their fully elaborated form they are the achievement of Homer himself. Likewise the parables, although they have precedents in the teaching techniques both of the great prophets and of first-century Rabbinic practice, seem in important ways to be the distinctive and individual creation of Jesus. Speculation about the earlier forms that may lie behind the extant works is one of several similarities between the ways in which the two sub-genres have been interpreted. In each case modern readings react against an influential earlier insistence that the simile or parable has a single point of comparison with the world, elaborated simply for literary effect or didactic impact. Yet in each case too that purist approach was itself a reaction: against too easy an assimilation of Homer to the literary epic of Virgil (whose similes typically involve elaborate multiple correspondence), and against the patristic and medieval tradition of reading the parables as allegories (where with mechanical ingenuity every detail in the story was assigned a meaning).[18] The correctives were salutary but too rigid, and too evidently also the product of dogmatic oral theory tending both to fragment the text and to cast it as in some sense primitive.

Modern criticism stresses in contrast that the parables frequently have complex associations and layers of meaning, and thereby returns to a more traditional way of reading them. Charles Dickens called the Prodigal Son the best short story in the world, and used its narrative pattern in several of his own novels, most obviously *Great Expectations*. The characters in the parable are unnamed. They belong broadly to the world of the original hearers (being reduced to feeding pigs is especially shocking in a Jewish context), but beyond that they appear to be fictitious. In fact, rather in the same way that the invented myths of Plato or the ostensibly original plots of Aristophanes frequently echo traditional Greek narratives, the story throughout makes implicit reference to the Old Testament. Indeed the reader is assigned a role like that of a Neoanalyst critic of Homer, looking for the shadow of other stories; and because the parable depends on the complex interplay of multiple sources, its method is analogous also to a characteristic technique of Virgil. Primarily it evokes Jacob and Esau (Gen. 25:21-34):[19] the selfishly assertive but enterprising younger brother and his more stolid elder, given cause for resentment. But this pair themselves already echo Cain and Abel (Gen. 4:1-16), in a story where the firstborn who tills the ground has to see his offering rejected whilst that of his nomadic younger sibling is accepted. Also in Genesis we think of Joseph, especially in relation to Judah among his older brothers, and another account of a journey to a far country and of eventual return: it is now the father in the parable rather than the Prodigal himself who is cast as Jacob, rejoicing in old age to find his son alive (Gen. 45:28).

The parable draws on the combined associations of these Genesis stories about brothers, and seems to be a new one within the same tradition. But (by the now familiar equating of nation and individual) yet another source is Isaiah's picture of Israel wilfully going its own way but led back to healing and comfort by a longsuffering God (Isa. 57:3-19). Already in Genesis, Jacob and Esau represented two communities (the flourishing Israelites and the less prosperous Edomites). By analogy this suggests a further resonance in the parable, of the upstart younger son as a figure for the new Christian movement. His experiences at the bottom of the social pile make him akin to the outcasts whom Luke constantly shows Jesus as welcoming. Paul in Galatians uses yet another Genesis pair, Isaac and Ishmael (Gen. 21:1-20), as an allegory of the new faith in relation to the old (Gal. 4:21-31): this is a tendentious piece of rhetoric, for it is in this case because he is the legitimate heir that the younger son supplants his older half-brother. If Luke intended his parable to be read in a similar way, the Genesis theme of the wayward youngster who prevails will have had the sort of uncanny suitability for its new purpose that the traditions of the Julian house did for Virgil. And if the story of the Prodigal Son was interpreted in this way by its earliest hearers, it will have been particularly disturbing to the Pharisees among them by implicitly appropriating for the new and radical cause the figure of Jacob, who by convention represented their own tradition.

The parable of the Prodigal is a spare narrative, fraught with background indeed, but also owing much of its power to unanswered questions. Does the elder brother join in the feast at the end? The story of Cain and Abel casts the shadow of a chilling alternative (Gen. 4:8). Perhaps we are deliberately left wondering what we would do in his position. Certainly this story, with its *peripeteia* from great misery to rejoicing, is about hospitality as a symbol of forgiveness. Jacob was returning home in anxiety about how his brother would react to him when he fought his unknown adversary at the Jabbok, ending in a recognition scene (Gen. 32:22-30). That part of his story is echoed here. The Prodigal at the depth of his degradation 'came to himself' (Luke 15:17): an internalised recognition, though the truly decisive moment is perhaps when he sees his father, and the rehearsed words of repentance are made his own. Rembrandt's great picture of their embrace, painted after the death of his own beloved son Titus, shows why this story has traditionally been regarded as *evangelium in evangelio*, the gospel within the gospel. As in the *Odyssey*, homecoming means the recovery of identity.

We come now to a passage which is central to the subject of this book. The story of the sheep and goats in Matthew 25 is not strictly a parable (though usually classed as one), but a word picture of the Last Judgement. It comes at a late and crucial stage in the account of Jesus' ministry: immediately after it, events move quickly to the Passion.

> When the Son of man comes in his glory, and all the angels with him, then he will sit on his glorious throne. Before him will be gathered all the nations, and he will separate them one from another as a shepherd separates the sheep from the goats, and he will place the sheep at his right hand, but the goats at the left. Then the King will say to those at his right hand, 'Come, O blessed of my Father, inherit the kingdom prepared for you from the beginning of the world; for I was hungry and you gave me food, I was thirsty and you gave me drink, I was a stranger and you welcomed me, I was naked and you clothed me, I was sick and you visited me, I was in prison and you came to me.' Then the righteous will answer him, 'Lord, when did we see thee hungry and feed thee, or thirsty and give thee drink? And when did we see thee a stranger and welcome thee, or naked and clothe thee? And when did we see thee sick or in prison and visit thee?' And the King will answer them, 'Truly, I say to you, as you did it to one of the least of these my brethren, you did it to me.' (Matt. 25:31-40)

These words, some of the most haunting in the New Testament, remind us that ancient authoritative texts compel us to think about how we relate to the everyday world around us.[20] The setting of this transfigured theoxeny is aggressively supernatural, but its content is radically demythologised. Beginning in the language of apocalyptic, the ancient story of a divine visitor who comes in disguise is restated as an account of ordinary charitable behaviour, of response to the depth of human need in others.

There is a remarkable parallel in the Egyptian Book of the Dead. That very ancient collection of spells is essentially a guide to the next world, a set of tips and passwords for coping with the hazards of the journey thither. Various versions of it, written on papyrus, were buried with the mummified dead, and lay there for 3,000 years until discovered by nineteenth-century archaeologists. Herodotus (2.86-8) famously describes several grades of mummification, and similar social grading applied to versions of the guidebook. Rich people had a scribe write an individualised text on fine papyrus. The poor relied on a short mass-produced version with a few blanks to fill in their personal details. But some central elements of the journey and story remain constant. The dead are judged by the underworld god Osiris in the Hall of Two Truths, and it is said of someone who has passed the judgement: 'The god has welcomed him, as he wished. He has given food to the hungry, drink to the thirsty, clothing to the naked.'[21]

In Matthew as in the *Odyssey*, moral worth is tested by response to a humble stranger, and accepting or rejecting him is tantamount to accepting or rejecting one subsequently revealed as ruler and judge. The prayer book collect for the first Sunday in Advent uses the same ideas, with its contrast between 'the time of this mortal life, in which thy son Jesus Christ came to visit us in great humility' and 'the last day, when he shall come again in his glorious majesty, to judge both the quick and the dead'. Matthew's story need not however be read as narrowly Christian. It has been suggested indeed that the use of 'my brethren' implies in particular needy believers, and it is true that the concerns of the nascent church feature more prominently in Matthew than in the other gospels. But John Locke in *The Reasonableness of Christianity* (1695) observed that the people on trial are not interrogated about what they believed.[22] In the spectrum of New Testament theology, the stress here is firmly on works. The Epistle of James has a similar emphasis, scorning the attitude which says to the needy ' "Go in peace, be warmed and filled", without giving them the things needed for the body' (James 2:16). Matthew's story is about recognition, or rather initial non-recognition (for charity was offered disinterestedly) followed by perception of the unsuspected truth.

In J.B. Priestley's play *An Inspector Calls* the wealthy manufacturer Arthur Birling and his family are celebrating his daughter's engagement.[23] The year is 1912, and Birling has been enthusing about an unsinkable new ship called the *Titanic* when the doorbell rings and the mysterious Inspector Goole arrives: he reports the suicide of a wretched young girl, Eva Smith, and proceeds to interrogate each member of the family in turn. It seems that they all (unknowingly, and unknown to each other) had a hand in her death. Birling had dismissed a girl from his factory for trade union agitation. She got a job in an up-market dress shop, but inadvertently offended Birling's daughter, who had her sacked for insolence. Unemployed, she became the mistress of the daughter's fiancé, but he abandoned her. Birling's son picked her up in a seedy bar and made her pregnant. She came before a charity committee chaired by Birling's wife, but no charity was forthcoming, so she killed herself. Inspector Goole makes an enigmatic last speech ('We don't live alone, we are members of one body', echoing Rom. 12:5) and leaves. They are all guilty – or are they? The younger members of the family, at first the most obviously contrite, begin to pick holes in the story: several of them were shown a photograph of a girl they recognised, but were they all shown the same one? Goole admitted that Eva Smith used several false names, so what proof is there that the same girl was involved in all these incidents? Indeed is Goole a real police inspector? A phone call to the Chief Constable confirms that there is no such person. And was the body of a suicide in fact brought to the local hospital? No. And so a rather muted family celebration resumes. But there is a final twist: the phone rings, and Birling speaks the last lines of the play: 'That was the police. A girl has just died on her way to the Infirmary after swallowing some disinfectant. And a police inspector is on his way here to ask some questions.' Priestley in this play used a very old story pattern, but he created an extra character: for in Matthew's version, Eva Smith and Inspector Goole are one and the same person.

Passion and Resurrection

We saw in Chapter 2 that the story of the final days and death of Jesus seems, like the equivalent story of Socrates, to have assumed a fairly fixed form at a stage before its incorporation into extant texts. Mark's gospel in particular seems to rush onwards to the Passion narrative, and in many episodes the shadow of the cross is cast forward. We noted similarities both to the *Iliad* and to Greek tragedy in a story which moves inexorably towards the death of its hero: Achilles treads an ordained course, and Agamemnon makes an ominous triumphal entry. Luke, who stresses in particular the prophetic status of Jesus, reminds the reader constantly in the central section of his gospel that Jerusalem is where prophets die (for example Luke 13:34). We saw too that the Last Supper is linked in different ways by the evangelists to the Passover: in the synoptic gospels it is a Passover meal ushering in a new Exodus, whilst in John the killing of the paschal lambs coincides with the crucifixion of the Lamb of God. Jesus in John's account utters no words of institution (where the bread and wine are identified as his body and blood), but he has earlier described himself both as the bread of life and as the true vine (John 6:35 and 15:1): implicit eucharistic reference pervades this gospel, which characteristically puts its meaning across by clues and allusions. Despite these differences Jesus himself is in all the accounts equated to an element of a meal. In terms of the Odyssean triangle of hospitality, the host voluntarily becomes the food (a play on 'host' in English would be apt, but based on false etymology: the giver of a meal is Latin *hospes,* host or guest according to context, like the Greek *xenos,* whilst consecrated bread is Latin *hostia,* a sacrificial victim). In all the gospels the Last Supper is the culmination of a series of meals where important encounters have taken place: in broad terms it is comparable to the Greek symposium used as a setting in the Socratic literature by Plato and Xenophon. John Drury shows how this fraught and mysterious meal contrasts with the calm and revelatory ones which follow the Resurrection.[24]

Henry Hart Milman's hymn for Palm Sunday 'Ride on, ride on in majesty' imagines angels watching as Jesus rides into Jerusalem:

> The wingèd squadrons of the sky
> Look down with sad and wondering eyes
> To see the approaching sacrifice.

Their physical vantage is that of the Homeric gods, but their combination of pitying foreknowledge and inability to intervene makes them more like the audience of a Greek tragedy. Throughout the Passion narrative we have a sense that things might so easily have turned out differently: Jesus could have been acquitted, as Socrates could at several points have escaped his fate. The thief released by Pilate at the people's request is Barabbas. His Aramaic name seems to mean 'son of the father': perhaps in the sense 'any father's son', like A.N. Other, but surely also with ironic reference to the status of Jesus himself. We feel to have got into the wrong side of a story about parallel universes: events should be taking another course, as they should for Andromache when she anticipates the home-coming of the already dead Hector, or for Iphigenia when she prepares for an illusory marriage. This sense illogically but powerfully co-exists with the idea (ratified by our existing knowledge of the story) that the pattern is preordained, that only one destined person can occupy this role. The other significant thief in the story, the penitent on the cross, was identified by later Christian tradition as the rich young ruler who had gone away sorrowful when told to sell all he had and give it to the poor (Luke 18:18-25): that reading imposes a narrative economy worthy of Sophocles, for whom the man who witnessed the killing of Laius was the shepherd who took the infant Oedipus to Cithaeron and in due time revealed the truth about his life.

The trilingual inscription on the cross of Jesus, in Hebrew, Latin, and Greek (John 19:20) reminds us that his crucifixion took place in the cockpit of the ancient world, when Graeco-Roman and Near Eastern cultures were drawing decisively together.[25] The account of the Passion ends with darkness and desolation, and with the cry 'My God, my God, why hast thou forsaken me?' (Mark 15:34, quoting Ps. 22:1). The curtain of the Temple is torn in two (Mark 15:38): this has been taken to symbolise the end of Jewish cult, but the implication may be rather that a barrier separating God and humanity is now removed, enabling an ampler vision. It is thus the context for the recognition scene in the following verse, where the centurion says 'Truly this man was the Son of God' (Mark 15:39; 'a righteous man' at Luke 23:47). The supernatural has otherwise been markedly in abeyance during most of this narrative, only to return with supreme drama at the Resurrection.

The gospel story acquires at this point a further resemblance to both the Homeric epics, as the account of an absent hero and his return. The four gospels treat the events of the first Easter Day in revealingly different ways. Mark has three women go to the tomb intending to anoint the body with spices. Finding the stone door rolled away, they enter to find a young man dressed in white who tells them that Jesus is not there because he has risen: they should take the message to Peter and the disciples that he is going to Galilee where they will see him. They hurry away, trembling with astonishment, and say nothing: 'for they were afraid' (Mark 16:8). According to the authoritative text the story ends here (several different continuations, generally regarded as spurious, are found in some manuscripts). Although it is almost unprecedentedly abrupt for the Greek word *gar* ('for') to end a sentence (let alone a book) as it does here, modern critics increasingly accept that the effect is deliberate and that the onus is on the reader to make sense of the text as it stands. Mark, like Xenophon or Caesar, is now typically read as a more sophisticated writer than he at first appears (the Ernest Hemingway of the New Testament): he ends with an explosive silence, and we are invited to ponder the sequel.

The technique here may be compared to puzzling and apparently unresolved endings in classical literature. Aeneas finally yields to the passion that he has habitually resisted and kills the Italian Turnus, who is a sympathetic character (equated to Hector in the *Iliad*) but who provocatively wears a sword-belt taken as spoil from the dead Pallas, the young son of Evander and ally of Aeneas: the epic ends with this act, and with the soul of Turnus going down to the Underworld (*Aen.* 12.940-52). Herodotus ends his *Histories* with the Athenians embarking on a quasi-Persian career of imperial conquest, capturing Sestus on the Hellespont where Xerxes had built his bridge and impaling the Persian governor Artayctes (9.114-20). In these cases we are invited to reflect on the events we know to have followed. Reluctance to accept closure often in modern criticism subserves a darker reading than the overt sense of the text, but need not always do so. At the end of the *Aeneid* the mood may be gloomy for a season, but we are perhaps intended to reflect that the ultimate outcome which is Rome justifies retrospectively the price paid. In Mark likewise the initial numbness of the women must have been temporary. Mark consistently shows Jesus as a reliable prophet: all the predictions of the Passion predict also the Resurrection, and the promise in the penultimate verse of a renewal of the relationship with him must surely in Mark's eyes have been fulfilled. That meeting is significantly to be in Galilee (Mark 16:7), the place where discipleship starts. As at the end of Herodotus, but in this case more optimistically, we have the sense of a cycle beginning again. The *Oresteia* with its concluding triumphant procession, or an Aristophanes play ending with revelry for the characters, blends what happens on stage into the Athenian experience of the audience. Mark similarly here invites us to believe that his story continues in the lives of his readers, themselves cast as disciples. As with the painful episodes of recent Roman history for Virgil (perhaps at some level alluded to by the final actions of Aeneas), we are not offered a panacea that will enable preceding events to be forgotten but a faith in the power of restoration, an optimism that acknowledges human failure.

The other evangelists differ over the location of the Resurrection appearances. Matthew modestly expands the hints in Mark: the disciples do indeed meet Jesus in Galilee (Matt. 28:16-20). The scene in John 21 is set in Galilee too, but the effect is quite different. Here the disciples are back at their long-abandoned occupation of fishing. We are not meant to ask literal-minded questions about the plausibility of this: it is like the reprise of an earlier theme at the end of a piece of music. John puts here the miraculous draft of fishes, which in Luke is an incident in the earthly ministry of Jesus (John 21:11 and Luke 5:1-7). The story works well in its new place, suggesting that the new Christian movement will enjoy comparable success, though our reading is complicated by the fact that chapter 21 may well be a later addition to the original text.

The preceding chapter already has three Resurrection appearances (to Mary Magdalene, to the disciples met behind locked doors, and to Thomas). By the classical device of ring-composition it takes up from the prologue of the gospel ('as many as received him') the themes of recognition and welcome. The first of these intersecting episodes about the passage from ignorance to understanding is a dramatic masterpiece (John 20:1-18). Mary arrives while it is still dark to find the stone removed. She runs to fetch Peter and the beloved disciple: they find the tomb empty, the grave-clothes folded. Though we are told they did not yet understand the scripture, the beloved disciple at least sees and believes, and the two go home. Why is Mary abandoned? Perhaps they leave her alone with her grief. But the answer may rather be that it creates a more effective setting for the recognition which follows, for in this encounter of a woman and a man in a garden (mentioned only by John) we are surely once more in Eden.[26] Here again John revisits Genesis, and shows the end as the beginning restored; and as in the *Odyssey*, that restoration is symbolised by a woman recognising a man returned. As she stands weeping, Mary sees two angels. Like Abraham at Mamre, she is unperturbed by her visitors. Asked the reason for her tears, she replies 'Because they have

126

taken away my Lord, and I do not know where they have laid him.' Turning again, she sees Jesus himself standing before her: as yet she does not know him, but takes him for the gardener, and asks if he has removed the body. And now (whether through the naturalistic tokens of voice and gesture, or by other means) the recognition takes place: 'Jesus said to her, "Mary". She turned and said to him in Hebrew, "Rabboni!" (which means Teacher)' (20:16).

Piero Boitani in *The Bible and its Rewritings* shows how this encounter lies behind scenes of recognition that haunt the western imagination.[27] They typically centre on a woman, and one character has usually assumed the other dead. T.S. Eliot described the recognition scene in Shakespeare's *Pericles* (Act V Scene i) as the finest ever written. The reunion after sixteen years of Pericles and his lost daughter Marina takes place in an atmosphere created by the associations of this passage in John. *Pericles* is not now well known, but as the first of the late plays it adumbrates themes that run also through *Cymbeline*, *The Winter's Tale* and *The Tempest*: children lost and found, shipwreck and rescue, recognition and redemption. At the climactic moment in *The Winter's Tale* (Act V Scene iii) Leontes recognises that the supposed statue of Hermione, the wife he had thought long dead, is her living self. The scene evokes and enacts the important ancient idea of a statue as the vehicle of epiphany. It is in an obvious sense an artificial contrivance, yet the encounter takes place in a chapel, and seems to enact also the idea of resurrection.[28] Recognition and recovery of the lost, in the late Shakespeare plays as in the stories of Joseph and the Prodigal Son, gives the uncanny sense of a return from the dead.

The themes of late Shakespeare are strikingly also those of late Euripides, of the plays often described (like their Shakespearian equivalents) as 'romances', especially *Helen*, *Ion* and *Iphigenia among the Taurians*: typically with a happy ending, and pointing forward to fourth-century New Comedy. These remain nominally tragedies, but Euripides returns in them to themes he had treated long before in *Alcestis* (438 BC), his earliest surviving work (though this was entered in the dramatic contest in place of a satyr play, the mythological burlesque which usually accompanied a set of three tragedies). Admetus king of Pherae is granted by Apollo a reprieve from his fated day of death if he can find a substitute; his wife Alcestis agrees to die in his place, yet her loss makes the life thus bought worthless for her husband. A roistering quasi-satyric Heracles arrives and is hospitably welcomed, Admetus concealing the reason for the evident mourning of the house. When he discovers the truth, Heracles fights a personified Death and wins Alcestis back. Practising on his host a benign counter-deception, he brings before Admetus a veiled woman whom he claims to have won as a prize for wrestling, and at the climax of a dialogue rich in dramatic irony reveals her as Alcestis (*Alc.* 1006-126). The physical recognition mirrors the access of self-knowledge attained by the previously egocentric Admetus.

The scenes in *Pericles* and *The Winter's Tale* seem close to Euripides as well as to John, perhaps because John is himself indebted to a classical tradition stretching back to Homer.[29] In the *Odyssey* the recognition of a god was a model for the recognition of a significant person, though in the meeting of the hero with his son the human seemed paradoxically more miraculous than the divine. In *Helen* Euripides has the heroine, reunited with her husband Menelaus, link human and divine in a powerful epigram: 'To recognise those we love is a god' (*Helen* 560). John describes a recognition of a familiar person which is simultaneously a recognition of his divinity, and the theme of recognition is here restored to the highest seriousness.

The road to Emmaus

The Resurrection appearances in Luke take place in or near Jerusalem. The story of the road to Emmaus is one of the most powerful in the whole Bible. Here supremely the themes of hospitality and recognition come together. It is towards evening on the day when the women (in this version) have found the empty tomb. The followers of Jesus are as yet unbelieving. Two of them, not named at this point, set out for the village of Emmaus. As they are talking over what has happened, Jesus draws near and walks with them: 'But their eyes were holden that they should not know him' (Luke 24:16). The reader in contrast has been told his identity by the narrator: the dramatic irony thus created is the first of several echoes of the account of Abraham at Mamre (Gen. 18:1).

Abraham's visitors were strangers. Odysseus and Joseph went plausibly unrecognised because they had not been seen for a long time. These realistic criteria cannot apply here. Commentators have invoked fading light, and artists have shown Jesus wearing a hood, but these expedients miss the point. This is to be (at least outwardly) a recognition scene of the Homeric kind, where the divine visitor is recognised when he chooses to be, but it makes a point also about the perceptiveness of the other characters. The failure of recognition represents a failure of understanding. The stranger asks about the conversation of his companions. They stop in amazement: one, now named as Cleopas (Luke 24:18), asks if he can be the only visitor to Jerusalem who does not know about the dramatic events of recent days. And so, like Odysseus among the Phaeacians, Jesus is told a story about himself. But it is a distorted and incomplete story: this prophet who had seemed so powerful in word and deed was delivered up by the chief priests and rulers, condemned and crucified, yet he was the one they had hoped would redeem Israel.

The location of Emmaus cannot be established with certainty, but the strong probability is that it is the place of that name referred to in 1 Maccabees (for example 3:40) and in Josephus (*Jewish War* 2.71). This requires reading (with some manuscripts) 160 rather than 60 stades as the

128

distance from Jerusalem (Luke 24:13), and even that is a slight under-estimate. Other sites nearer to the city have been claimed, but without firm evidence.[30] It is however much more likely that Luke intends a symbolic point than that he is preoccupied with the minutiae of geography or that there were two places of the same name. Emmaus was the place where, almost exactly 200 years before the traditional date of the crucifixion, the Jewish rebel leader Judas Maccabaeus won his first major victory over the Syrian king Antiochus IV Epiphanes, who had tried to destroy Jewish worship and identity (1 Macc. 3:38-4:25). Luke surely expects us to pick up the clue: the two companions are walking to a site steeped in memories of an earlier redeeming of Israel. They expect a conquering hero, and their preoccupation with battles long ago prevents them from seeing the significance of what Luke presents as the greater victory won by the unrecognised stranger who walks with them.

Yet the women of their company report amazing things: an empty tomb (since confirmed), a vision of angels saying he was alive (as yet unconfirmed).

> And he said to them, 'O foolish men, and slow of heart to believe all that the prophets have spoken! Was it not necessary that the Christ should suffer these things and enter into his glory?' And beginning with Moses and all the prophets, he interpreted to them in all the scriptures the things concerning himself. So they drew near to the village to which they were going, but they constrained him, saying, 'Stay with us, for it is toward evening and the day is now far spent.' So he went in to stay with them. When he was at table with them, he took the bread and blessed, and broke it, and gave it to them. And their eyes were opened and they recognised him; and he vanished out of their sight. They said to each other. 'Did not our hearts burn within us while he talked to us on the road, while he opened to us the scriptures?' (Luke 24:25-32)

Significant things happen on roads in Luke: we may think back to the man going down to Jericho in the parable of the Good Samaritan, or forward to Paul on the Damascus road in Acts. More distantly in the background perhaps is Tobias in the book of Tobit, accompanied on his journey to Ecbatana by the disguised archangel Raphael (Tobit 5-6). Recognition and miraculous departure are closely connected and almost simultaneous, as they were in the story of Telemachus and Athene, though here the recognition comes first.

Luke's gospel makes important use of ring composition. The divine visitor at Emmaus corresponds to Gabriel at the Annunciation (though he is in effect the message of that scene as well as the messenger), and the recognition scene here echoes the recognition of the unborn Jesus by the unborn John, who leaps in the womb of Elizabeth when she is visited by the expectant Mary (Luke 1:41). Recognitions of Jesus thus extend beyond the span of his life at both ends, as indeed do failures of recognition or acceptance, the impaired vision on the Emmaus road perhaps balancing the striking dumb of Zechariah (1:20). The two companions here also echo the shepherds, who likewise go eagerly into town with news after a divine visitation (2:15-18). At the end of his gospel as also at its opening, Luke deliberately adopts the style and manner of the Septuagint.

Like Odysseus in Scherie, Jesus takes over as a more informed and authoritative narrator of his own story. As with the songs of Troy sung by Demodocus, recognition is precipitated by retrospective narrative. The disciples only now learn the true sense of familiar passages of scripture (and also the true sense of earlier sayings of Jesus himself), as characters in Herodotus or Sophocles grasp only with hindsight the meaning of oracular pronouncements. A pattern in history is recognised because a person has been recognised. That pattern is on a grand scale: it is the perspective of Luke himself.[31] Like Solon in Herodotus, Jesus here speaks for the author. If Jesus is like Luke, the two companions are like his readers. As we have seen often in classical literature, the emotions and experiences of the characters are also ours. The two are shown a new trajectory in and from the scriptures, and the reader likewise sees a pattern not just in the Hebrew texts, but in what he has read so far of the gospel. The story offers indeed a parable about the interpretation of texts, about the perspective and imagination which that process demands. In this story Luke conveys the sense that we stand at an intersection, a crucial turning-point of time. This idea is basic to his theology; it is also very similar to a central theme in Virgil.

We saw that in the parable of the Prodigal Son it is unclear when the true moment of insight comes. Here the recognition is in two stages, or expressed in two ways: an increase of understanding as the scriptures are explained on the road, then full and personal recognition at the table. The request to 'stay with us' has a clear resonance beyond its immediate context, anticipating the symbolic importance of the scene which follows. The divine guest enters (at evening, as in many classical theoxeny stories) what we infer to be the humble home of Cleopas: taking the initiative in blessing and breaking the bread, just as he took over as narrator, he is in effect acknowledged as the host. Full recognition comes now, the opening of the 'holden' eyes a symbol of deeper understanding. The passage is coloured strongly by eucharistic language: again there is a moment of recognition for the reader too, for we realise as we read that this is the first Christian communion service, the first re-enactment of the Last Supper (Luke 22:7-38). We now retrospectively see that narrative as the *aition* of the later rite: it is recalled here, and its returned hero shown once again present with his companions. We realise too that the order of events in the house of Cleopas reflects the structure of a simple liturgy: the scriptures are read and expounded, then the bread is shared. The earthly life of Jesus has ended, a new stage has begun, and the theme of Luke's second volume is advertised in advance. Like many classical theoxeny stories, this is an account of a significant beginning. Like the account of the hospitality of Abraham, it is instinct with promise for the future.

The mysterious stranger met at the ford of the Jabbok (again we return to that passage) conferred on Abraham's grandson Jacob a new identity as Israel: ancestor, eponym and personification of the future nation. The mysterious stranger met on the road to Emmaus confers on the disciples a new identity as the Christian church, constantly seen by New Testament authors as a new Israel. Charles Wesley's 'Traveller unknown' implicitly associated these passages of Genesis and Luke. His brother John in his journal entry for 24 May 1738 famously alluded to the Emmaus story to describe his own conversion experience:

> In the evening I went very unwillingly to a society in Aldersgate-street, where one was reading Luther's preface to the epistle of the Romans. About a quarter before nine, while he was describing the change which God works in the heart through faith in Christ, I felt my heart strangely warmed. I felt I did trust in Christ, Christ alone, for salvation; and an assurance was given me, that He had taken away *my* sins, even *mine*, and saved me from the law of sin and death.[32]

The two companions when Jesus has left them return at once to Jerusalem despite the late hour, to share with the other disciples (full already of the news of an otherwise unrecorded appearance to Peter) their experience of 'what had happened on the road, and how he was known to them in the breaking of the bread' (Luke 24:35). Jesus appears among them, his physicality attested by the eating of some broiled fish, and repeats for this larger gathering the claim that in him is fulfilled what is written 'in the law of Moses and the prophets and the psalms' (24:44). The command to wait in Jerusalem until they are clothed with power from on high (24:49) provides a clear forward link to the opening scenes of Acts, but in the New Testament as we have it we come first to John. The meditation on the Incarnation that forms his prologue, its account of the 'true light' rejected by his own but received to empowering effect by some (John 1:11-12), felicitously echoes and generalises the theme of Luke's account of Emmaus. It has been thought indebted to a pre-existing hymn: John speaks of the Word as many writers in Hellenistic Judaism speak of a personified Wisdom. In the book of Ecclesiasticus that figure of Wisdom describes her own coming forth from on high and visiting every people and nation, seeking a resting place, a territory in which she might lodge (Ecclus. 24:3-7). She is cast in a role like that of many divine visitors we have considered: Demeter in the *Homeric Hymn*, or Jupiter and Mercury in the story of Baucis and Philemon. When the prologue to the fourth gospel records how 'the Word ... dwelt among us' (John 1:14), the word used is *eskênôsen*, literally 'pitched his tent': an image from a nomadic world, but also a specific allusion to the Tent of Meeting in Exodus, the portable sanctuary carried by the Israelites through the wilderness. The

Emmaus story is echoed again in Revelation, where John (traditionally identified with the evangelist but now generally thought to be another) receives on the Greek island of Patmos a vision of the risen Christ ordering him to write to the seven churches of Asia Minor (Rev. 1:9-11). The Laodiceans, reproached as lukewarm in commitment and blind to their own failings, are challenged to offer hospitality. This is the scene depicted by Holman Hunt in *The Light of the World,* whose title and iconography link it also to John's prologue: all these passages combine to suggest a new and decisive theoxeny.

> Behold, I stand at the door and knock; if any one hears my voice and opens the door, I will come in to him and eat with him, and he with me. (Rev. 3:20)

Reading Acts

Here we reach the most obvious site of interaction between the biblical and classical worlds. Acts was traditionally the only New Testament text prescribed for Classical Honour Moderations at Oxford. It is a great adventure story that repays being read at a sitting, perhaps the best narrative of any book in the Bible. Its generic affiliations are endlessly debated. Many critics in the past have stressed Luke's adherence to the conventions of classical historiography, particularly in his formal prefaces (both in his gospel and here) and in his use of speeches. More recently comparisons have been drawn with other types of prose treatise,[33] but it is probably wrong to look for a single model: David Aune in *The New Testament in its Literary Environment* describes the text as 'a popular general history written by an amateur Hellenistic historian with credentials in Greek rhetoric'.[34] In his gospel Luke was operating not only within the broad expectations of classical biography, but within the more specific and recent framework imposed by the existing versions of the story which he aimed to surpass. In Acts he had greater freedom because he was doing something entirely original, and it is not surprising that there are similarities to many different types of writing. The variety of the text derives from changes of generic gear as well as from the drama inherent in the story. Exciting last-minute escapes from peril take us into the world of the Greek novel; elsewhere we seem closer to Herodotus (Acts too is a prose epic) or to Plutarch.

Above all, this Mediterranean *periêgêsis* resembles the *Odyssey.* The title of Acts is misleading, because relatively few characters are involved and the second half of the story focuses almost entirely on Paul, putting him in the role of an epic or tragic hero. His successive arrivals at different places, with accounts of the people he meets and the good or bad treatment he receives, are broadly equivalent to the adventures of Odysseus. Paul has perhaps also something of Alexander: his international missionary ambition has no obvious precedents within Judaism, but it echoes the

Macedonian export of Hellenism. In baptising whole households and moving quickly on, presumably leaving the ensuing practicalities to local congregations, Paul replicates the pattern by which Alexander won allegiance through symbolic conquest: he founds churches as Alexander founded cities.

A debt to Greek literature is entirely plausible for Luke. It is much less likely that he knew the *Aeneid*, but there are striking analogies. Here too we have the story of an apparently defeated remnant destined to rebuild their community. This process in both cases involves re-formulation of the pilgrim people, who have to leave behind what is familiar: the Trojans become proto-Romans, and a Jewish movement becomes the Christian church. It also means incorporating former enemies, success depending on inclusivity. Aeneas gains Greek allies, and his descendants will merge their identity with that of the Italians. Likewise Roman officials are converted to the new faith, and Luke intends us to conclude from his story that the faction wanting to confine the Christian message to the Jews was necessarily and rightly defeated. In the *Aeneid* and also in Acts we are shown an enterprise commanded by heaven, which despite setbacks cannot be stopped by human opposition. Both are tales of two cities (Troy or Jerusalem and Rome), each tracing a journey from the old world of an eastern city to the new one represented by the western metropolis.[35] In both cases the journey to Rome is proleptically symbolic of a rise to world-historical importance, already accomplished for Virgil (though not for Aeneas) and enriched by hindsight for later readers of Luke. Both texts end in dark mood (Aeneas heedless of the Roman aspiration to be merciful to the defeated, Paul in prison awaiting sentence), but in both cases our reading is coloured by knowledge of events to follow.

Luke recapitulates from the beginning of his gospel the formal address to Theophilus (ostensibly a patron in classical style, but perhaps rather a figure for the reader: the name means 'dear to God') and gives him a gentle reminder of the contents of his first volume (Acts 1:1-4). From its end he recurs to the post-Resurrection period, giving a second and more detailed account of the Ascension. Jesus appearing to the apostles tells them that they will receive the Holy Spirit, and be his witnesses 'in Jerusalem and in all Judea and Samaria and to the end of the earth' (1:8). Like much in the early chapters, this is programmatic for what follows: the list of places represents the gradual outreach presently to be narrated. After giving this commission, Jesus is lifted up before their eyes: two men in white ask them why they are looking up. The advice of the angels to the apostles is to wait for Jesus to return; the message of Luke to the reader is not to look up but to read on.

The recruitment of Matthias in place of Judas is followed by the account of the Day of Pentecost (2:1-41). As with Passover in the gospels, a new significance is given to a traditional Jewish festival: this is the occasion of the promised empowerment. Luke in his gospel switched from the formal classical tone of the preface to an atmosphere evocative of Hebrew tradition for the birth stories. He repeats this contrast at the beginning of Acts: the description of the coming of the Spirit evokes a whole range of Old Testament passages, but in particular the appearance of God at Babel (Gen. 11:5-9) and at Sinai (Exod.19:3-24). Pentecost in first-century Judaism was closely linked to the giving of the Law: Luke implies that the event now narrated has a similar importance in the sacred history of the new Israel. The theophany is typically described by comparison rather than directly ('like a rushing mighty wind, tongues as of fire': Acts 2:2-3), but whatever its nature it is enough to draw a crowd of the pilgrims in Jerusalem for the festival. This is a miracle of hearing: some indeed apparently perceive only a confusion of ecstatic or (they suspect) drunken voices, but most hear intelligible speech in a cosmopolitan variety of languages (2:12-13). Pentecost rectifies Babel: the confusion of tongues originating there is reversed. We now have another and more elaborate list of places, a catalogue of the Jewish diaspora from where the pilgrims come. Babel had indeed been partly rectified already by the spread of the Greek language in the wake of Alexander, but the point here is rather a symbolic one: the exotic place-names foreshadow the outspreading of the Christian movement in Acts and beyond, and the attuned hearing represents the way in which people from far and near can find unity in its message.

Further programmatic themes dominate the following chapters. The healing at the Temple gate by Peter and John of a beggar lame from birth (3:1-10) demonstrates how the apostles have the power to perform miracles, and thus how a characteristic feature of the ministry of Jesus still continues: the episode echoes the past as well as pointing forward. The account of Stephen (6:8-7:60) gives us the prototype of the Christian martyr. His speech to the Sanhedrin in answer to a charge of blasphemy offers a remarkable potted (and slanted) history from Abraham to Solomon, going further than the New Testament usually does in suggesting that the worship of the Jerusalem Temple has not merely been superseded but was misguided from the outset. Not entirely relevant to its context, it should perhaps with other speeches in Acts be read rather as part of a cumulative presentation to the reader, illustrating the development of Christian apologetics. It has often been observed that the use of speeches in Acts is broadly comparable to the technique of Thucydides.[36] The similarity includes (for example) the demarcation of important events by formal direct speech attributed to historical characters, and the apparent blending of fact and fiction in its content. But we can see here a more specific analogy. Thucydides explores themes such as the changing nature of Athenian imperialism by having the words of one speaker echoed or varied by another in a different time and place: the echoes are not strictly realistic, but are intended to make a point to the reader. Luke likewise has his speakers address the reader at the same time as they address the inscribed audience.[37]

Now comes the resonant story of Philip and the Ethiopian eunuch. An angel prompts the apostle to go down to the desert road (again the location of a significant encounter) from Jerusalem to Gaza:

> And behold, an Ethiopian, a eunuch, a minister of Candace the queen of the Ethiopians, in charge of all her treasure, had come to Jerusalem to worship and was returning; seated in his chariot, he was reading the prophet Isaiah. And the Spirit said to Philip, 'Go up and join this chariot'. So Philip ran to him, and heard him reading Isaiah the prophet, and asked, 'Do you understand what you are reading?' And he said, 'How can I, unless someone guides me?' And he invited Philip to come up and sit with him. Now the passage of the scripture which he was reading was this:
>
> > As a sheep led to the slaughter or as a lamb before its shearer is dumb, so he opens not his mouth. In his humiliation justice was denied him. Who can describe his generation? For his life is taken up from the earth.
>
> And the eunuch said to Philip, 'About whom, pray, does the prophet say this, about himself or about someone else?' Then Philip opened his mouth, and beginning with this scripture he told him the good news of Jesus. (Acts 8:27-35, quoting Isa. 53:7-8)

When they shortly afterwards come to some water, the eunuch asks to be baptised; this done, Philip is caught up by the Spirit and disappears, and the eunuch goes his way rejoicing. This story is a meditation on the act of reading: the moment of encounter between text and reader, and its mysteriously great potential power (a theme we shall return to in Chapter 5). The Greek words for reading (*anagnôsis*) and for recognition (*anagnôrisis*) are closely linked,[38] but here one becomes the other only through an intermediary. There are numerous echoes of the Emmaus story: the stranger met on the road, the invitation for him to stay, his role in revealing the sense of scripture, his enacting of a Christian rite, and finally his disappearance. As with Peter and John in the healing miracle, Philip here takes on the character of Jesus: we have moved beyond the stage represented by the Resurrection appearances, but we are shown that their effects continue. The encounter with Jesus at Emmaus is re-written as more explicitly an encounter with a text: the figure miraculously risen from the tomb becomes the figure no less miraculously risen from the page. In the developing story of Acts, the eunuch (an exotic eastern figure but a worshipper in the Jerusalem Temple) occupies the 'conceptual space'[39] between the purely Jewish converts and the Roman centurion Cornelius, whose conversion will be narrated at length (10:1-48): it is the test case for the mission to the Gentiles, a new direction not initially taken for granted but decisive for the future, and made possible by the intervening experience of Saul on the Damascus road (9:3-9).

Paul in Athens

Biblical and classical themes intersect most powerfully when Paul arrives in Athens.[40] His visit is invested with high symbolic importance: a decisive stage in the story, and in Luke's argument that Christianity must engage with the world.[41] The new faith is to be revealed as an enlightened position that intelligent people can support.[42] Martin Dibelius, the great German interpreter of Acts who stressed repeatedly the affiliations of the text with classical historiography, thought Paul's speech on the Areopagus entirely fictional.[43] We may prefer to envisage a literary re-casting of history, though we have seen that the speeches in Acts are addressed to the reader as well as to their original audiences. The winning of Greece is the beginning of the mission to the world: this is the first momentous encounter between Christian belief and classical culture. In Rome the apostle will come to the place epitomising the power of the classical world. Here he comes to the city which embodies its spirit.

Older books make Roman Athens sound like Edwardian England (late afternoon glory, an Indian summer) or like Matthew Arnold's Oxford (a university city living on its past, a finishing school for the ruling class).[44] This whimsy could claim some warrant in scholarly views formerly held both about Greece under Roman rule (inert, depopulated) and about Greek religion (in terminal decline). Susan Alcock in *Graecia Capta* offers a more up-beat picture of life in the Roman province of Achaea, and Robin Lane Fox in *Pagans and Christians* shows that traditional religion continued vigorous long after this date.[45] Nonetheless a traveller arriving in Athens in AD 50 (the approximate date of Paul's visit) would most obviously be struck by evidence of a great classical past lying all around. The city was much as it had been left by Augustus.[46] Major restoration and new building projects were to come a century later under the wealthy benefactor Herodes Atticus, in the age of Greek revival. The literary side of that movement, the Second Sophistic, is read now as an expression of Hellenic self-assertion, even of subversiveness towards Rome, but it remains true that such revivalism is founded ultimately on nostalgia.

Paul has come from Beroea (Acts 17:10-15), a flourishing commercial town on the Via Egnatia in northern Greece, and already a centre of the imperial cult.[47] Athens will present a strong contrast. He travels by sea (the usual way of getting between places on or near the coast of mainland Greece): he will thus have arrived at the Piraeus, and made his way up the Hamaxitos, a relatively new road from port to city. He left his companions Silas and Timothy in Beroea, but has now summoned them to join him.

> Now while Paul was waiting for them at Athens, his spirit was provoked within him as he saw that the city was full of idols. So he argued in the synagogue with the Jews and with the devout persons, and in the marketplace every day with those who chanced to be there. Some also of the

Epicurean and Stoic philosophers met him. And some said, 'What would this babbler say?' Others said, 'He seems to be a preacher of foreign divinities' – because he preached Jesus and the Resurrection. And they took hold of him and brought him to the Areopagus, saying, 'May we know what this new teaching is which you present? For you bring some strange things to our ears; we wish to know therefore what these things mean.' Now all the Athenians and the foreigners who lived there spent their time in nothing except telling or hearing something new. (Acts 17:16-21)

Paul will of course have seen pagan shrines elsewhere, but Athens had been famously religious already in the time of Sophocles (*Oedipus at Colonus* 1006-7) and was crowded with statues and dedications. According to the formulaic pattern of his arrival in a new place, he goes first to the synagogue. The remains of a building below Hymettus once claimed to be this (because of an inscription quoting Psalm 118) are now identified as a much later Christian church, but there will certainly have been a synagogue in Athens at this date: Jews formed on average a tenth of the population of Eastern Mediterranean cities.[48] But this time the synagogue is insufficient, and the next bit of Paul's walk symbolises the fact that he is to find growing acceptance instead in the Gentile world.[49]

He goes to the Agora, still the crowded city centre it had been in the days of Aristophanes. He meets adherents of the main philosophical schools, both originally founded in Athens. Their attitude seems to be that of the 'cultured despisers' addressed by Schleiermacher in the eighteenth century. The word rendered 'babbler' is *spermologos*, a gatherer of seeds (usually used of birds): Paul seems to his hearers a magpie-minded syncretist. The comment about 'foreign divinities' is clearly intended by Luke to recall the charge against Socrates, of introducing new gods. Paul is implicitly cast as a new Socratic figure: a hugely influential template, to which allusion can be made as easily as to a familiar passage of the Old Testament.[50] The plural 'divinities' may in part be explained by the Socratic echo. It is however a tempting suggestion, first made by the fourth-century church father John Chrysostom (*Homily on Acts* 38.1), that *Anastasis* ('Resurrection') is taken by Paul's hearers as the proper name of a goddess: 'Jesus and his Anastasis' would then be envisaged as a divine couple (husband and wife, or son and mother) of a sort widely paralleled in the religion of the Near East.

Paul is taken to the Areopagus ('hill of Ares', both location and institution). In classical times it had been a court dealing specifically with religious offences. By this date its venerable name seems to have been applied to what was in effect the city council, but the older and Aeschylean associations are not necessarily irrelevant for an educated reader of Luke. Apollo in *Eumenides*, a play set on the Areopagus and embodying its charter myth, says in the trial of Orestes: 'When the dust once drinks the blood of a dead man, there is no *anastasis*' (*Eum.* 647-8). Uncanny coincidence, or does Paul implicitly contradict him? At any rate, the Athenians (whose intellectual curiosity, indolence and love of novelty are traditional characteristics attested elsewhere) settle down to listen: this is probably not a formal trial, but the Socratic association equates it to one, and we are perhaps to infer that the Areopagus has the equivalent of a public gallery. The apostle now takes a more formal tone than he had in the Agora, and embarks on a rhetorical display. Older commentators slap him (or rather Luke) jovially on the back at this point: it just goes to show he could write scholarship Greek prose when he wanted to.

This is the magnificent passage that can be read today on a bronze plaque on a rocky outcrop just below the Acropolis.

> So Paul, standing in the middle of the Areopagus, said: 'Men of Athens, I perceive that in every way you are very religious. For as I passed along, and observed the objects of your worship, I found also an altar with this inscription, "To an unknown god". What therefore you worship as unknown, this I proclaim to you. The God who made the world and everything in it, being Lord of heaven and earth, does not live in shrines made by man, nor is he served by human hands, as though he needed anything, since he himself gives to all men life and breath and everything. And he made from one every nation of men to live on all the face of the earth, having determined allotted periods and the boundaries of their habitation, that they should seek God, in the hope that they might feel after and find him. Yet he is not far from each one of us, for "In him we live and move and have our being"; as even some of your poets have said, "For we are indeed his offspring". Being then God's offspring, we ought not to think that the Deity is like gold, or silver, or stone, a representation by the art and imagination of man. The times of ignorance God overlooked, but now he commands all men everywhere to repent, because he has fixed a day on which he will judge the world in righteousness by a man whom he has appointed, and of this he has given assurance to all men by raising him from the dead.' (Acts 17:22-31)

Paul takes his starting-point from his walk through the city, his conciliatory tone contrasting with his initial inward reaction. There has been much debate about the inscription he claims to have read. No such altar has been found: that of course is not decisive, but dedications to 'unknown gods' in the plural are very common. It must remain an open question whether Paul saw an exceptional example, or Luke retouched the story to suit his argument. The underlying idea is nonetheless extremely widespread: a polytheist agenda always allows for Any Other Business, and fosters the precaution of which we catch a distant echo in the dedication by a soldier on Hadrian's Wall to 'whatever god lives in this place'. Paul elevates the unknown god from afterthought to unique centrality. We meet again here the theme of a visitor bringing or revealing something present already, like Socrates uncovering innate ideas, or Aeneas carrying his household gods to a naturally numinous Italy. Far from introducing foreign deities, Paul preaches a god unwittingly worshipped already,[51] but an intermediary is needed (again like a Socratic midwife, or like Philip

138

expounding scripture to the Ethiopian eunuch) to reveal the true meaning of something ostensibly familiar.

This sense of recognition applies not just to the inscription but to fundamental patterns of thought. Paul's account of the nature of God will have seemed at once conventional and provocative. Ideas about Zeus had long tended in a monotheist direction, and the Greek philosophical deity shared with the God of Israel oneness, universality, and self-sufficiency (the last a theme much stressed in Hellenistic philosophy). Insisting that God does not dwell in shrines made by human hands allows Paul rhetorically to deny (it is tempting to imagine with a sweeping gesture) the rationale of the great temples around him, yet that idea was already a commonplace to educated pagans: Zeno, the founder of Stoicism, had declared temples superfluous (the true temple being the human intellect), and Chrysippus, a later head of the same school, had said that it was childish to represent gods in human shape.[52]

Paul uses language and arguments already forged by Greek-speaking Jews to commend their religion to outsiders. Such apologetic argued that, whilst the images and cults of paganism were unworthy of God, all people in their own traditions could have some intimation of his nature, and the poets and philosophers of Greece had often come near to the truth. Judaism and philosophy are blended through most of his speech. The claim that God 'made the world and everything in it' echoes the beginning of Genesis, but Stoic philosophers also proclaimed God as the creator of all things: both accounts insist that he is the maker not the made. This 'natural theology', the idea that knowledge of God can be gained simply by looking at the world, is important in the Old Testament: 'The heavens declare the glory of God, and the firmament sheweth his handiwork' (Ps. 19:1). The notion of divine self-sufficiency underlies a frequent criticism of Temple ritual (for example Ps. 50:8-11), as well as being a philosophical commonplace. Creation of all nations from one stock expresses the Hebrew idea of descent from Adam, but chimes too with the unity of mankind stressed by Stoicism. 'Allotted periods and the boundaries of their habitation' evokes Hebrew myths about creation over a sequence of days, with the pushing back both of chaos and of the sea, but also echoes Stoic ideas about the succession of ages and the providential ordering of the earth which made some parts fit for human occupation. The name of the God of Israel suggested 'to be' ('the great I Am'), and the name of Zeus had been connected with *zaô* ('I live').[53] Such wordplay seems to be involved in the confession (which both traditions could make) that 'In him we live and move and have our being.'

This is punctuated in the RSV as a quotation, and usually attributed to the Cretan Epimenides. A shadowy and semi-mythical figure of perhaps about 600 BC, reputedly the author of a *Theogony* and other mystical works, Epimenides was credited with the character of a shaman, claiming out-of-body experiences, a miraculous sleep of fifty-seven years, and extreme longevity.[54] We approach him here by a circuitous trail. A Syriac commentary on Acts, thought to be based on the work of the church father Theodore of Mopsuestia (writing about AD 400), claims that Paul quotes an address by King Minos of Crete to his father Zeus, protesting against a local tradition that the god had been savaged by a wild boar, and was dead and buried:

> The Cretans carve a tomb for you, high and holy one! Liars, evil beasts and slow bellies! For you are not dead for ever; you are alive and risen; for in you we live and move and have our being.[55]

The disguised Odysseus in Ithaca casts himself as a Cretan in three of the five false stories he tells about his life: it is likely that Homer wittily invokes as familiar (rather than creating) a reputation for mendacity. It seems originally to have focused specifically on these claims about Zeus, outrageous to pious sentiment.[56] Paul quotes the phrase 'Liars, evil beasts and slow bellies!' in his Epistle to Titus as a description of Cretans by 'a prophet of their own' (Titus 1:12). Another church father, Clement of Alexandria (writing about AD 200), attributes that quotation specifically to Epimenides, and it is therefore often supposed that the whole speech put into the mouth of Minos comes from a poetic work by the Cretan author. Callimachus in his *Hymn to Zeus* (10-12) has a shorter but similar passage about Cretan liars and the tomb of Zeus,[57] and he too may be drawing on Epimenides. Paul (or Luke) perhaps intends the quotation in the Areopagus speech to bring associations of its original context when he applies it to another figure proclaimed to be alive and risen. Certainly the gist of the quotation in Titus, or the tradition behind it, was famous: it is the basis of the paradox (on which whole books were written in the ancient world) 'Epimenides the Cretan said all Cretans are liars': as he is a Cretan himself, must he not be lying in making the claim?[58]

Epimenides may have a second connection with Acts 17. Diogenes Laertius in his *Lives of the Philosophers* (1.110), written in the third century AD, relates how the Cretan sage was summoned as a religious expert to deal with a crisis in Athens. An attempted coup by the aristocrat Cylon (traditionally dated 632 BC) had been foiled by the Athenians under the magistrate Megacles at the cost of incurring religious pollution when some associates of the would-be tyrant were killed while taking refuge as suppliants at an altar of Athene (this was the origin of a famous curse on Megacles' family the Alcmaeonids, often invoked against them later by political opponents, and a significant factor in classical Greek history). The pollution also caused a plague, and it was to purify the city from this that Epimenides was reputedly consulted. His proposed solution was to let sheep graze on the then grassy Areopagus: any that lay down were to be sacrificed to 'the appropriate' (that is, unspecified local) god, and the plague was duly stayed. Diogenes concludes the story by saying that still in his time altars could be found in different parts of Attica with no name on them, as a memorial of this atonement: could it have been one of these that Paul saw as he passed along?

We are on firmer ground with his second quotation, 'For we are indeed his offspring.' Immediately recognisable as part of a hexameter, this comes from the fifth line of Aratus' *Phaenomena*, a Hellenistic didactic poem about the heavenly bodies dating from the early third century BC. It exemplifies the fashion in that age for polished poems on technically difficult subjects: poets saw a challenge in turning prose treatises into lucid and elegant verse, as well as aspiring to write in the tradition of Hesiod. In some cases, such as Nicander in his *Alexipharmaca* on antidotes to poisonous snakes, the aim was perhaps to savour a contrast between fine manner and ludicrously mundane matter (like Tom Lehrer singing the periodic table of the elements as a Gilbertian patter-song). But in the case of Aratus we should not underestimate the direct interest of the subject. Inhabitants of the ancient world told the time by the sun, navigated by the stars, and (as we find Jane Austen's characters still doing) planned journeys to coincide with a full moon.[59] Furthermore Aratus wrote from a Stoic perspective: Paul pays a graceful compliment to the Stoics in his audience, for whom the heavenly bodies were part of a familiar argument from design. The proem from which the quotation comes is a hymn to Zeus, and the most obviously Stoic part of the work. It is sometimes claimed that the *Phaenomena* is a systematic attempt to depict a benign deity supervising an ordered cosmos: that may go too far, but it can be safely said that the role of Zeus in the prologue neatly sums up his dual identity as the Stoic guiding principle who is still also the traditional sky god.

The poem was popular in antiquity and Luke could well have read it, or Paul himself (if the historicity of the speech extends to such detail) may have known and paid tribute to the work of a fellow Cilician. Equally however the phrase may have been already a familiar quotation, in oral tradition or as part of a published collection. The same applies to another well-known example of a classical author quoted by Paul: the phrase in 1 Corinthians rendered by the Authorised Version as 'evil communications corrupt good manners' (1 Cor.15:33, formerly attributed to Euripides, but now known to come from Menander's comedy *Thais*) seems an obvious candidate for circulation as a gnomic piece of popular wisdom.[60] On the other hand we should not play down too much Paul's direct acquaintance with Greek literature. 1 Corinthians shows the clear influence of classical rhetoric, with its diatribe style, its imaginary interlocutor objecting to the idea of bodily resurrection (15:12-58), and the analogy of the mutually dependent body parts as a model for society (12:12-31): this has many classical parallels, but is most familiar as the fable of Menenius Agrippa in Livy (2.32.8-12).

It is also perhaps significant that Paul attributes the quotation from *Phaenomena* to plural 'poets'. A very similar phrase occurs in the *Hymn to*

Zeus of Cleanthes, another Stoic work (Cleanthes was head of the school between Zeno and Chrysippus) to which Aratus himself may already be referring.[61] That hymn has often been seen as the high water mark of a conception of Zeus comparable to Judaeo-Christian ethical monotheism. James Adam in *The Religious Teachers of Greece* (1910) described the Cleanthes hymn as 'perhaps the noblest tribute of religious adoration in the whole range of ancient literature'.[62] Adam's tone may seem dated, but the conception of Zeus which he commends needs due emphasis for understanding Paul's rhetorical technique. Only with much common ground established does he come finally to the specifically Christian content of his sermon. In obvious respects this would be startling: the urgent call to repentance, the appointed man who is the Son of Man, and his bodily resurrection (in contrast to the Greek philosophical tradition which saw the body as a prison or tomb from which the immortal soul sought escape). Yet even here there are some shared ideas. We have seen that repentance, coming to oneself, is a version of recognition. The appointed man is the visitor who will also be the judge. The Platonist idea of the immortality of the soul as expounded in *Phaedo* and the Christian idea of the resurrection of the body have profound differences, but they share the underlying assumption that human life exists in a larger context. As in the account of the sheep and goats in Matthew 25, we have here a story about an unknown god which both is and is not specifically Christian.

Paul gets a mixed reception: some mock the idea of bodily resurrection, others enigmatically say they will hear him further on the subject (Acts 17:32). Like David Livingstone in Africa, Paul does not attract a quantity of converts commensurate with the symbolic importance of his visit. There is no Pauline equivalent of an Alexandria founded here, and no Epistle to the Athenians.[63] The Parthenon would eventually be converted into a church, but Christianity seems to have been slow to take root in Athens. Nonetheless we read that some join Paul and believe, 'among them Dionysius the Areopagite and a woman named Damaris and others with them' (17:34). Dionysius gave his name to the broad pedestrianised street which now runs below the Areopagus, but we know nothing about him. He is perhaps singled out for mention because Luke likes to stress that Paul made contacts with the educated élite as well as ordinary people in the cities he visited. He was traditionally regarded as the author of a corpus of mystical writings including a treatise on the ranks of angels which shaped medieval ideas of heaven (and provided Athelstan Riley in 'Ye watchers and ye holy ones' with his rich vocabulary: 'Bright Seraphs, Cherubim and Thrones ... Dominions, Princedoms, Powers'[64]). These texts, blending Christian and Neoplatonist elements in indiscriminate abundance,[65] are now known to belong to a much later period, but their anonymous author made an apposite choice when he attached to them the name of a man converted by a programmatic expression of the new faith and Greek philosophy in combination.

142

Paul's speech seems prophetic of much to come: that is partly why scholars have been sceptical of its historicity. It foreshadows a style of apologetic characteristic of the Greek fathers of the later second century, though Acts itself is unlikely to have been written later than the end of the first, if only because its pro-Roman stance would be less easily explicable after the persecution under Domitian. Nonetheless many German scholars traditionally assigned a date of AD 120 or later. This is the background to Eduard Norden's classic *Agnostos Theos* (1913): he argued (in a style analogous to later Neoanalyst criticism of Homer) that the account of Paul in Athens is an adaptation of a story originally told with a different central character, the wandering and wonder-working Pythagorean philosopher and mystic Apollonius of Tyana (born about 4 BC). There are indeed compelling thematic connections between the story of Apollonius and the New Testament, but Norden surely put the cart before the horse.[66] The more obvious parallel to Apollonius is not Paul but Jesus, and this perception is in a crucial way retrospective. Apollonius would not stand out from the many other holy men of the time but for the biography of him written by Philostratus about AD 200. By that date opponents of Christianity sought a pagan narrative to set against the life of Jesus in the gospels.[67] Specific parallels in the text are therefore unsurprising, because the natural assumption is that Philostratus had the gospels before him as a model.

Damaris lost even her fleeting appearance in the text when she was omitted by western copyists from an important group of manuscripts, but like Dionysius she has a symbolic importance. The role of women in the New Testament has in recent decades attracted much attention from new perspectives, but it has always been acknowledged that Luke (both in his gospel and in Acts) is an honourable exception within the male-centred presentation of the earliest church: his female characters are treated with unusual consideration, and even their silence attests not masculine disregard but wisdom (Luke 10:38-42).[68]

Young churches

Athens represented the Greek intellectual legacy. In Corinth, his next port of call, Paul confronts the practicalities of the first-century Roman world, and we can trace links with familiar historical events. He meets a Jewish couple, Aquila and Priscilla, and goes to stay with them: Luke repeatedly records hospitality to bearers of the Christian message (Acts 18:2-3). Paul's hosts are refugees from Rome after the expulsion of Jews by Claudius in AD 49 (Luke alone among New Testament authors mentions any of the Roman emperors by name). He is able to earn his keep because they are tent-makers as he is: only anachronistic prejudice sees a problem in the apostle as simultaneously artisan and learned Rabbi. The trade probably extended to sails and awnings, the latter in demand for the

Isthmian games nearby. Paul stayed in Corinth for eighteen months, and the athletic imagery of his letters may derive from direct observation as well as rhetorical convention.

As an archaeological site Corinth brings us closer than any other city to the events of Acts.[69] Although some of its excavated buildings belong to a later period, the view over the Lechaion road and market gives a fine sense of a thriving Graeco-Roman city. Already in Homer described by the formulaic epithet 'wealthy' (for example *Il.* 2.570), Corinth had been the main trading rival of Athens in the fifth century BC (a major cause of the Peloponnesian War), and as a cosmopolitan port with harbours on both sides of the Isthmus developed a louche reputation. Already in Aristophanes (*Frogs* 354) the verb *korinthiazomai* means 'fornicate', and the city became famous for its prostitutes (Plato *Republic* 404d), many reputedly attached to a shrine of Aphrodite on the rocky summit of Acrocorinth. It has seemed to many commentators an easy jump to the rebukes hurled by Paul in 1 Corinthians at a prevailing culture of immorality (1 Cor. 5:1-13). It can indeed be pointed out that Corinth is famous also for its sack by the Roman general Mummius in 146 BC, after which it lay desolate for a century before being re-founded as a colony by Julius Caesar: hence it is questioned whether we can legitimately assume continuity of reputation. On the other hand, just as the archaic temple of Apollo survived to form part of the Roman city, the literary tradition may have seemed still relevant when similar social conditions again prevailed.

Corinth was probably at this date the administrative centre for the province of Achaea. It has a similar centrality for the apologetic purpose of the text. At first Paul's method in Corinth is his usual one: 'Every Sabbath he reasoned in the synagogue, trying to persuade Jews and Greeks' (Acts 18:4). But then (emboldened perhaps by the arrival of Silas and Timothy from Macedonia) he seems to have devoted himself to preaching in a more concentrated and uncompromising way. When the Jews oppose him and become abusive, he shakes out his clothes in protest and says to them: 'Your blood be on your own heads! I am clear of my responsibility. From now on I will go to the Gentiles' (18:6). Though Paul continues to attract Jewish converts, this is a major thematic turning-point, anticipated in Athens and marked by a nocturnal divine vision urging him to remain steadfast (18:9-10). The Jews then make a united attack on Paul and bring him to the tribunal (the stone platform survives) before the proconsul Gallio (18:12).

This is L. Iunius Gallio Annaeanus, the brother of the Stoic philosopher Seneca the Younger. Originally Annaeus Novatus, he was adopted by the orator and senator L. Junius Gallio by whose name he was thereafter known. Our evidence about him not only illustrates the intersection of Roman history and New Testament studies, but provides a textbook example of the use of epigraphy to fill gaps in a literary text: Acts conforms in many respects to the conventions of ancient historiography, but is

144

conspicuously lacking in absolute indications of date.[70] An inscription found at Delphi in 1905 records privileges granted to the city by the emperor Claudius on the basis of a report sent to him by his 'friend and proconsul Lucius Iunius Gallio', at a time when (according to the fragmentary but formulaic imperial titles heading the stone) he had been acclaimed as emperor twenty-six times. Although such acclamations were made not at fixed intervals but in response to military victories, by cross-reference to other preserved inscriptions and to a letter of Seneca recording Gallio's return to Rome through illness part way through his twelve months of office (*Epistles* 104.1), we can date his encounter with Paul to the second half of AD 51. This pleasingly confirms what had been inferred on other grounds about the chronology of Acts.[71]

Gallio takes the line that Paul is involved in a debate about Jewish law, not a contravention of Roman. He thus refuses to consider the case brought against him by the Jews (18:14-16). Although this ruling is followed by a violent outburst about which Gallio takes no action, Luke leaves us in no doubt that the proconsul has on the main issue made the right decision. Once again the text defends Roman rule and insists that the message of Paul offers it no threat. A similar perception underlies the anonymous (and certainly spurious) letters which survive, purporting to be a correspondence between Paul and Seneca.[72] Their author presumably saw a literary opportunity in bringing together two great letter-writers of the period: the apostle who wrote to the young churches he had founded or supported, and the Roman moralist and statesman who cast much of his teaching in the form of letters to a real or imaginary friend Lucilius. The church father Tertullian (*Apology* 20) describes Seneca as *saepe noster* ('often ours'), and in the Middle Ages it was commonly believed that the philosopher had been a Christian.[73]

The theme of civil unrest features more prominently in Acts 19, when Paul comes to Ephesus. No text better illustrates city life under Rome in the Greek east: the local loyalties, the integration of religion and the economy, the violence only just held in check. Ephesus was probably by this date the third largest city in the empire after Rome and Alexandria. Its temple of Artemis (four times the size of the Parthenon) was from Hellenistic times usually listed as one of the Seven Wonders. The cult was untypically expansionist, and the goddess herself was unusual: in origin perhaps a local fertility deity, a world away from the virgin huntress of literary tradition. A thriving tourist trade had developed, specialising (it appears, though none has been found) in miniature models of the shrine.

About this time there arose no little stir concerning the Way. For a man named Demetrius, a silversmith, who made silver shrines of Artemis, brought no little business to the craftsmen. These he gathered together, with the workmen of like occupation, and said, 'Men, you know that from this occupation we have our wealth. And you see and hear that not only at

145

Ephesus but almost throughout all Asia this Paul has persuaded and turned away a considerable company of people, saying that gods made with hands are not gods. And there is danger not only that this trade of ours may come into disrepute but also that the temple of the great goddess Artemis may count for nothing, and that she may even be deposed from her magnificence, she whom all Asia and the world worship.' When they heard this they were enraged, and cried out, 'Great is Artemis of the Ephesians!' (Acts 19:23-8)

The Ephesians fill the theatre (the natural political focus of an ancient city) and keep up their chant for two hours: they are quieted only when the city clerk points out the risk of being charged with rioting. The attack on Paul is oblique testimony to his success. Here again is the theme of the Areopagus speech, about the unreality of gods made with hands; and retrospect opens up the larger view of a time when the scarcely conceivable happened, the ancient gods indeed deposed from their magnificence.

After these chapters in which Paul carries the gospel to the provinces bordering the Aegean comes his last journey to Jerusalem, his arrest there, and his journey to Rome under armed guard to have his case (as a Roman citizen) heard by the emperor. With the account of the voyage and shipwreck in chapter 27, followed by the landing in Malta and arrival at Rome in chapter 28, Acts comes to a powerful but enigmatic climax. The transition to first-person narrative as Paul sets sail has been much discussed. The simplest reading suggests an incorporated passage from a diary kept by Luke. Or perhaps (as has been claimed, without very firm evidence) there was a literary convention of using a first-person authorial voice to give immediacy to accounts of voyages:[74] that at any rate is the effect Luke achieves, with the narrator temporarily becoming a character in his own narrative. If a recognised stylistic device of this kind did exist, it would further attest what we know from many sources: that sea-travel in the ancient Mediterranean world was as fearfully hazardous as it was indispensable, and that a rich literary tradition grew up around the theme of voyages and in particular of storms and shipwrecks. It has been argued that the language of Acts 27 has specific echoes of the *Odyssey*,[75] and we have seen already that there are more general similarities. Hazardous voyages and shipwrecks are the stuff of the Greek novel, and that genre too (itself ultimately descended from Homeric epic) has parallels in Acts. The dangers of the deep are important also in many biblical stories. In the new earth of John's vision there is no more sea (Rev. 21:1). He implicitly endorses what Hesiod had said long before, that going to sea is disagreeable, and it is a fearful thing to die among the waves (*Works and Days* 618 and 687).

Paul's voyage is a lesson in ancient geography, and in sailing conditions. The Alexandrian grain ship bound from Lycia to Italy is diverted from its intended course by the wind (Acts 27:7) as the ships of Odysseus involuntarily leave behind places that can be found on a map (*Od.* 9.80-4). The unheeded warning of Paul that it is dangerously late in the year (Acts

27:9-12) underlines the seasonal nature of ancient seafaring. In that incident he appears in a benign and secular role. People whose actions had made them polluted so that they might provoke divine wrath were however understandably shunned as fellow passengers, and one reason why the ensuing shipwreck is related at such length is surely to stress that the escape of all the passengers amounts to a confirmation of Paul's innocence (27:44).[76] Landing in Malta, they are welcomed by the inhabitants. A viper fastens itself on Paul's hand as they gather firewood: the islanders initially take this as a bad omen, but when he shakes it off into the flames without harm they conclude that he is a god (28:3-6). In contrast to the incident at Lystra, this false recognition does not provoke an immediate denial. We are redirected instead to the true nature of Paul's mission (and to recurrent themes of Acts) when immediately afterwards he is hospitably received by Publius, the chief official of the island, whose sick father he heals by prayer and the laying on of hands (28:7-8).

After three months Paul and his companions set sail in another Alexandrian ship via Syracuse and Rhegium to Puteoli. The ship has as its figurehead the heavenly twins Castor and Pollux (28:11). Why does Luke pause to tell us this? Castor and Pollux (the Dioscuri) were guardians of truth and punishers of perjurers, so the point about the innocence of their passenger is implicitly reiterated. They were also however connected importantly with the imperial cult, and so perhaps there is a hint here about the trial in Rome which still lies ahead when Acts ends, and more generally about rival claims to allegiance. The final section of the book presents a mixed picture. Welcomed by local Christians as he approaches the city, Paul cannot enter the Roman Forum as he entered the Athenian Agora: throughout the second half of Acts Paul the prisoner looms as large as Paul the missionary.[77] But he is allowed under house arrest to receive visitors (it is tempting to see an echo of Socrates in prison) and to preach for two years (28:15-31). Here the narrative breaks off, rivalling the end of Mark in its abruptness.[78] Here too we are to infer that there is more of the story to come. Like the *Iliad*, Acts funnels down to a concentration on its main character and his impending death, but leaves that death itself undescribed. Like the *Aeneid*, it ends in a manner ostensibly puzzling and unsatisfactory, but requiring the perspective given by later events. Like the *Oresteia*, it leaves us with a sense of vast distance already travelled, and also has a momentum thrusting beyond the text into the lives of its audience. The journey from Jerusalem has been accomplished: the message of the gospel has leapt like a beacon light from community to community through the Mediterranean world, and has entered the gates of Rome.

5

Spots of Time

In this final chapter I trace some of the themes we have been considering in authors of the Roman imperial period, and look at aspects of their reception in the eighteenth and nineteenth centuries.

The death of Pan

Plutarch's dialogue *On the Decline of Oracles* is set at Delphi in about AD 83. Its author is the most important Greek writer of the Roman period: a prolific biographer, historian and moral philosopher. He held a priesthood at the shrine, and seems to have regarded it as a second home.[1] Delphi had been the leading oracle of the ancient world since the eighth century BC. A group of learned men here discuss how oracular prophecy works, and why oracles have become less vocal and important than in the classical past. The conversation turns to *daimones* (divine spirits, spoken of by Hesiod and Plato as intermediaries between gods and men), and the question whether divine beings can die elicits from a historian named Philip the haunting story of the death of Pan. He tells his interlocutors how Epitherses, a teacher and the father of a mutual friend, was once sailing from Greece to Italy on a ship full of passengers and cargo. In the evening the wind dropped as they were passing the Echinades islands in north-west Greece; becalmed, the ship drifted towards a further pair of small islands called Paxi. With most of the passengers still awake and enjoying their after-dinner wine, a voice was suddenly heard from one of these islands, calling out 'Thamus'. Unknown to most of the passengers, this was the name of the ship's Egyptian helmsman who kept silent at the first two calls, but responded to a third, whereupon he was told that when they reached Palodes (the harbour of the city of Buthrotum familiar from Virgil) he should announce that Great Pan was dead. Astounded, he resolved that if there was a wind he would sail past and do nothing, but if sky and sea were calm he would comply. This duly happening, he had no sooner uttered the prescribed words than there arose a great groaning and cry of amazement, as if from many people. News of the incident quickly spread to Rome, and Thamus was summoned to give an account to the emperor Tiberius (Plutarch *Moralia* 419b-e).

This story is known from no other source. It has been variously explained. Several different theories depend on the near-identity in Greek of the name of the god and *pan* meaning 'all'. Thamus has been linked to the

148

Mesopotamian Tammuz, one of the dying and rising fertility gods made central to the explanation of all religion by Frazer in *The Golden Bough*. Thus it is suggested that the story garbles a ritual cry which accompanied the annual commemoration of his death: its original form would have had not Thamus as addressee, but Tammuz as subject, and would have honoured not Great Pan, but the 'all-great' vegetation god identified by Frazer with the Greek Adonis.[2] In contrast to all this is the explanation offered by Christian legend from the church father Eusebius onwards. Because the events described took place during the reign of Tiberius, it was claimed that they coincided in time with the Crucifixion. The story thus represented the demise of paganism, the replacement of its regime of evil spirits: not Pan but Christ was truly 'all', because from him everything derived and he was everything to the world.[3] Interpreted in this way, the story has had considerable literary influence. Thus Milton in his 'Hymn: On the Morning of Christ's Nativity':

> The oracles are dumb,
> No voice or hideous hum
> Runs through the arched roofs in words deceiving.

As we saw in Chapter 4, modern scholarship stresses the health and longevity of pagan religion, and resists seeing decline and desolation as the dominant characteristics of Roman Greece. The Delphic oracle survived for another three centuries after the conversation recorded by Plutarch, but his story foreshadows the poignant account of the very last oracular response, delivered in the fourth century (via his doctor Oribasius) to the emperor Julian, named by Christian writers 'the Apostate' for his counter-reformation attempt to restore the pagan past after the conversion of Constantine.[4]

> Tell the king: the decorated court has fallen to the ground;
> Apollo no longer has a cell, or a prophetic laurel,
> Or a babbling spring: even the chattering water is dry.
> *(Palatine Anthology* 3.6.122)

The mysterious story which Philip tells, whatever its original significance, has in retrospect an important symbolic meaning. The replacement of classical paganism by Christianity is the one massive exception to the general rule that religions (for example Zoroastrianism, the creed of ancient Persia) do not die but live precariously on in attenuated form.[5] At some point in perhaps the sixth or seventh century AD, the last person died who had believed literally in the old gods.

Elizabeth Barrett Browning in 'The Dead Pan' (1844) reworked Plutarch:

> And that dismal cry rose slowly,
> And sank slowly through the air,

Full of spirit's melancholy
And eternity's despair.

Her poem ostensibly depicts with imaginative sympathy an event distant in time, viewed from the safe perspective of Victorian piety. Yet for many nineteenth-century writers there was a disturbing implied question about whether the demise of religion was to be re-enacted in their own society. This is the road to Matthew Arnold's 'Dover Beach', with the 'melancholy long withdrawing roar' of the sea of faith, echoed a century later by Philip Larkin musing in a country church about who would be 'the last, the very last, to seek this place for what it was'.[6] Richard Jenkyns in *The Victorians and Ancient Greece* shows how Mrs Browning was writing in response to Friedrich von Schiller's 1788 poem 'The Gods of Greece'.[7] This was a lament for the Greek deities who had died because something in the human spirit had died: nature had once been alive with gods, and the sun seen as the golden chariot of Helios. Scientists explaining it as a ball of gas had spoiled the sacred story, repeating the offence of the Ionian philosopher Anaxagoras who had long ago explained it as an incandescent rock. Schiller's poem was taken by some Victorian readers as an attack on Christianity, a manifesto for recovering the spirit of classical paganism, but its target seems rather to have been the spiritual deadness of the modern world.

The powerful theme of the decline of religion can be traced back a long way. Schiller in imagining the Olympian gods leaving the earth had implicitly equated their departure with the end of mankind's belief in them, and with the end of the ancient world. But classical authors themselves frequently used the idea of divine withdrawal to point up the contrast between the heroic past and their own prosaic present. Already in the *Odyssey* when Alcinous, speculating about the identity of his guest, describes the free communication of the gods with the Phaeacians (in contrast to the subterfuge that would have to be assumed if their unidentified guest were a god in disguise), Homer implies that this is something no longer available (*Od.* 7.199-206). The description of the impious Iron Age in Hesiod (*Works and Days* 174-201) ends with the withdrawal from earth of the white-robed goddesses Aidôs and Nemesis (something like 'Modesty' and 'Moral Disapproval'). Aratus in recounting the stories behind the heavenly bodies relates how Justice, the virgin daughter of Astraeus, mingled happily with men and women in the Golden Age, tolerated the Silver, but departed in disgust with the advent of the Bronze (*Phaenomena* 96-136). Catullus at the end of Poem 64, his miniature epic in Hellenistic style written about 60 BC, after contrasting happy and unhappy love in the interlaced stories of Peleus and Ariadne, explains how the events narrated (in which the gods interacted freely with human characters) had been able to take place:

For of old, before religion was despised, the heavenly ones in bodily presence used to visit the pious homes of heroes and show themselves to mortal company. (64.384-6)

Theoxeny is seen to belong to a vanished age. The poem until this point has been a highly polished and self-conscious treatment of two myths: though not indeed lacking darker tones, it has seemed to many critics elegantly detached and lacking real passion. Its epilogue in contrast is unrelievedly serious and sombre: ever-increasing human wickedness in the period between the heroic age and his own day has produced a catalogue of crimes.[8] Catullus perhaps expresses a gloom especially characteristic of the late Republic, but he uses a familiar idea in contrasting the contemporary world with a more glamorous and vibrant past.[9] He ends by returning once more to the gods, in a lament for lost enchantment which seems proto-Romantic in feeling:[10]

Therefore they no longer condescend to join men's feasts and festivals, nor endure the touch of glaring daylight. (64.407-8)

The second-century AD travel writer and historian Pausanias may seem a curious pair for Catullus: author of the immensely detailed *Periegesis* of Greece, a guidebook concerned in particular with religious antiquities, he was in the past valued mainly as a source for classical archaeology. But he is now taken more seriously as a literary writer, and the sensibility he brings to his task seems similarly to anticipate Romanticism. Pausanias is in general self-effacing: his expressions of opinion and feeling are the more powerful for their relative infrequency. Arcadia, offering a concentration of the oldest and most mysterious Greek lore, prompts him to fundamental questions about the distant past and to a renewed conviction of the wisdom and truth embodied in myth. Like Catullus, he uses the language of theoxeny:

For the men of those days, because of their justice and piety, were *xenoi* (hosts/guests) of the gods, eating at the same table (*Paus.* 8.2.4)

In those days, he goes on to say, men even turned into gods (he instances Aristaeus, Heracles and others), and stories of metamorphosis (Lycaon into a wolf, Niobe into stone) can also be believed. The contrast between this rich past and a duller, darker present is introduced by a tellingly recurrent phrase:

But in my time, since wickedness has increased to the highest degree and spread over every land and all cities, no one turns from man to god, except in words and flattery addressed to despotic power. (8.2.5)

This cynical dismissal of the Roman imperial cult is a product of his

151

nostalgia for Greek freedom, the sense of a lost classical past. Pausanias invites being read as the literary equivalent of a painting by Caspar David Friedrich, as a study of ruined shrines in a sacred landscape. It is true indeed that for every deserted temple Pausanias describes ten fully functioning; he is however preoccupied with the themes of grandeur and decline. He can seem also Virgilian: underlying the vast catalogue of monuments is the sense of an obscure anxiety, a quest never entirely fulfilled. Our reading is inevitably coloured by hindsight: travelling in the security of the Antonine age, Pausanias saw those monuments just in time.[11] He seems nonetheless uncannily to anticipate the Romantic idea of impending inevitable loss as even more poignant than past loss, and his longing gaze at an irretrievable ideal made him a congenial guide to early nineteenth-century travellers whose cult of ruins he seemed to confirm.[12]

In the rest of this chapter we shall see other ideas in ancient authors which foreshadow the age of Wordsworth. Virgil is a rich source of them. Yet it is also Virgil who alludes obliquely to the peroration of Catullus 64 only in order to reverse its message, envisaging in the fourth *Eclogue* a time when 'a new generation descends from heaven on high' (*Ecl.* 4.7). This is the language of panegyric, yet it implies a possibility not closed off for ever, a potential for enchantment even in modernity; and indeed we shall see that the themes both of theoxeny and of *anagnôrisis* have proved remarkably enduring in new guises.

Fathers and heretics

We saw that Paul's speech in Athens anticipates the strategies of preachers a century after its dramatic date. Luke may already write for a partly non-Christian audience, but the second century is the great age of apologetic, of works consciously addressed to outsiders.[13] In this section I consider the important tradition in the early church represented by the Greek apologists of the second and third centuries, and some links between them and contemporary pagan authors. The hospitable openness of the Greek fathers to classical culture (or at least to some aspects of it) contrasts markedly with the attitude of their Latin contemporaries, most obviously Tertullian, who famously asked 'What has Athens to do with Jerusalem?' (*Against Heretics* 7). This was a question expecting the answer 'Nothing', but (as Henry Chadwick put it) the Greek fathers would have replied 'Much in every way';[14] they might have begun by observing that Tertullian's rhetoric was itself classical. The Greek fathers were concerned with a question of central importance for educated Christians in the early centuries AD: what should be made of the pagan past and its literature?

The first important figure here is Justin:[15] we met in Chapter 2 the comparison between Socrates and Jesus which pervades his writings. Like many of the apologists, Justin was a convert. The Christian idea of conversion draws importantly on concepts we have explored: the sense of coming to oneself which is internalised recognition, and the radical change of perspective precipitated by that experience. A.D. Nock in his classic study *Conversion* (1933) showed that there is a more specific model in the tradition of conversion to philosophy as a new way of life.[16] It is in these terms that Justin describes his own early career in his *Dialogue with Trypho the Jew* (the title a reminder that early Christian apologists were addressing Jewish as well as pagan critics).[17] He tells how he went first to study with a Stoic philosopher, but learned nothing about God, a subject which indeed seemed to bore him. He turned then to a Peripatetic (a follower of Aristotle), but found the man preoccupied with his fee: this echoes criticism of the fifth-century Sophists, but had become a cliché specifically about Aristotelian tutors. Next he went to a Pythagorean, who seemed interested solely in mathematical theorems. Only upon attaching himself to a Platonist did he for the first time feel to be making progress: his mind had been given wings, and he hoped in time to attain the goal held up in the *Phaedrus*, namely to see God.

Then one day while walking along a beach (Justin tells us he likes solitary walks, not a typical ancient enthusiasm) he met an old man and fell into conversation about Plato (*Dialogue with Trypho* 3). It was a strange meeting: the seventeenth-century French historian Tillemont commented that the old man must have been an angel.[18] Unlike Plato, who taught that the soul was immortal and had life in itself, the old man described the soul's life as a gift from God, the source of all life. Justin sensed that the old man was talking about things he had not heard before: who could teach this way of life? The old man replied that long before the Greek philosophers there had lived prophets who wrote about the beginning and end of things, proceeding not by argument but by bearing witness to what they had seen and heard. Their predictions (especially in the Suffering Servant passages of Isaiah) had been fulfilled in the virgin birth of Jesus, his Passion and descent to Hades, his Ascension and his title 'Son of God'. The old man departed with a prayer that the gates of light would be opened for Justin, who indeed came to see that the way of life his companion had described was alone sure and fulfilling.

This is a moving account, and also a highly polished one in a recognisable tradition (Lucian and Galen describe in a pagan context their pilgrimage from one philosophical school to another[19]): hence inevitable but unanswerable questions about historicity. The leading themes are Justin's sustained exploration of his own experience, and the fact that true transformation comes only after several unsuccessful encounters. Conversion and autobiography go naturally together: the most celebrated ancient example is Augustine, whom we shall look at in the next section. But the ideas of a restless quest (Justin was both physically and intellectually itinerant) and of transformation are characteristic also of the Greek novel. That genre is now a fashionable area of study, and although some claims made for the five surviving examples may be exaggerated, it can readily be conceded that these texts were unfairly neglected in the past. The novels attest what Simon Goldhill (echoing Michel Foucault) has called 'a new internalising "care of the self" – part of the milieu from which Christianity emerged'.[20] Some of the novels are difficult to date: the genre probably had its formal origin in the Hellenistic period, though Xenophon's *Cyropaedia* provides an important earlier precedent. We saw in the previous chapter that Acts (and indeed the gospels) have some features in common with the novel in its developed form, though this is not necessarily an indication of direct debt. G.W. Bowersock in *Fiction as History* presents an intriguing case for influence the other way round, arguing that we can see in the novel a Graeco-Roman response to 'the extraordinary story coming out of Palestine in the mid-first century'.[21] Thus for example in Chariton's *Chaereas and Callirhoe* (3.3.1) the hero comes to the tomb of the heroine to find it empty, the stone rolled away. On this reading, some at least of the novels may (like the *Life of Apollonius of Tyana*) be seen as a pagan response to the gospels, and part of the rivalry between paganism and Christianity becomes a tussle over who has the better stories.

If Christian texts influenced the novel, unsurprisingly there was in due course demand for Christian novels. The *Clementine Recognitions* survives only in fragments, and most of these in a Latin translation, but seems in origin to have been a Greek text of the early third century AD.[22] Its hero and narrator is a young man called Clemens, probably intended to be identified with Clement of Rome (traditionally the second successor of Peter as head of the church), to whom a number of letters are attributed. The text seems broadly to have followed the usual formula for a Greek novel. The protagonist's family breaks up when his mother, slandered because a wicked uncle has designs on her, leaves with his twin brothers and is shipwrecked. Clement initially stays with his father but they too become separated. The novel appears to have traced the sequence of events by which the family is eventually re-united, and bound together by Christian allegiance. It may have drawn on an apocryphal *Acts of Peter*: Clement travels with the apostle, who discovers that a beggar woman is his companion's lost mother. In Antioch two prominent members of the Christian community are recognised as his twin brothers, previously captured by pirates and sold to a Jewish woman convert. Finally an elderly astrologer cured by Peter of doctrinal error is revealed as the father. As in the life of Justin, there seems to have been be a focus on charismatic individuals, the holy men prominent in both pagan and Christian contexts in later antiquity; and the presentation of Christianity as the fulfilment rather than the antithesis of classical culture aligns the text with the Greek apologists. What Northrop Frye called the 'earnest clumsiness' of the narrative serves only to emphasise its preoccupations.[23] The title is a reminder of the ultimate source of all ancient novels in the *Odyssey*, which provides the story pattern of physical and spiritual travels through multiple hazards to a hard-won return, as well as the unifying theme of *anagnôrisis*. The restored family at the end of the novel seems to have been presented as an allegory of the Last Judgement, imagined as one vast recognition scene.[24]

Here demonstrably a pagan and popular genre has been appropriated, classical and Christian themes conjoined. There were indeed Hellenistic Jewish precedents, catering for a similar demand: the books of Tobit and Judith are essentially novels. If the Christian novel did not develop further in later antiquity, that may be because its place was increasingly taken by equally dramatic and edifying but non-fictional (if no doubt often re-touched) lives of saints and accounts of martyrdoms.[25] Justin, who saw Socrates as a pattern for Christian martyrs, was himself to be martyred in Rome in AD 165, and (unlike Clement and Origen, his less orthodox successors in the Hellenic tradition of the church) he is venerated as a saint.

Justin in sampling competing creeds has a semi-fictional counterpart in Lucius, the hero of Apuleius' *Metamorphoses* (the only Latin novel surviving complete, but probably based on a Greek original). The work echoes Ovid in its range of literary registers as well as in its title and central theme, for in the course of his picaresque adventures Lucius undergoes the transformation alluded to by the alternative title *The Golden Ass*. After a successful performing career in this guise he is restored to human form by the intervention of the Egyptian goddess Isis. Finally (and now more overtly identified with Apuleius himself) he is initiated into the mysteries of the goddess and her consort Osiris (*Metamorphoses* 11.1-30).[26] Eastern religions and mystery cults were characteristic of the age: Lucius finds his rest there as Justin does in Christianity. For a reverse example we can cite the historical figure Peregrinus, an apostate Christian and fanatical Cynic who in Lucian's account theatrically burns himself alive at Olympia (*Peregrinus* 36).[27] But perhaps the best parallel for Justin in imaginative literature comes from a novel set in the second century but written in the nineteenth. Walter Pater's *Marius the Epicurean* stands out from the large body of Victorian ancient historical fiction as a study of Christian conversion not through high drama but through reflection.[28] The young Roman aristocrat is at first content with the warmly familiar paganism of household and country gods: the Virgilian description of this 'religion of Numa' is memorable.[29] But the deaths of his mother and of his unbelieving best friend set Marius off on a spiritual quest. He first becomes an Epicurean, then after meeting and serving as secretary to the philosophic emperor Marcus Aurelius rises to Stoicism. He meets Lucian. In time increasingly interested in the still illegal new religion, he is arrested at a Christian meeting and dies for the faith to which he does not yet formally belong.[30]

Like Mrs Browning's poem on Pan, Pater's novel obliquely reflects nineteenth-century spiritual dilemmas. Richard Jenkyns shows that the Victorians were drawn to the second century for other reasons too. Gibbon had famously begun his *Decline and Fall* by declaring the Antonine age the happiest in human history, and a century later there was a more obvious parallel between Rome and Britain at the high noon of empire. Both the second century and the nineteenth were great ages of cultural revival.[31] Victorian interest both in the ancient world and in the Gothic Middle Ages is paralleled by the Second Sophistic, the second-century movement emulating the literary style (and sighing for the political independence) of classical Athens. Among the church fathers Melito of Sardis can plausibly be claimed as part of this.[32] His Easter sermon on the eucharist, formerly known only in fragmentary form but published from papyri in 1940, has the florid and mannered rhetorical style characteristic of contemporary Sophists, as well as a use of allegory and typology pioneered by Justin. Melito addressed a defence of Christianity to Marcus Aurelius (as Justin did to the previous emperor Antoninus Pius), in which he sees Christ's birth as providentially coinciding with the establishment by Augustus of the *pax Romana*, thus anticipating the idea of *praeparatio evangelica* developed by Eusebius.

Justin in his two *Apologies* (the first addressed to the emperor, the second to the Senate) makes much use of the notion of a 'spermatic' *logos*, identifiable with Christ or linked to him, which instructs every man in wisdom, so that even pagan philosophers foreshadowed Christian truth.[33] The concept of *logos*, used in a variety of ways in the Greek philosophical tradition, comes more directly to Justin from John's prologue (John 1:1-14). But the fourth gospel does not much develop the idea thereafter:[34] it was Justin himself who made it part of Christian theology. He has a wider range of general culture then any previous Christian author: he claims that the *logos* is to be seen both in the Old Testament and in Greek philosophy. Of Jesus, 'born 150 years ago, under Cyrenius', Justin says:

> He is the Word of whom the whole human race are partakers, and those who lived according to reason are Christians, even though accounted atheists. Such among the Greeks were Socrates and Heraclitus and those who resembled them; of the barbarians, Abraham, ... Elijah and many others. (*First Apology* 46)

Abraham and Socrates alike were thus Christians before Christ, and the parable of the Sower (Mark 4:1-9) could be applied to the seeds of philosophical truth scattered by Providence along the wayside. Justin remained positive towards Platonism, which he describes as 'not radically different from Christianity but not quite the same' (*Second Apology* 13). He accepts the argument of Jewish scholars such as Philo that Plato had used the first chapter of Genesis in his account of creation in the *Timaeus*. Like the other Greek fathers, Justin is less sympathetic to traditional myth than to philosophy: he recognises in it similar themes to those of scripture (miraculous birth, divine sonship), but sees them as demonic distortion (the first statement of this influential idea) and material for rhetorical points: 'no son of Jupiter imitated being crucified' (*First Apology* 55). But criticism of myth was nothing new, and overall Justin does a great deal to explain and enhance the attractiveness of Christianity for an educated Graeco-Roman audience.

In much of this he anticipates the next important Greek father, Clement of Alexandria.[35] Born like Justin to pagan parents and perhaps initiated into one of the mystery cults, Clement's conversion seems to have come early. Like a contemporary orator or the hero of a novel he travelled widely in the Mediterranean world, but in his case it was to seek instruction from different teachers of a faith already adopted. Like Melito, he exemplifies traits of the Second Sophistic: his *Protrepticus* or 'Hortatory address to the Greeks', seeking to persuade his audience of the superiority of Christianity to pagan cults and lifestyle, has much in common with the methods of rhetorical teachers advertising their wares. Clement read very widely: his *Stromateis* ('Miscellanies') in particular, setting out to construct a Christian philosophy, abound in quotations from classical authors. Some may indeed come (like the quoted passages in Paul and Luke) from published collections of apophthegms, but they preserve much that is unknown from elsewhere, notably the extracts from Presocratic philosophers. Like Justin, he aims explicitly to attract pagan converts. He combines the Bible with anything he finds useful from classical sources. He cites Homer some 250 times, and as an advocate of allegorical interpretation knows existing figural readings of the epics.[36] The twelfth chapter of the *Protrepticus* exemplifies his style and method. It begins with an exhortation to shun the 'custom' of pagan tradition, equated to the hazards both of Scylla and Charybdis and of the Sirens in *Odyssey* 12. Clement uses the image we noticed in Chapter 1, of the Christian bound to the cross like Odysseus to the mast: the Word is his pilot, and the Holy Spirit guides him into the harbour of heaven, of whose joys 'ear hath not heard' (1 Cor. 2:9). Next Clement turns to *Bacchae*. He apostrophises both Pentheus (urging him to cast off his Dionysiac headband and fawnskin) and Teiresias (holding out the promise of restored sight): like a hierophant he offers an alternative initiation into the true 'holy mysteries'.[37]

Third and perhaps greatest of the early Greek fathers is Origen, born late in the second century and living beyond the middle of the third.[38] We met him in Chapter 2 as the author of the counter-blast to Celsus, the pagan critic whose discussion of *Bacchae* Clement in effect reverses. Origen's Alexandrian setting puts him, like Clement, in a tradition continuous with the liberal Judaism of Philo two centuries earlier. Like Clement, he is broadly tolerant and universalist to the point where the bounds of Christian orthodoxy are strained; like him, he resorts readily to allegorical explanation and sits loose to the historicity of the texts he discusses. Echoing the encounter of Philip and the Ethiopian eunuch, he has much to say on the nature of reading, a theme we shall consider

157

further in the next section: for Origen the same spirit inspires the reader as inspired the writer,[39] and past events are preserved and are significant insofar as they happen again for us as we read.[40] He thus anticipates existentialist theology by combining radical demythologising with an emphasis on epiphanic present encounter. Origen belongs in a tradition of Greek learning and makes it Christian.[41] He alone among early Christian authors explicitly compares the experience of reading Homer and reading the gospels (*Contra Celsum* 1.42).[42] It is with him decisively that the classical traditions of textual criticism and exegetical scholarship are applied to the Bible, making the commentary on scripture a permanently familiar literary form.[43] Frances Young in *Biblical Exegesis and the Formation of Christian Culture* shows that Origen and scholars in his tradition created a new *paideia*, a new form of literary education with all the scholarly apparatus of the old, but centred on a different body of texts.[44]

Is the successful achievement of this transformation surprising? Commenting on literature was the basis of ancient education and it remained so. On purely stylistic grounds most of the New Testament authors would not score highly, but in other respects much was recognisable. For educated people intertextuality was an important feature of literature: a text achieved its status by its relation to authoritative earlier ones.[45] We saw in Chapter 3 that the New Testament has much in common here with classical literature. This process of assimilation to tradition was especially important at a time when Christian documents were being formed into a canon, and were gradually being raised to the same inspired status as the Jewish ones that lay behind them. Appeal to tradition was also a way in which Christian apologetic dealt with the preconception (addressed long before in *Bacchae* and in the Socratic literature) that nothing could be both new and true.

Literary texts were in ancient education routinely assumed to provide moral exemplars. Narratives of great deeds and heroic characters offered models for imitation, giving shape and meaning to more ordinary lives. This is made explicit only in some authors (Plutarch is an obvious example), but the idea of the poet as a teacher was of very general currency. The Greek tradition in the early church ensured that the study of pagan literature did not die out. In the fourth century Basil of Caesarea, one of the Cappadocian fathers (heirs of the apologists we have considered here), wrote *An Address to Young Men*, about the use of classical literature in the Christian curriculum.[46] It is utterly level-headed: he assumes students can be trusted to read the great authors of the past without taking too much notice of morally dubious mythology. Basil finds edifying content in Homer, Hesiod and Plato. He looks to Odysseus among the Phaeacians as the model of a man looked up to by others for his wisdom, a wisdom that came from seeing the cities of many men and getting to know their minds (*Od.* 1.3). Basil's essay was a charter for Christian higher education for centuries to come; and perhaps it can speak to us still.

A curious early Christian narrative illustrates many features of the world we have been considering, and takes us back once more to the Odyssean themes of disguise and (in this case posthumous) recognition. Alexius lived in the fifth century, the only son of a wealthy Roman senator.[47] His father was a Christian, but opposed to the extreme forms of devotion favoured by his son, for whom an advantageous marriage was arranged. Immediately after the exchange of vows he took flight (apparently with his bride's consent) and lived at Edessa in Syria where he became revered as a holy man. Celebrity in this role being paradoxical and unwelcome, he came back to his own home in disguise as a beggar. Unrecognised, he became (like the heroine of Mrs Henry Wood's 1861 novel *East Lynne*) a servant to his own family. Alexius lived in a corner under the stairs for seventeen years, pursuing a life of devotion and what circumstances allowed of witness and benevolence. After his death a note found on his body revealed his identity. St Alexius is a patron of beggars and travellers, recognised iconographically by holding a ladder to represent his staircase. His story, reminiscent of an ancient novel, became highly popular in the western church: in the eleventh century his adventures were made the subject of an epic poem, and also of the remarkable frescoes which adorn the lower church of San Clemente in Rome. And his own house (like the cottage of Baucis and Philemon) became a shrine: in the church of Alexius and Boniface on the Aventine visitors are shown, built into an eighteenth-century altar, the wooden stairs under which this ancient Harry Potter once slept.

Romantics and Victorians

In this final section I look briefly at two ancient authors (Longinus and Augustine) whose interests foreshadow a later age, then at some more recent writers (from Wordsworth to Matthew Arnold) in whom the themes we have been considering are reflected.

And God said, 'Let there be light'; and there was light. (Gen. 1:3)

The splendour of these words bursts upon us like the light they describe: it is for this that they are quoted, in a way unique in any pagan writer, by the author of the critical treatise *On the Sublime*. His name and date are uncertain, but he is traditionally called Longinus (the name's dubious status now often indicated by inverted commas) and he probably wrote in the first century AD.[48] We have seen that an implicit theory of literature is important already in Homer. Critical judgement of poetry is involved in the censure or allegorising of Homeric mythology practised widely from the sixth century onwards. Explicit discussion of texts occupies much of the contest between Aeschylus and Euripides in Aristophanes' *Frogs* (830-1481). Systematic criticism achieves magisterial authority in Aris-

159

totle's *Poetics*. From the Hellenistic and Roman periods a great deal of critical writing survives, though to the modern reader it can often seem arid in content or wayward in judgement. In this whole tradition the Greek essay *On the Sublime*, described by G.M.A. Grube as a 'mysterious masterpiece',[49] has no real parallel. In its focus and assumptions it seems frequently to anticipate Romanticism, in particular offering a foretaste of Coleridge in its concern with the imagination.[50] It gives serious attention to the author, as few critics since Plato had done. It applies Platonist ideas of poetic inspiration (themselves proto-Romantic in tendence) to a subject often preoccupied with the minutiae of rhetorical rules: Longinus like Aristotle is nominally advising aspirant writers. It 'soars above pedantry'[51] and reaffirms the literary greatness of Plato himself.

For Longinus the apprehension of the sublime in literature is a version of recognition: 'Our spirits are elevated by the truly excellent and, acquiring a sort of vigorous exaltation, are filled with a sense of joy and pride, as though they had produced what they hear' (*On the Sublime* 7.2). We shall hear later echoes of this paradoxical feeling of familiarity in the encounter with a classic text, and of the sense in which it becomes our own. This sits alongside the description of a classic as a permanent public possession. Longinus is concerned throughout with the effect of particular passages, but his tests are those which others have applied to whole texts: true sublimity becomes increasingly apparent with repeated hearing or reading, and the recognition of it is common to people of different 'occupations, habits, ideals and ages' (7.4).

Longinus was much studied in the seventeenth and eighteenth centuries. He importantly influenced Robert Lowth in his pioneering study of Hebrew poetry (foreshadowing modern literary readings of biblical texts), and his subject was taken up by Edmund Burke in his *Enquiry into the Sublime and the Beautiful* (1757). M.H. Abrams in *The Mirror and the Lamp* demonstrates his far-reaching influence on the Romantics, for whom he replaced Aristotle (admired by the preceding age of Neo-classicism) as the most influential ancient literary critic.[52] Criticism in this tradition unashamedly weighs poetry in the balance, like the literary contest in *Frogs*. Longinus seeks to show (and here too the Romantics echo him) that faulty genius outshines flawless mediocrity. His work is thus a manifesto against the Callimachean ideal of a perfect small-scale masterpiece: with authors as with the works of nature, we admire the mighty rivers rather than the tiny pellucid spring (*On the Sublime* 35.4).

This belief in the imaginative power of the greatest authors, expressed in an impassioned digression towards the end of the treatise, provides the context for the earlier discussion of Genesis. Chapter 9 (described by Gibbon as 'one of the finest monuments of antiquity'[53]) discusses the nature of genius, and the idea (again Romantic in flavour) of sublimity as the echo of a noble mind. Longinus has been describing successful and unsuccessful ways of representing supernatural beings and of arousing awe. He is impressed by the picture in the *Iliad* of the thundering horses pulling the chariot of Hera and Athene, their stride as great as the distance to which a man on watch can scan the sea (*Il.* 5.770-2). The battle of the gods (21.383-513) is remarkable but 'blasphemous and indecent unless it is treated allegorically' (*On the Sublime* 9.7). The best Homeric example is found in the description of Poseidon: hills and forests, the city of Troy and the Greek ships tremble under the immortal feet of the god as he goes on his way; he drives over the waves, the sea-monsters come up from the deep and recognise their king, and the sea parts in joy (*Il.* 13.18-31). And then:

> Similarly, the lawgiver of the Jews, no ordinary man – for he understood and expressed the power of God in accordance with its worth – writes at the beginning of his *Laws*: 'God said' – then what? – '"Let there be light", and there was light; "Let there be earth", and there was earth'. (*On the Sublime* 9.9)

It has been questioned whether this passage is genuine or a later insertion. But there are also several resemblances in language and thought between Longinus and Philo: it is plausible to assume that he had Jewish contacts as well as Greek and Roman ones, and that he obtained through them this superbly apposite example of the sublime from the Hebrew scriptures.[54]

A similarly striking anticipation of Romantic interests is provided by the late fourth-century *Confessions* of St Augustine. Cicero and he are the two figures from classical antiquity whom we know in the richest detail: Cicero from his letters, and Augustine from this first full-scale autobiography. His conversion narrative (a vastly expanded equivalent to the passage in Justin) is a spiritual Odyssey, and a story of internalised recognition: its controlling image is the Prodigal coming to himself (Luke 15:17), mediated by the theology of Paul.[55] The work is permeated by scriptural references, but Augustine substitutes the story of his own life for the biblical grand narrative of human history and salvation, or rather sees one within the other.[56] This is a momentous move. We saw already in Virgil an implicit analogy between the development of the poet and the larger account of development he gives us in the prophesied history of Rome. Augustine makes this inner narrative central, and it is surely significant that he was strongly influenced by Virgil. In the early parts of his great defence of Christianity *The City of God*, written in response to the fall of Rome to Alaric and the Goths in AD 410, he quotes Virgil frequently and pays tribute to the *Aeneid* as the supreme literary celebration of the now fading earthly city (*De Civitate Dei* 1.1-5 and 3.12-14).[57] He takes up its own haunting hints of transience, and applies its story pattern anew: Rome itself now stands, as the ruined Troy once did, in contrast with the vision of a promised and greater city. The work develops into an exposition of the whole spiritual development of mankind, yet remains rooted in Augustine's own life and times: it thus re-directs the theme of the *Confessions* back onto a bigger story.

Virgil in the *Aeneid* rewrote the two Homeric epics, and Milton created a still bolder new unity by rewriting both the *Aeneid* and the Bible in *Paradise Lost.* When Wordsworth rewrites Milton in *The Prelude*, making the development of the poet's imagination the subject of a long narrative poem and applying to the individual what had in the earlier work been the history of humanity, he replicates what Augustine had already done with the Bible. Stephen Prickett in *Romanticism and Religion* demonstrates the overt similarities of *The Prelude* to the *Confessions.* Augustine is concerned not only with the themes of spiritual crisis and conversion, but with a quest for wholeness of life, and by echoing him Wordsworth 'located himself in a tradition of religious sensibility interested in self-discovery'.[58] Autobiography of the heart and mind is a characteristic Romantic interest. Even allowing for the fact that we inevitably now read Augustine through lenses provided by the Romantics, we see in the *Confessions* in unmistakable embryo what Keats called 'the Wordsworthian or egotistical sublime'.[59]

Augustine and Milton are in different ways intermediaries between Virgil and Wordsworth: two poets remarkably akin in sensibility, in interests and in development. The words of Anchises in the Underworld about the inner spirit sustaining the world (*Aen.* 6.724-7) echo in 'Lines composed above Tintern Abbey' (93-102), and the transition from *Eclogues* to *Aeneid* (broadly Epicurean to Stoic) is mirrored in the evolution of the adventurer in revolutionary France into the sage of Rydal Mount. Each poet brings a sense of wonder to humble things and makes the ordinary seem extraordinary, finding (as the New Testament also does) the radiance of the eternal in the particular. Each rediscovers a spiritual dimension in natural landscape, with a countryman's perception of man and nature mysteriously joined, and a patriotism expressed by evident love of particular places. Each rediscovers also a high conception of the poetic calling: Wordsworth's language ('that I should be, else sinning greatly, a dedicated spirit': *Prelude* 4.336-7) echoes the idea of the *vates* in Augustan Rome, and attests equivalent ambition in broadly similar historical circumstances, where revolutionary upheaval ushered in a great age of poetic creativity. The Romantics typically saw Milton as the last great example of the poet as a public and prophetic voice, but they aspired to regain this role, and John Keble wrote in commemoration of Wordsworth that he 'in perilous times was raised up to be a chief minister ... of high and sacred truth' (memorial in Grasmere church). The sense here of deliverance, and of the poet as a national voice, seems very close to Virgil and to Augustan ideals.

Literary criticism and theology were in the nineteenth century closely intertwined: M.H. Abrams in *Natural Supernaturalism* shows how many of the great central themes in Wordsworth and the other Romantic poets are biblical in origin.[60] The idea that children have a special insight or wisdom (and are thus ideal readers because they enter fully and disinterestedly into an imagined world) is in effect a blend of Wordsworth and the New Testament: 'the Child is father of the Man'[61] echoes and restates 'unless ye be converted, and become as little children, ye shall not enter into the kingdom of heaven' (Matt. 18:3). Indeed the Romantic re-reading of the Bible here shows once more how powerfully a later interpretation can affect our perception of earlier texts. Becoming as little children is very different from remaining little children, like the unappealing Mr Skimpole in *Bleak House*: it describes rather (in Blake's terms) a new sort of innocence on the far side of experience. Expressed like that, the pattern is obviously biblical: the story of loss and redemption becomes an account of poetic vision unconsciously enjoyed in childhood but lost in adolescence, the visionary gleam departing like the gods leaving the earth. The 'Immortality Ode' laments its passing, yet by its own existence attests that it is regained in a new (if fragile and fleeting) form in the creative years of the young adult.

We saw in Chapter 2 that Wordsworth uses the Platonic idea of *anamnêsis*, the recollection of the soul's pre-natal experience, as a metaphor for imaginative insight. We saw too that *anamnêsis* itself is a form of *anagnôrisis*, and this takes us to a central theme of *The Prelude*:

Such moments worthy of all gratitude,
Are scatter'd everywhere, taking their date
From our first childhood: in our childhood even
Perhaps are most conspicuous. Life with me,
As far as memory can look back, is full
Of this beneficent influence. (*Prelude* 11.274-9)

Transient but transcendental, the 'spots of time' are another version of the classical and biblical theme of internalised recognition.[62] Both in *The Prelude* and elsewhere in Wordsworth they are often precipitated by incidents which resemble the encounter with disguised divine visitors in theoxeny stories.[63] Beggars, vagrants and solitaries – 'wanderers of the earth' (*Prel.* 12.156) – recur throughout Wordsworth's poetry, and in starkly intensified form reveal something about the human condition. In 'Resolution and Independence' (1802) the aged leech-gatherer met on the lonely moor, enviable for his child-like absorption in nature and admirable for his firmness of mind despite physical decrepitude, seems

... like a man from some far region sent
To give me human strength, by apt admonishment. (111-12)

Wordsworth speculates that this strange meeting came about by 'a peculiar grace': the old man has about him a visionary and almost supernatural quality. When the poet describes encountering in a London street a blind

163

beggar, whose pathetic self-description on a piece of paper seems like an emblem for 'the utmost that we know', similar language is used: 'I looked, as if admonish'd from another world' (*Prel.* 7.618 and 622). Each of these figures somehow tests the poet, and is thus another version of the humble visitor who is also the judge.

The Prelude is ostensibly and in original intention preliminary to an even more ambitious philosophical poem, but it in fact describes the preparation of a masterwork which proves to be itself. Here too is a theological point restated: in literature as in life, the journey rather than the arrival ultimately matters (Cavafy's 'Ithaca' makes the same point), and eschatological language becomes a coded description of present reality. *The Prelude* is autobiographical in several senses: the revised version of 1850 is a meditation on the texts of 1799 and 1805, which already themselves meditate on events up to the start of their composition. Wordsworth's poems frequently have this self-referential dimension. In 'Tintern Abbey' (1798) he describes revisiting the Wye Valley after several years. In the renewed presence of a remembered scene he explores both his changing response to nature through successive stages in his life, and also the means by which this response can be recreated in the imagination (famously described in the preface to *Lyrical Ballads* as 'emotion recollected in tranquillity'). Wordsworth explores his own experience as he comes to a fuller understanding of his poetic self, and of the reciprocity between the external world and his own mind.[64] At the same time (by a transference we have traced from Homer onwards) he describes also the experience of the reader, in recognising and imaginatively recreating the scene and the feelings described, and also in revisiting this (or any) poem at different times in his or her life.

'Tintern Abbey' is addressed to Coleridge, whose central concern is the nature of imagination. His *Biographia Literaria* was ranked by George Saintsbury (along with the *Poetics* and *On the Sublime*) as one of the three abidingly influential works of literary criticism.[65] It encourages us to reflect on the act of reading, on how meaning is generated in the reader's mind. Coleridge began his essay after studying Wordsworth's prefaces, and it engages with his poetry throughout. He takes it for granted that neither Wordsworth nor Plato believed literally in the recollection of pre-natal experience. That *anamnêsis* is a potent metaphor for imaginative insight will be plain, he says, to readers interested in modes of being 'to which they know that the attributes of time and space are inapplicable, but yet which cannot be conveyed save in symbols of time and space':[66] the idea of recollection is fertile because it ascribes to the human mind a deep source of creative power, explaining and vindicating the activity of the artist.[67] Platonist too is his identification of a shared quality of imagination in poet, prophet and mystic (Isaiah features prominently, and Coleridge interestingly adds the historian, described as 'a poet facing backwards'). The poet employs an 'esemplastic power' to re-form the world, creating a new imaginative unity from the metamorphosis of disparate elements. The reader in turn responds by mentally re-enacting the poet's experiences and thus sharing them: I.A. Richards wrote of how according to Coleridge 'acts of Imagination ... literally are *recognised*: the *all in each* finds again in them the same enlargement'.[68] This seems very close to the process described by Longinus and Origen.

The imagination is of profound religious importance to Coleridge: he sees it as something unaccounted for in materialist explanations of the world, and as the repetition in finite human beings of God's eternal and infinite act of creation.[69] The theological thinker and the literary critic are throughout his works inseparable. In his *Confessions of an Enquiring Spirit* (1825) he attacks the constrictive futility of too literal a reading of the Bible, and insists that it should be read in the same way as other books: 'In short, whatever *finds* me bears witness for itself that it has proceeded from a Holy Spirit.'[70] The combination of indefinite article and upper case may seem evasive, but expresses a point lost on contemporary critics shocked by this apparent blurring of the concept of inspiration. It was not widely appreciated how seriously and sensitively Coleridge read other books; and he does indeed give the Bible special status, because there is in it 'more that *finds* me than in all other books put together': it is exactly by reading the Bible like other books that the reader comes to recognise its uniqueness. Coleridge's language here is also carefully calculated in another sense. In the recurrent emphasis on finding, he deliberately uses the biblical image of call and response: this hallmark of God's dealings with mankind from Genesis to Acts, the challenge that evokes 'Here am I, send me!' (Isa. 6:8), becomes also a description of the act of reading.[71]

Decisive moments of recognition are in a very different context an important concern of a near-contemporary of Wordsworth and Coleridge, not always acknowledged as one of the great religious writers of the English church:

> Her own conduct, as well as her own heart, was before her in the same few minutes. She saw it all with a clearness which had never blessed her before. How improperly she had been acting by Harriet! How inconsiderate, how indelicate, how irrational, how unfeeling had been her conduct! What blindness, what madness had led her on! It struck her with dreadful force, and she was ready to give it every bad name in the world. (*Emma* ch. 47)

C.S. Lewis in a classic essay showed that this moment of coming to oneself, this acknowledgement of previous folly, is the recurrent experience of Jane Austen's heroines.[72] Sometimes the treatment is closer to comedy than to tragedy, but the underlying theme is constant: a realisation that the cause of deception lies within. Contemporary readers would sense that whilst not cast in overtly religious terms these are moments of *metanoia*, of internalised recognition and repentance. Jane Austen's treatment of the church and its clergy is typically satirical (Mr Collins in *Pride and Preju-dice*, Mr Elton in *Emma*): the serious religious points are instead made obliquely, through the ironic moralism of the narrator, censuring pride and commending cheerful moderation. In *Emma* the theme of recognition is also used in another way. Emma imagines that her protégée Harriet Smith will turn out to be of gentle birth. Northrop Frye points out that she thus wants her to follow the rules of romance, imagining an outcome in the tradition of New Comedy. She looks for one sort of recognition scene but experiences another. Yet the moment of self-knowledge itself has classical as well as biblical resonances. Virginia Woolf in her essay 'On Not Know-ing Greek' juxtaposes *Emma* and Sophocles' *Electra* in order to comment on the constricted lives of their protagonists,[73] but there is a further similarity. Thomas Hardy is the English novelist we more obviously compare to the Greek tragedians, yet Jane Austen's heroines also in their quieter way resemble the Sophoclean central character who typically sees at a climactic moment the true pattern of his life.

In the second generation of Romantic poets, Keats explores ideas which echo those we saw in 'Tintern Abbey'. He is both reader and poet in his sonnet 'On First Looking into Chapman's Homer' (1816), and indeed hero too:

> Much have I travell'd in the realms of gold,
> And many goodly states and kingdoms seen.

Equating reading to seafaring (the 'realms of gold' represent classical literature, perhaps evoking the gold tooling and page-edging of the vol-umes that contain it), Keats casts himself as an experienced traveller, like Odysseus (the second line echoes *Od.* 1.3).[74] But this is a voyage of discovery. Keats knew no Greek: he was familiar with the Homeric poems in Pope's translations, but (like the Romantics generally) saw in them only polished pomp. The 'loud and bold' voice of the Elizabethan translator George Chapman revealed to him for the first time the power of Homer. He compares his sense of discovery to the experience of an astronomer finding a new planet, or an explorer an unknown ocean. It resembles also the moments of insight and recognition which are a central theme of the *Odyssey* itself. To a modern reader indeed the 'gnarled rhetoric'[75] of Chap-man may seem no less a potential barrier than Pope's heroic couplets, but Keats in reaching back beyond the eighteenth century finds in his mystical ardour a revelatory authenticity. Chapman took seriously an allegorical dimension in Homer, and Keats himself famously wrote in a letter that 'A man's life of any worth is a continual allegory.'[76] The poet's own discovery of Homer draws on and replicates an earlier engagement with the text: Keats contemplates one work of art through a second, and in the process creates a third. He evokes for us the experience of intellectual and emo-tional discovery in the act of reading, so that our encounter with his poem parallels his own self-discovery in reading of Chapman, which in turn illuminates Homer. The sonnet also anticipates the more ambitious 'Ode on a Grecian Urn' by showing how art can give fixity to fleeting emotion and insight.[77]

In the literature of the high Victorian period the interaction of the classical and biblical traditions is represented above all by the contrasting Oxonian figures John Henry Newman and Matthew Arnold: I turn finally to them. Among Newman's papers preserved at Birmingham Oratory is a single sheet which he kept from the age of eleven until the end of his long life. It begins in a child's hand:

> John Newman wrote this just before he was going up to Greek on Tuesday, June 10th, 1812, when it wanted only 3 days to his going home, thinking of the time (at home) when looking at this he shall recollect when he did it.[78]

The natural schoolboy anticipation of holidays is combined with the unusual sensibility of *olim meminisse iuvabit*, envisaging a future moment of recollection. Later entries made the memories many-layered: he is back at school, on vacation from Oxford, back in Oxford; then in 1829 in his rooms at Oriel, as a fellow of the college and vicar of St Mary's 'having suffered much, slowly advancing to what is good and holy, and led on by God's hand blindly'; seventeen years later a Catholic and 'expecting soon to set out for Rome'; in due course a priest of the Oratory. Finally, in shaky letters in the tiny space left at the bottom of the page: 'And now a Cardinal. March 2, 1884'. Thus is summed up one of the most remarkable lives of the Victorian age. Newman's *Apologia pro Vita Sua* (1864), provoked by a slur on his veracity by the militantly Protestant Charles Kingsley, is one of the great English autobiographies, and a tragic story even though in its author's eyes his reception into the Roman church is a happy homecoming.

Newman was impelled in his quest by study of the early church. His book *The Arians of the Fourth Century* (1833) is an authoritative account of the heresy which denied the full divinity of Christ, but (like many works of nineteenth-century scholarship) comments also on a contemporary controversy: he saw Arian ideas resurgent in modern theological liberalism. Preoccupied with the issue of authority, Newman in 1839 while studying the aftermath of the Council of Chalcedon in AD 451 famously experienced an alarming recognition: 'I saw my face in that mirror, and I was a Monophysite.'[79] Not because he literally adhered to this other heresy (which attributed to Christ only one nature, instead of the orthodox duality of God and Man), but because he saw the Anglican church in an analogous position of disobedient distance from Rome. That change of perspective still lay ahead when in 1833 he set off on his formative travels to Mediterranean lands. Like many classically educated Englishmen of his era he relished his first sight of the central sea, the scene of events two millennia old yet closely familiar. In Italy he witnessed (with initial revulsion) Catholic piety in its colourful fullness. He was captivated by the evidence of the pagan classical past, and the tension between it and Christianity remained for him as lively an issue as it had been in the early church. He described his visit to the lonely and unfinished Doric temple at Egesta in Sicily as the most memorable day of his life, reflecting 'Such was the genius of ancient Greek worship – grand in the midst of error, simple and unadorned in its architecture: it chose some elevated spot, and fixed there its solitary witness, where it could not be hid.'[80] He thus in part answered the question posed in his poem 'Why, wedded to the Lord, still yearns my heart towards these scenes of ancient heathen fame?'[81]

Newman experienced severe illness and mystical visions in Sicily, and wrote 'Lead, kindly Light' when on his homeward journey the boat carrying him to Marseilles was becalmed in the Straits of Bonifacio. Shortly after his return, John Keble preached the sermon on 'National Apostasy', attacking the Church of England for failing to fulfil its prophetic mission, which inaugurated the main twelve years of the Oxford Movement, ended by Newman's conversion to Rome in 1845.[82] His *Essay on the Development of Christian Doctrine*, written in that year, traces the gradual emergence of Catholic belief, even and especially where it is acknowledged to go beyond what is sanctioned by the New Testament. The theme of organic growth is sometimes said to anticipate Darwin on evolution, but a more persuasive analogy lies closer to hand. The account of church history in the *Essay on Development* is remarkably parallel to the later account of the formation of Newman's own views in the *Apologia*. As in Virgil, the writer's development and his subject mirror each other; and as in Wordsworth's rewriting of Milton, a pattern previously discerned in history is applied to the growth of an individual mind. Newman's *Apologia*, like *The Prelude*, stands in a tradition of conversion narratives deriving from Augustine. Newman's sensibility has much in common with the Romantic poets, especially in his introspectiveness and in his preoccupation with childhood experience. His sense of 'two luminously self-evident beings, myself and my Creator'[83] echoes Wordsworth's characteristic feeling of being alone with the visible phenomena of nature, and his description of his first home at Ham as 'remnant of a pre-existent state' uses again the language of the 'Immortality Ode'.[84] The high ideal of priesthood in the Oxford Movement, the rekindled sense of apostolic succession, is recognisably akin to the prophetic role of the poet in *The Prelude* and in turn to the concept of the *vates* in Augustan Rome. His autobiographical writings are marked throughout by a sense (both Romantic and Virgilian) of wistful exile from a past happy state.

Newman's mature reflections on the nature of faith and the mind produced in 1870 a classic treatment of religious belief, *An Essay in Aid of a Grammar of Assent*. It shows how complex are the forces shaping our convictions. It includes much about the nature of reading, including this famous passage describing a moment of revelatory insight in returning to an ostensibly familiar text:

Let us consider, too, how differently young and old are affected by the words of some classic author, such as Homer or Horace. Passages, which to a boy are but rhetorical commonplaces, neither better nor worse than a hundred others which any clever writer might supply ... at length come home to him, when long years have passed, and he has had experience of life, and pierce him, as if he had never known them before, with their sad earnestness and vivid exactness. Then he comes to understand how it is that lines, the birth of some chance morning or evening at an Ionian festival, or among the Sabine hills, have lasted generation after generation, for thousands of years, with a power over the mind, and a charm, which the current literature of his own day, with all its obvious advantages, is utterly unable to rival. Perhaps this is the reason of the medieval opinion about Virgil, as if a prophet or magician; his single words and phrases, his pathetic half lines, giving utterance, as the voice of Nature herself, to that pain and weariness, yet hope of better things, which is the experience of her children in every time.[85]

Modern literary theory about the radical fluidity of texts says nothing new. The Presocratic philosopher Heraclitus observed that you cannot step into the same river twice, because next time it will have moved on and so will you. A book or poem has not itself changed when the reader sees new meaning in it, but it seems to have done so because new experience is brought to it. Newman's language of 'piercing' echoes Coleridge's 'finding', and the whole passage provides another version of the theme of 'Tintern Abbey'. Revisiting a text like revisiting a place precipitates recognition and new insight, and what is ostensibly familiar seems for the first time fully known.

The *Grammar of Assent* gives a central role to two concepts: what Newman calls 'real assent', where we come to make an idea our own, to know it in the full Platonic sense of the word, and (as a route to this) the 'illative sense': a process of hidden or telescoped inference, by which the mind puts together scattered hints and clues. In a much earlier sermon he described the process with this analogy:

The mind ranges to and fro, and spreads out, and advances forward ... and thus it makes progress not unlike a clamberer on a steep cliff, who, by quick eye, prompt hand, and firm foot, ascends how he knows not himself, by personal endowments and by rule, leaving no track behind him, and unable to teach another.[86]

Newman is concerned specifically with how religious conviction is reached, but we seem very close here to Coleridge's description of the 'esemplastic' imagination, bringing many things into one.[87] In both writers the concept of *anamnêsis* is used as a description of how in reading we come to recognise what we had somehow thought all along. And the perception of ever richer and deeper meaning on subsequent encounters with a text, which for Longinus was one of the criteria of literary greatness, is another version of the story of gradual discernment which shapes both the *Essay on Development* and the *Apologia*. It draws too on the Platonist idea of uncovering innate knowledge, and more broadly it is analogous to the discovery of something already in place which was the experience of Aeneas at the site of Rome and of Paul in Athens. Newman rather stiffly censured Coleridge for having 'indulged a liberty of speculation that no Christian can tolerate',[88] but acknowledged the larger vision he had opened up beyond the materialist philosophy of the eighteenth century. His own developed thought is inconceivable without Coleridge's exploration of symbolic language.[89] Matthew Arnold, more obviously the heir of Coleridge in his theological liberalism, attests from the other side this sense of affinity despite differences in formal doctrine: in 1872 he named Newman along with Goethe, Wordsworth and the French critic C.A. Sainte-Beuve as a pantheon of writers from whom he had learned 'habits, methods, ruling ideas'.[90]

Hebrew and Hellene as explanatory categories, as symbols of contrasted approaches to life ('all men are either Jews or Greeks'), were borrowed by Arnold from the German poet Heinrich Heine and became central to his own social and literary criticism.[91] They are rooted in but go beyond the historical cultures over whose compatibility Justin and Tertullian argued. Both are ideals for human improvement, but Hebraism is concerned with conduct and morality, Hellenism with aesthetic 'sweetness and light' (another Arnoldian borrowing, from Jonathan Swift). They perhaps also represent two sides of Arnold himself, the aesthete and poet making his living as an inspector of elementary schools, and finding among the provincial middle classes abundant Hebraism but a woeful lack of Hellenism.

Classics and Christianity appear from our own perspective to have been equally and impressively vigorous in Victorian England, but Arnold envisaged a future decline of both and suggested strategies to cope with it, looking to literature for the emotional sustenance traditionally provided by religion, and steering readers with no Greek to 'Milton and parts of Wordsworth'.[92] In aristocratic ages 'vast ideas are commonly entertained of the dignity, the power, and the greatness of man',[93] but because aristocracy is also passing away, the provision of inspiring models must fall instead to literature. In his critical writing Arnold is concerned above all with nobility and the 'grand style'. His late essay 'The Study of Poetry' (1880) encapsulates his ideas.[94] It is reminiscent of *On the Sublime* in both content and method. Like Longinus, Arnold insists that nobility is to be recognised rather than defined: he conveys the quality of the best poetry only by what he calls the 'touchstones' of greatness. He offers eleven short extracts from Homer, Dante, Shakespeare and Milton.[95] Like Longinus, he takes his Homeric examples from the *Iliad*. The first is the passage where Helen, identifying to Priam from the walls of Troy the various Greek heroes, fails to see her brothers Castor and Polydeuces, and speculates whether their absence may be attributable to the disgrace she has brought upon them:

170

So she spoke; but the life-giving earth already held them
in Lacedaemon, in their dear native land. (*Il.* 3.243-4)

This was something of a Victorian favourite: John Ruskin famously commented on the pathos in its context of the description of the earth (which has the flavour of a recurrent standard epithet, though in fact it occurs only one other time).[96] The second passage is the address of Zeus to the horses of Peleus as they mourn for Patroclus:

Ah, unhappy pair, why did we give you to king Peleus,
a mortal, when you are ageless and immortal?
Was it so that among wretched men you should have sorrows?
(17.443-5)

The third comes from the great speech of Achilles to Priam, where he has been lamenting his own father left sad and alone:

And of you too, old man, we hear that you were once happy. (24.543)

All three passages express the pathos of the *Iliad*, the tragic dimension stressed also by modern critics; but this is only part of the Homeric picture, and it is tempting to see these choices as typically Arnoldian.

A gentle melancholy characteristic of late Romanticism has often been discerned in Arnold's own poetry, but such was not his aim. In his 1853 collection of poems he suppressed his earlier 'Empedocles on Etna', in which the lonely Sicilian sage in existential despair cast himself into the crater of the volcano, for its mood of dejection. He substituted an ambitious new narrative poem. The story of the Tartar Sohrab 'whom his great father did in ignorance kill' ('Sohrab and Rustum' 793) came to Arnold (via a French translation, discussed in an essay by Sainte-Beuve) from the Persian poet Firdousi, but the treatment is consciously (and successfully) Homeric. The episode is told in a plain narrative style but with fine extended similes (Virgilian in their tenderness) and richly Sophoclean dramatic irony, for the Persian warrior Rustum is unaware that he has a son: the woman he loved and left told him she had produced a daughter, to prevent the boy being enlisted in the Persian army. Sohrab consciously seeks his father, but his challenge to the Persians to provide a champion for single combat is taken up by Rustum only reluctantly (the role belonging to a younger man) and with arms bearing no insignia. Advancing into combat, Rustum pities his adversary, urging him not to fight but 'quit the Tartar host ... and be as a son to me' (330-1). Sohrab suspects his true identity: 'Art thou not Rustum?' (344). Rustum however fears that if his heroic fame is revealed, Sohrab will offer Homeric tribute of praise and gifts, and later boast of their parting in peace. So they fight: the Persian invokes the name 'Rustum' as he mortally wounds the young man, but still denies it is his own. But Sohrab's claim that his father Rustum will avenge his death at last precipitates the scene of tragic recognition, for when the Persian in cold incredulity says 'The mighty Rustum never had a son', Sohrab replies 'Ah yes, he had! and that lost son am I' (578 and 580). The recognition is confirmed by 'that seal which Rustum to my mother gave' pricked on his arm 'in faint vermilion points' (659 and 671): we inevitably think here of the scar of Odysseus. The story is in one sense *Oedipus Tyrannus* in reverse, and the final exchange between a father and the son whose death he has caused has echoes of the conversation between Theseus and the dying Hippolytus in Euripides (*Hippolytus* 1405-15). But the overall theme of 'Sohrab and Rustum' is purely Iliadic: the pathos of a young man doomed to an early death.

> Unwillingly the spirit fled away,
> Regretting the warm mansion which it left,
> And youth, and bloom, and this delightful world. (854-6)

'Sohrab and Rustum' is no less tragic than 'Empedocles', but in Arnold's view it succeeded where that poem had failed. It was a story of action rather than ennui, and did not rest in melancholy but aimed 'to *animate* and *ennoble*'. Arnold granted that its manner contained conscious imitation of Milton, and it specifically aspired to rank among poems that might give English readers something of the feeling of Homer. It implied a reading of the *Iliad* which anticipates his later list of 'touchstones' and which also informs the famous series of lectures *On Translating Homer*, which he delivered as Professor of Poetry at Oxford in 1861.[97] Rather as Aristotle in the *Poetics* surveyed the genre of tragic drama by nominally advising aspirant writers of it, Arnold in giving guidance to future translators of Homer not only discusses existing translations (from the sixteenth century onwards), but in effect offers a general survey of English versification and poetic language. Homer is for him characterised by four qualities: rapidity, directness of diction, plainness of thought, and nobility. Most translations failed to convey at least one of these: the rhetorical heroic couplets of Pope could not achieve directness of diction, but Chapman (who for Keats had revealed authenticity behind this eighteenth-century façade) with his Elizabethan love of fanciful complexity failed to attain directness of thought. Arnold's elegantly ironic satire is however chiefly directed at an unfortunate recent translation by F.W. Newman, the erudite but eccentric brother of the theologian: he had sought to represent Homeric language (which is indeed an amalgam formed over centuries) by a self-conscious archaism which for Arnold revealed only the tastes and tendencies of his own age in its bizarrely faddist and arbitrary effect, so that the 'grand style' could here be recognised by its absence.

Since Arnold's time, many of his assumptions and many of the ideas considered in this chapter have fallen from favour. Modern books on Greek tragedy routinely disclaim the traditional humanist idea of the plays as aesthetic masterpieces, timeless in their universality, stressing instead the immediate historical circumstances of their original production. The Romantic conception of the creative artist with privileged visionary insight (so attractive to the Victorians) has been assailed by revisionist stress on the social and political context of the Romantics themselves, as well as by critical methods which have sought to approach texts with no context at all. In all this there has been gain: the removal of Romantic prejudice enables us to see once more the merits of Pope and of the Hellenistic poets, and the playful irreverence of postmodernism helps us to appreciate Ovid. The reception history of a text is now seen as inescapably and enrichingly part of its meaning. But reception studies can play on us the same trick as the parable of the Pharisee and the tax collector: in demonstrating how previous generations were the prisoners of their preconceptions, we may forget that the same is necessarily true of our own perception both of them and of the original text. The moral is perhaps to beware the vanity of dogmatising, but there is danger too in relativism: a levelling reluctance to assess the merits of ancient authors, or commendation only of their clever manipulation of words, implicitly denies them serious views on important subjects, the very wisdom in pursuit of which they were for centuries read.

Italo Calvino, often claimed as a typical voice of postmodernism, in *Why Read the Classics?* offers a list of criteria for recognising a text as belonging to that category.[98] They are strikingly traditional, echoing ideas we have traced from Plato and Longinus to Newman and Arnold. One of them defines a classic as a book which even when we read it for the first time gives the sense of re-reading something we have read before. In the case of a work canonical in our own culture, this might simply be because we know it already from allusions. But Calvino answers this reductionist objection in considering another distinctive mark: a classic is a book whose unexpectedness and originality are in direct proportion to our sense of knowing it by hearsay. And (a third test) it is one which on each re-reading offers as much of a sense of discovery as it did when first encountered.

Classical literature and the Bible alike offer the rich intrinsic fascination of reading what has been read before: by previous generations, and by our earlier selves. Analysis of the act of reading resorts naturally to the language of theology and to the metaphors of hospitality and recognition, the themes that have taken us from Eumaeus to Emmaus. George Steiner in his essay 'The Uncommon Reader' discusses Chardin's painting *Le Philosophe Lisant* (1734). Tracing the iconography of the seated figure with a book open on a table (from depictions of St Jerome in his study, through the great age of Dutch domestic interiors), and observing the formal garb and manner of Chardin's subject, he comments:

Reading, here, is no haphazard, unpremeditated motion. It is a courteous, almost a courtly encounter, between a private person and one of those 'high guests' whose entrance into mortal houses is evoked by Hölderlin in his hymn 'As on a festive day'.[99]

Books are here equated to divine visitors in a theoxeny story. Hölderlin himself compared the supper at Emmaus to a Homeric epiphany.[100] Steiner writes elsewhere of the coming of these guests as unbidden and unexpected, but irrevocable.[101] We form with apparently inert and static texts a relation which acquires the lasting and reciprocal quality of Homeric guest-friendship:[102] their meaning is like oil or wine miraculously replenished. These guests may come in disguise, but they tell us stories in which we recognise ourselves. Robert Louis Stevenson in *The Ebb Tide* (1894) describes a man lost on a distant island, resorting with a tattered text to the *sortes Virgilianae*, the random consultation of the poetic magus. He finds no counsel for his immediate predicament, but is stirred to thoughts of home:

> For it is the destiny of those grave, restrained and classic writers with whom we make enforced and often painful acquaintanceship at school to pass into the blood and become native in the memory; so that a phrase of Virgil speaks not so much of Mantua or Augustus, but of English places and the student's own irrevocable youth.[103]

Notes

1. Homer

1. Rutherford (2001a).
2. Eric Milner-White: Christmas bidding prayer.
3. T.S. Eliot, 'Little Gidding' (1942), fifth canto.
4. Burkert (1985), 130; Dowden (2006), 78-80.
5. Beye (2006), 157-8.
6. Seaford (1994).
7. Wilamowitz, quoted by Stanford (1959), 206.
8. Murnaghan (1987), 11-12.
9. Murnaghan (1987), 91-117.
10. Kearns (1996); Hollis (1990), 341-54; West (1997), 123.
11. Louden (1999), 132.
12. Kearns (1982); Murnaghan (1987), 11-12.
13. Grafton, Most and Zetzel (1985), 85 and 145-6.
14. Boitani (1999), 10.
15. Bogan (1658), 152.
16. Boitani (1999), 2.
17. Alter (2004), 85-90.
18. Alter (1981), 49-51.
19. Boitani (1999), 6.
20. Boitani (1999), 2.
21. Pritchard (1955), 149-51.
22. Alter (2004), 85.
23. Boitani (1999), 3; Alter (2004), 85.
24. Hansen (2002), 217-18 and 223.
25. West (1997).
26. Aune (1989), 42.
27. Bogan (1658), 371.
28. Alter (2004), 91.
29. Burkert (1992), 41-2.
30. Lamberton (1989), 189; Brown (1999), 191.
31. Steiner and Fagles (1962), 12.
32. Cave (1988), 22.
33. Murnaghan (1987), 13.
34. Drury (1985), 6.
35. Austin (1975), 139.
36. Clarke (1981), 60-105; Lamberton (1989).
37. Hardie (1986), 326.
38. Stanford (1963), 121-5.
39. Bultmann (1960), 195.
40. Long (1992), 43.

41. Kermode (1979).
42. MacDonald (2000), 44-54.
43. Rahner (1963), 328-86; Pelikan (1999), 43.
44. Cave (1988), 41 and 45-6.
45. Lamberton (1989), 234-5 and 318-24.
46. Clarke (1981), 96.
47. Lowe (2000), 144.
48. Norton (1993), 30.
49. Alter (1981), 94.
50. Richardson (1983), 228.
51. Boitani (1999), 16.
52. Josipovici (1988), 85.
53. Murnaghan (1987), 45-51.
54. Auerbach (2003), 3-23.
55. Murnaghan (1987), 5-6 and 23.
56. Turner (1981), 158.
57. Lowe (2000), 128.
58. Griffin (1980a), Macleod (1982).
59. Alter (1981 and 1992), Alter and Kermode (1987), Drury (1985 and 1999), Josipovici (1988), Boitani (1999).
60. Weil (1957), 24-55; Schein (1985), 82-4.
61. Brittain (1979), 291.
62. West (1997), 123.
63. Jenkyns (1996), 1.
64. Schein (1985), 69.
65. Fragment 2.1-4: Campbell (1967), 226-7.
66. Alter (1992), 98-9.
67. Alter (1981), 38.
68. Josipovici (1988), 130.
69. Jasper (2004), 27.
70. Barthes (1977), 125-41; Barton (1984), 116-19.
71. Propp (1968), 25-117.
72. Macleod (1982), 115.
73. Burkert (1985), 157-8.
74. van Nortwick (1996), 79.
75. Drury (1985), 45.
76. Landow (1980), 49 and 130.
77. Griffin (1980b), 53.
78. Rutherford (2001b), 265.
79. Edwards (1987), 195.
80. Cairns (2001), 25.
81. Murnaghan (1987), 70.
82. Rutherford (2001b), 283-4.
83. Rutherford (2001b), 261-2.
84. Jenkyns (1980), 340.
85. John Arkwright, 'O Valiant Hearts.'
86. West (1978), 3-25.
87. West (1997), 307.
88. West (1978), 229.
89. Lloyd-Jones (1971), 28-54.
90. Murnaghan (1987), 12.

91. Foley (1994), 79-178.
92. Rutherford (2005), 274.
93. Lowe (2000), 82.
94. Foley (1994), 40.
95. Parker (2005), 342.
96. Lowe (2000), 81.
97. Compare the words of Jesus: John 12:24.

2. History, Tragedy and Philosophy

1. Rogerson (1984), 65.
2. Feeney (1991), 1; Parker (2005), 136.
3. Dancy (2001), 779.
4. White (2005), 382.
5. Dancy (2001), 17.
6. Steiner (1963), 4; Humphreys (1985), 1-20; Exum (1992), 1-15.
7. Josipovici (1988), 72.
8. Nielsen (1997).
9. Flower and Marincola (2002), 315-19.
10. Rosenbloom (2006), 40.
11. Birch, Brueggemann, Fretham and Peterson (2005), 127-71.
12. Alexander (2005a), 165.
13. Nielsen (1997), 162.
14. Hart (1982), 27-32.
15. Momigliano (1990), 5-28.
16. Dodds (1951), 30.
17. Romm (1998), 2.
18. Harrison (2000).
19. Harrison (2000), 91.
20. Exum (1992), 51.
21. Servius on *Aen.* 3.122: Williams (1962), 80.
22. Brown (1999), 256; Dean (1959), 590.
23. Fragment 8 (West): Goward (2005), 46.
24. Cave (1988), 47-54.
25. Dodds (1973), 45-63.
26. Parker (2005), 141.
27. Hardie (1991), 29-30.
28. Lloyd-Jones (1971), 84-103.
29. Goward (2005), 78.
30. Hardie (1991), 29.
31. Parker (2005), 138.
32. Humphreys (1985), 134.
33. Exum (1992), 16-42
34. Humphreys (1985), 24.
35. Humphreys (1985), 38.
36. Exum (1992), 39.
37. Humphreys (1985), 40.
38. Norton (1993), 167.
39. Frye (1982), 182.
40. Humphreys (1985), 139; Exum (1992), 23.
41. West (1997), 550-1.

42. Josipovici (1988), 201.
43. Humphreys (1985), 37.
44. Exum (1992), 17.
45. Mold (1985), 201; Dean (1959), 274-310.
46. Ginzberg (2001), 560-4.
47. Drury (1985), 48.
48. Hurst (2006), 205
49. Cave (1988), 146 and 232; Grossvogel (1979), 23-38.
50. Barton (1984), 228.
51. Goldhill (2005), 303.
52. Frazer (1994), 9-16.
53. Frazer (1994), 228-53 and 557-668.
54. Vernant and Vidal-Naquet (1981), 97; Seaford (1994), 312.
55. Wiles (2000), 148.
56. Halliwell (2002), 223.
57. Goldhill (2005), 298.
58. Goldhill (2005), 306.
59. Alter (1981), 33.
60. Prickett (1986), 60.
61. Humphreys (1985), 94 and 105.
62. Humphreys (1985), 98.
63. Dancy (2001), 779.
64. Humphreys (1985), 104.
65. Humphreys (1985), 113.
66. Dodds (1973), 74.
67. Seaford (1994), 240.
68. Dodds (1951), 193-5; Dodds (1960), xxiii-v.
69. Zeitlin (1990), 135-6.
70. Burnett (1970).
71. Seaford (1994), 385.
72. Stibbe (1992), 131-47.
73. Chadwick (1953); Alexander (2005b), 222.
74. Jacobson (1983).
75. Josipovici (1988), 173.
76. Dodds (1960), 245; Seaford (1996), 144-5.
77. Hunter (2006), 48.
78. Seaford (1997).
79. Seaford (2006), 123; Bolton (1973), 134.
80. Feeney (1991), 21.
81. Lamberton (1989), 10-21.
82. Fragment 13.1-5: Campbell (1967), 341.
83. Lloyd-Jones (1971), 132.
84. Taplin (1989), 98.
85. Rutherford (2005), 61.
86. Taplin (1989), 191.
87. Burkert (1985), 162.
88. Otto (1965), 79-85.
89. Neill (1966), 309-10; Bultmann (1971).
90. Hunter (2006), 43.
91. Steiner (1996), 402.
92. Brickhouse and Smith (2002), 117-21.

93. Burnyeat (2002), 144.
94. Steiner (1996), 381.
95. Dodds (1951), 17.
96. Pelikan (1999), 188.
97. Barnard (1967), 56.
98. Garrison (1997), 95-104.
99. Gooch (1996), 197.
100. Barth (2001), 190.
101. Burnyeat (2002), 144.
102. Josipovici (1988), 160.
103. Cave (1988), 144.
104. Ryle (1966), 17-19 and 110-45.
105. Nightingale (1995), 60-92.
106. Frye (1982), 80.
107. Parker (1996), 199-217.
108. Prickett (1986), 58.
109. Harrison (1925), 83.

3. Virgil Between Two Worlds

1. Jaeger (1961), 5; Momigliano (1994), 147-61.
2. Caird (1980), 122-3.
3. Young (1983), 3-14.
4. Taylor (1931), 8-13.
5. Price (1984), 1-22.
6. Price (1984), 11-15.
7. West (1997), 33.
8. Deissmann (2004), 252-392; Young (1977).
9. Caird (1980), 122-8; Dines (2004), 27-40.
10. Lane Fox (1975), 55-67.
11. Lewis (1942), 12-50.
12. Hutchinson (1988), 58-63; Hollis (1990), 1-10 and 341-54; Nisetich (2001), 3-19.
13. Fragments numbered as in Hollis (1990), 67-131.
14. Hollis (1990), 343-4.
15. Hollis (1990), 344-5; Nisetich (2001), 130-7.
16. Hollis (1990), 345-7; Seaford (1994), 301.
17. Wilder (1971), 71.
18. Syme (1960), 191.
19. Millar and Segal (1984); Bowman, Champlin and Lintott (1996).
20. Martindale (1993), 42; Prickett (1996), 165.
21. Prickett (1996), 73.
22. Dancy (2001), 778.
23. Goulder (1974), 28-46 and 227-249.
24. Griffin (1985), 184-8.
25. Hardie (1986), 31.
26. 'To Virgil': Page (1898), xxxix.
27. Hardie (1993), 16.
28. Burrow (1997), 80.
29. Kennedy (1997), 153.
30. Prickett and Barnes (1991), ix.
31. Steiner (1984), 105.

32. Josipovici (1988), 77
33. Comparetti (1966), 98.
34. Eliot (1975), 115-31; Ziolkowski (1993), 119-29.
35. Gransden (1984), 216.
36. Clausen (1994), 126-8.
37. Page (1898), 124.
38. Weinfeld (1993), 1.
39. Hardie (1986), 1-156.
40. Weinfeld (1993), 1-21.
41. Norton (1993), 325.
42. Josipovici (1988), 72.
43. Brueggemann (2003), 110.
44. Jenkyns (1999), 535-7.
45. Warde Fowler (1917), 45.
46. Jenkyns (1999), 539.
47. Galinsky (1972), 131-52; Gransden (1976), 17-20.
48. Jenkyns (1999), 550.
49. Gibbon (1907), 160.
50. Martindale (1993), 42.
51. Price (1996), 830-4.
52. Austin (1971), 25-7.
53. Myers (1908), 144.
54. Hardie (1986), 40.
55. Henry Scott Holland, 'Judge Eternal, throned in splendour'.
56. Kugel (1997), 152.
57. Alter (1992), 51-2.
58. Anderson (1982), 438.
59. Lewis (1942), 34.
60. Feeney (1991), 188-90.
61. Frye (1982), 97.
62. Wallace-Hadrill (2005), 55.
63. Fränkel (1945).
64. Hinds (1998), 106.
65. Galinsky (1975), 197.
66. Barchiesi (2001), 51.
67. Feldherr (2002), 166.
68. Hollis (1970), 108.
69. Hollis (1970), 109.
70. Hollis (1970), 127; Lane Fox (1986), 99-100.
71. Hurst (2006), 149-50.
72. Gabel, Wheeler and York (2000), 44-7.
73. Heidel (1946), 109.
74. Frazer (1923), 46-143.
75. Hollis (1970), 109-12.
76. Kenney (1986), xxviii.
77. Barchiesi (2001), 51.
78. Barchiesi (2001), 52.
79. Bull (2006), 383-4; Hall (1979), 224-5 and 293.
80. Watson (2002), 196-7.
81. Fantham (2004), 144.
82. Hollis (1970), 110.

83. AD 6, or an otherwise unattested earlier tenure and census before the death of Herod the Great in 4 BC.

4. Foolishness to Greeks

1. Burridge (1992).
2. Hengel (2005), 72.
3. Auerbach (2003), 24-49.
4. Russell and Winterbottom (1972), 504-7.
5. Alter (1981), 147-8.
6. James (1924), xi-xiii.
7. Pagels (1979).
8. Jenkins (2001), 178-216.
9. Griffin (1977).
10. Graziosi and Haubold (2005).
11. Josipovici (1988), 40.
12. Josipovici (1988), 226.
13. Lowe (2000), 155.
14. Frye (1982), 216.
15. Byrne (2000), 53.
16. Drury (1987), 434.
17. Edwards (1987), 102-10.
18. Bailey (2003), 48-53.
19. Bailey (2003), 54-199.
20. Ashton (2000), 69.
21. Ewing (1899); Brandon (1973), 108-12.
22. Clarke (2003), 199.
23. Priestley (1947).
24. Drury (1999), 121.
25. Garrard (1965), 61.
26. Griffith-Jones (2001), 403.
27. Boitani (1999), 130-79.
28. Marx (2000), 8.
29. Boitani (1999), 145.
30. Evans (1990), 904-5.
31. Drury (1987), 424.
32. Garland (1992), vii.
33. Alexander (2005a), 1-42.
34. Aune (1989), 77.
35. Pelikan (1999), 18; Bonz (2000), 31-60.
36. Dibelius (2004), 49-86.
37. Alexander (1999), 21.
38. Cave (1988), 260; Goldhill (1991), 5; Boitani (1999), 10.
39. Ashton (2000), 175.
40. Barr (1993), 21-38; Pelikan (2006), 190-8.
41. Chadwick (1966), 3.
42. Drury (1987), 475.
43. Dibelius (2004), 108-33.
44. Frazer (1900), 2; Ramsay (1903), 237-8; Jaeger (1961), 39; Williams (1964), 201.
45. Alcock (1993); Lane Fox (1986).
46. Wallace and Williams (1998), 212.

47. Wallace and Williams (1998), 13 and 212.
48. Conybeare (1898), 197; Meeks (1983), 34.
49. Gabel, Wheeler and York (2000), 189.
50. Alexander (1993), 57.
51. Alexander (1999), 33.
52. Dodds (1951), 240.
53. Witherington (1998), 523.
54. Dodds (1951), 141-2.
55. Williams (1964), 205.
56. Dowden (2006), 5.
57. Nisetich (2001), 20 and 201.
58. Grant (1988), 25-6.
59. Hopkinson (1988), 131-2; Grant (1988), 26-7.
60. Jaeger (1961), 112; Grant (1988), 25.
61. Williams (1964), 205.
62. Adam (1910), 27.
63. Garrard (1965), 83.
64. Watson (2002), 382.
65. Pelikan (1999), 124.
66. Norden (1956); Jaeger (1961), 112.
67. Alexander (2005b), 237.
68. Cameron (1990), 730.
69. Wallace and Williams (1998), 216.
70. Humphries (2006), 126-32.
71. Williams (1964), 34 and 211; Wallace and Williams (1993), 97-8.
72. Gabel, Wheeler and York (2000), 209; Pelikan (2006), 191.
73. Wallace and Williams (1998), 128.
74. Porter (1994); Cadbury (1958), 357-60; Alexander (2001), 1048.
75. Aune (1989), 129.
76. Rapske (1994), 43.
77. Alexander (1999), 42
78. Aune (1989), 118.

5. Spots of Time

1. Barrow (1967), 30-5.
2. Frazer (1994), 226; Boardman (1997), 42.
3. Bolton (1973), 149-50.
4. Clark (2004), 56.
5. Jenkyns (1980), 174.
6. Philip Larkin, 'Churchgoing'.
7. Jenkyns (1980), 175-7; Butler (1958), 164-73.
8. Jenkyns (1982), 147-8.
9. Martindale (2005), 96.
10. Jenkyns (1982), 149.
11. Frazer (1900), 2; Pretzler (2007).
12. Porter (2001), 84.
13. Young (1997), 3 and 47.
14. Chadwick (1966), 1.
15. Barnard (1967); Grant (1988), 28-49; Chadwick (2001), 93-9.
16. Nock (1933), 164-92.

17. Wilken (2003), 5.
18. Farrer (1889), 135.
19. Barnard (1967), 8 and 30.
20. Goldhill (2002a), 112.
21. Bowersock (1994), 74.
22. Bowersock (1994), 140-1; Hägg (1983), 162-4; Emmett (2003), 81.
23. Frye (1976), 142.
24. Frye (1976), 141.
25. Bowersock (1994), 141.
26. Nock (1933), 138-55.
27. Bowersock (1994), 71.
28. Benson (1906), 89-116.
29. Pater (1914), 3-12.
30. Highet (1949), 464-5.
31. Jenkyns (1980), 53-6.
32. Grant (1988), 92-9 and 178.
33. Farrer (1889), 149.
34. Chadwick (1966), 4.
35. Grant (1988), 179-81; Chadwick (2001), 124-9.
36. Lamberton (1989), 78; van der Poll (2001), 183.
37. Chadwick (1966), 57; Seaford (2006), 126.
38. Trigg (1983), 3-86.
39. Dawson (2002), 61.
40. Dawson (2002), 114.
41. Jaeger (1961), 57.
42. Lamberton (1989), 81.
43. Hanson (1959), 360.
44. Young (1997), 3.
45. Young (1997), 11.
46. Wilson (1975).
47. Hall (1979), 13.
48. Russell (1964), xxii-xxx.
49. Grube (1968), 340-53.
50. Richards (1934), 24-5.
51. Rutherford (2005), 27.
52. Abrams (1953), 72-8.
53. Russell (1964), 89.
54. Russell (1964), 92-4; Russell and Winterbottom (1972), 461.
55. Josipovici (1988), 246; Young (1997), 277-8.
56. Abrams (1973), 83-7; Clark (1993), 63-9.
57. Vance (1984), 185.
58. Prickett (1986), 97 and 104; Prickett (1976), 89-90.
59. Keats (1977), 157.
60. Abrams (1973).
61. Wordsworth, 'My heart leaps up.'
62. Paffard (1973), 36-48.
63. Abrams (1973), 86.
64. Bloom (1972), 95.
65. Engell (2002), 59.
66. Coleridge (1975), 268.
67. Lane (2001), 89.

68. Richards (1934), 98.
69. Engell (2002), 67; Lane (2001), 89.
70. Norton (1993), 161.
71. Prickett (1976), 28.
72. Lewis (1969), 175-86.
73. Hurst (2006), 221; Frye (1976), 138.
74. Ferris (2000), 70-6; Goldhill (2002b), 186-91.
75. Clarke (1981), 69.
76. Lord (1956), 78-126; Keats (1977), 218.
77. Bowra (1961), 142.
78. Gilley (1990), x.
79. Newman (1886), 114.
80. Ker (1988), 61-2.
81. Faber (1974), 289-95; Runcie (2003).
82. Newman (1886), 35; Faber (1974), 334.
83. Newman (1886), 4.
84. Gilley (1990), 8.
85. Newman (1979), 78-9.
86. Kenny (1992), 94.
87. Willey (1949), 92.
88. Newsome (1974), 57.
89. Holmes (1982), 80.
90. Honan (1981), 305.
91. Arnold (1960), 129-44.
92. Trilling (1949), 33.
93. Trilling (1949), 175.
94. Chambers (1947), 112.
95. Trilling (1949), 374-5; Martindale (2005), 45.
96. Clarke (1981), 271.
97. Arnold (1979), 97-216.
98. Calvino (2000), 3-9.
99. Steiner (1996), 2.
100. Shaffer (1975), 170
101. Steiner (1989), 180.
102. Steiner (1996), 8.
103. Manguel (1996), 210.

Bibliography

[For modern editions of older texts, the date of first publication is added in square brackets.]

Abrams, M.H. (1953) *The Mirror and the Lamp* (Oxford University Press).
—— (1973) *Natural Supernaturalism* (W.W. Norton).
—— (ed.) (1972) *Wordsworth: A Collection of Critical Essays* (Prentice-Hall).
Adam, J. (1910) *The Religious Teachers of Greece* (T. and T. Clark).
Alcock, S. (1993) *Graecia Capta: The Landscapes of Roman Greece* (Cambridge University Press).
—— Cherry, J.F. and Elsner, J. (eds) (2001) *Pausanias: Travel and Memory in Roman Greece* (Oxford University Press).
Alexander, L. (1993) 'Acts and Ancient Intellectual Biography' in Winter and Clarke: 31-63.
—— (1999) 'The Acts of the Apostles as an Apologetic Text' in Edwards, Goodman and Price: 15-44.
—— (2001) 'Acts' in Barton and Muddiman: 1028-61.
—— (2005a) *Acts in its Ancient Literary Context* (T. and T. Clark).
—— (2005b) 'The Four among Pagans' in Bockmuehl and Hagner: 222-37.
Alter, R. (1981) *The Art of Biblical Narrative* (Basic Books).
—— (1992) *The World of Biblical Literature* (SPCK).
—— (ed. and tr.) (2004) *The Five Books of Moses* (W.W. Norton).
—— and Kermode, F. (eds) (1987) *The Literary Guide to the Bible* (Collins).
Anderson, B.W. (1982) *The Living World of the Old Testament* (Longman).
Arnold, M. (1960 [1869]) *Culture and Anarchy* ed. J. Dover Wilson (Cambridge University Press).
—— (1979 [1853-61]) *On the Classical Tradition* ed. R.H. Super (University of Michigan Press).
Ashton, J. (2000) *The Religion of Paul the Apostle* (Oxford University Press).
Auerbach, E. (2003 [1953]) *Mimesis* (Princeton University Press).
Aune, D. (1989) *The New Testament in its Literary Environment* (Westminster Press).
Austin, N. (1975) *Archery at the Dark of the Moon* (University of California Press).
Austin, R.G. (ed.) (1971) *Virgil:* Aeneid *Book I* (Oxford University Press).
Bailey, K.E. (2003) *Jacob and the Prodigal* (Bible Reading Fellowship).
Barchiesi, A. (2001) *Speaking Volumes* (Duckworth).
Barnard, L.W. (1967) *Justin Martyr* (Cambridge University Press).
Barr, J. (1993) *Biblical Faith and Natural Theology* (Oxford University Press).
Barrow, R.H. (1967) *Plutarch and his Times* (Chatto and Windus).
Barth, K. (2001 [1947]) *Protestant Theology in the Nineteenth Century* (SCM Press).
Barthes, R. (1977) *Image, Music, Text* (Fontana).
Barton, J. (1984) *Reading the Old Testament* (Darton, Longman and Todd).

—— and Muddiman, J. (eds) (2001) *The Oxford Bible Commentary* (Oxford University Press).

Benson, A.C. (1906) *Walter Pater* (Macmillan).

Beye, C.R. (2006) *Ancient Epic Poetry* (Bolchazy-Carducci).

Birch, B.C., Brueggemann, W., Fretham, T.E. and Peterson, D.L. (2005) *A Theological Introduction to the Old Testament* (Abingdon Press, Nashville).

Bloom, H. (1972) 'The Myth of Memory and Natural Man' in Abrams: 95-106.

Boardman, J. (1997) *The Great God Pan* (Thames and Hudson).

Bockmuehl, M. and Hagner, D.A. (eds) (2005) *The Written Gospel* (Cambridge University Press).

Bogan, Z. (1658) *Homerus Hebraizon* (H. Hall, Oxford).

Boitani, P. (1999) *The Bible and its Re-writings* (Oxford University Press).

Bolton, J.D.P. (1973) *Glory, Jest and Riddle* (Duckworth).

Bonz, M.P. (2000) *The Past as Legacy: Luke-Acts and Ancient Epic* (Fortress Press).

Bowersock, G.W. (1994) *Fiction as History* (University of California Press).

Bowman, A.K., Champlin, E. and Lintott, A. (eds) (1996) *The Cambridge Ancient History* (2nd edn) vol. X: *The Augustan Empire, 43 BC – AD 69* (Cambridge University Press).

Bowra, C.M. (1961) *The Romantic Imagination* (Oxford University Press).

Brandon, S.G.F. (1973) *Religion in Ancient History* (George Allen and Unwin).

Brickhouse, T.C. and Smith, N.D. (eds) (2002) *The Trial and Execution of Socrates* (Oxford University Press).

Brittain, V. (1979 [1933]) *Testament of Youth* (Fontana).

Brown, D. (1999) *Tradition and Imagination* (Oxford University Press).

Brueggemann, W. (2003) *An Introduction to the Old Testament* (Westminster John Knox Press).

Budelmann, F. and Michelakis, P. (eds) (2001) *Homer, Tragedy and Beyond: Essays in Honour of P.E. Easterling* (Society for the Promotion of Hellenic Studies).

Bull, M. (2006) *The Mirror of the Gods* (Penguin).

Bultmann, R. (1960) *Primitive Christianity in its Contemporary Setting* (Fontana).

—— (ed.) (1971) *The Gospel of St John* (Westminster Press).

Burkert, W. (1985) *Greek Religion* (Blackwell).

—— (1992) *The Orientalizing Revolution* (Harvard University Press).

Burnett, A.P. (1970) 'Pentheus and Dionysus: Host and Guest' *Classical Philology* 65: 15-29.

Burnyeat, M. (2002) 'The Impiety of Socrates' in Brickhouse and Smith: 133-45.

Burridge, R.A. (1992) *What are the Gospels?* (Cambridge University Press).

Burrow, C. (1997) 'Virgils, from Dante to Milton' in Martindale: 79-90.

Butler, E.M. (1958 [1935]) *The Tyranny of Greece over Germany* (Beacon Press, Boston).

Byrne, B. (2000) *The Hospitality of God* (The Liturgical Press, Collegeville, Minnesota).

Cadbury, H.J. (1958 [1927]) *The Making of Luke-Acts* (SPCK).

Caird, G.B. (1980) *The Language and Imagery of the Bible* (Duckworth).

Cairns, D. (ed.) (2001) *Oxford Readings in Homer's* Iliad (Oxford University Press).

Calvino, I. (2000) *Why Read the Classics?* (Vintage).

Cameron, A. (1990) 'Women in Early Christian Interpretation' in Coggins and Houlden: 729-31.

Campbell, D.A. (ed.) (1967) *Greek Lyric Poetry: A Selection* (Macmillan).

Cave, T. (1988) *Recognitions* (Oxford University Press).

Bibliography

Chadwick, H. (1966) *Early Christian Thought and the Classical Tradition* (Oxford University Press).
—— (2001) *The Church in Ancient Society* (Oxford University Press).
—— (ed. and tr.) (1953) *Origen:* Contra Celsum (Cambridge University Press).
Chambers, E.K. (1947) *Matthew Arnold: A Study* (Oxford University Press).
Clark, G. (1993) *Augustine: The* Confessions (Cambridge University Press).
—— (2004) *Christianity and Roman Society* (Cambridge University Press).
Clarke, H. (1981) *Homer's Readers* (Associated University Presses).
—— (2003) *The Gospel of Matthew and its Readers* (Indiana University Press).
Clausen, W.V. (ed.) (1994) *Virgil:* Eclogues (Oxford University Press).
Coggins, R.J. and Houlden, J.L. (eds) (1990) *A Dictionary of Biblical Interpretation* (SCM Press).
Coleridge, S.T. (1975 [1817]) *Biographia Literaria* ed. G. Watson (Dent).
Comparetti, D. (1966 [1895]) *Vergil in the Middle Ages* tr. E. Benecke (George Allen and Unwin).
Conybeare, F.C. (1899) 'Athens' in Hastings vol. 1: 196-7.
Dancy, J. (2001) *The Divine Drama* (Lutterworth).
Dawson, J.D. (2002) *Christian Figural Reading and the Fashioning of Identity* (University of California Press).
Dean, W. (1959) *Handel's Dramatic Oratorios and Masques* (Oxford University Press).
Deissmann, A. (2004 [1923]) *Light from the Ancient East* tr. L. Strachan (Wipf and Stock).
Dibelius, M. (2004 [1956]) *The Book of Acts: Form, Style, and Theology* ed. K. Hanson (Fortress Press).
Dines, J.M. (2004) *The Septuagint* (T. and T. Clark).
Dodds, E.R. (1951) *The Greeks and the Irrational* (University of California Press).
—— (1973) *The Ancient Concept of Progress* (Oxford University Press).
—— (ed.) (1960) *Euripides:* Bacchae (Oxford University Press).
Dowden, K. (2006) *Zeus* (Routledge).
Drury, J. (1985) *The Parables in the Gospels* (SPCK).
—— (1987) 'Luke' in Alter and Kermode: 418-39.
—— (1999) *Painting the Word* (Yale University Press).
Edwards, M., Goodman, M. and Price, S. (1999) *Apologetics in the Roman Empire* (Oxford University Press).
Edwards, M.W. (1987) *Homer: Poet of the* Iliad (Johns Hopkins University Press).
Eliot, T.S. (1975) *Selected Prose of T.S. Eliot* ed. F. Kermode (Faber and Faber).
Emmett, L. (2003) 'A third-century Christian novel', *Classical Quarterly* 53.1: 81-2.
Engell, J. (2002) '*Biographia Literaria*' in Newlyn: 59-74.
Evans, C.F. (1990) (ed.) *Saint Luke* (SCM Press).
Ewing, W. (1899) 'Hospitality, Host' in Hastings vol. 2: 427-9.
Exum, J.C. (1992) *Tragedy and Biblical Narrative* (Cambridge University Press).
Faber, G. (1974 [1933]) *Oxford Apostles* (Faber and Faber).
Fantham, E. (2004) *Ovid's* Metamorphoses (Oxford University Press).
Farrer, F.W. (1889) *Lives of the Fathers* vol. 1 (A. and C. Black).
Feeney, D.C. (1991) *The Gods in Epic* (Oxford University Press).
Feldherr, A. (2002) 'Metamorphosis in the *Metamorphoses*' in Hardie: 163-79.
Ferris, D.S. (2000) *Silent Urns: Romanticism, Hellenism, Modernity* (Stanford University Press).
Flower, M.A. and Marincola, J. (eds) (2002) *Herodotus:* Histories Book IX (Cambridge University Press).

Foley, H.P. (ed.) (1994) *The Homeric Hymn to Demeter* (Princeton University Press).

Fränkel, H. (1945) *Ovid: A Poet Between Two Worlds* (University of California Press).

Frazer, J.G. (1900) *Pausanias and Other Greek Sketches* (Macmillan).

—— (1923) *Folklore in the Old Testament* (Macmillan).

—— (1994 [1900]) *The Golden Bough (A New Abridgement)* ed. R. Fraser (Oxford University Press).

Frye, N. (1976) *The Secular Scripture* (Harvard University Press).

—— (1982) *The Great Code* (Routledge and Kegan Paul).

Gabel, J.B., Wheeler, C.B., and York, A.D. (2000) *The Bible as Literature: An Introduction* (Oxford University Press).

Galinsky, G.K. (1972) *The Herakles Theme* (Basil Blackwell).

—— (1975) *Ovid's* Metamorphoses: *An Introduction to the Basic Aspects* (Blackwell).

—— (ed.) (2005) *The Cambridge Companion to the Age of Augustus* (Cambridge University Press).

Garland, R. (1992) *Introducing New Gods* (Duckworth).

Garrard, L.A. (1965) *Athens or Jerusalem?* (George Allen and Unwin).

Garrison, R. (1997) *The Graeco-Roman Context of Early Christian Literature* (Sheffield Academic Press).

Gibbon, E. (1907 [1796]) *The Autobiography of Edward Gibbon* ed. J.B. Bury (Oxford University Press).

Gill, D.W.J. and Gempf, C. (eds) (1994) *The Book of Acts in its First Century Setting* vol. 2: *Graeco-Roman Setting* (Eerdmans).

Gilley, S. (1990) *Newman and his Age* (Darton, Longman and Todd).

Ginzberg, L. (2001) *Legends of the Bible* (Robson Books).

Goldhill, S. (1991) *The Poet's Voice* (Cambridge University Press).

—— (2002a) *The Invention of Prose* (Oxford University Press).

—— (2002b) *Who needs Greek?* (Cambridge University Press).

—— (2005) *Love, Sex and Tragedy: Why Classics Matters* (John Murray).

Gooch, P. (1996) *Reflections on Jesus and Socrates* (Yale University Press).

Goulder, M.D. (1974) *Midrash and Lection in Matthew* (SPCK).

Goward, B. (2005) *Aeschylus:* Agamemnon (Duckworth).

Grafton, A., Most, G.W. and Zetzel, J.E.G. (eds) (1985) *F.A. Wolf: Prolegomena to Homer, 1795* (Princeton University Press).

Gransden, K.W. (1984) *Virgil's* Iliad (Cambridge University Press).

—— (ed.) (1976) *Virgil:* Aeneid *Book VIII* (Cambridge University Press).

Grant, R.M. (1988) *Greek Apologists of the Second Century* (SCM Press).

Graziosi, B. and Haubold, J. (2005) *Homer: The Resonance of Epic* (Duckworth).

Griffin, J. (1977) 'The Epic Cycle and the Uniqueness of Homer', *Journal of Hellenic Studies* 97: 39-53.

—— (1980a) *Homer on Life and Death* (Oxford University Press).

—— (1980b) *Homer* (Oxford University Press).

—— (1985) *Latin Poets and Roman Life* (Duckworth).

Griffith-Jones, R. (2001) *The Four Witnesses* (Harper Collins).

Grossvogel, D.I. (1979) *Mystery and its Fictions: From Oedipus to Agatha Christie* (Johns Hopkins University Press).

Grube, G.M.A. (1968) *The Greek and Roman Critics* (Methuen).

Hägg, Tomas (1983) *The Novel in Antiquity* (Blackwell).

Hall, J. (1979) *Dictionary of Subjects and Symbols in Art* (John Murray).

Bibliography

Halliwell, S. (2002) *Aesthetics of Mimesis: Ancient Texts and Modern Problems* (Princeton University Press).

Hansen, W. (2002) *Ariadne's Thread* (Cornell University Press).

Hanson, R.P.C. (1959) *Allegory and Event* (SCM Press).

Hardie, P. (1986) *Virgil's* Aeneid*: Cosmos and Imperium* (Oxford University Press).

———— (1991) 'The *Aeneid* and the *Oresteia*', *Proceedings of the Virgil Society* 20: 29-42.

———— (1993) *The Epic Successors of Virgil* (Cambridge University Press).

———— (ed.) (2002) *The Cambridge Companion to Ovid* (Cambridge University Press).

Harrison, J. (1925) *Reminiscences of a Student's Life* (Hogarth Press).

Harrison, T. (2000) *Divinity and History* (Oxford University Press).

Hart, J. (1982) *Herodotus and Greek History* (Croom Helm).

Hastings, J. (ed.) (1899) *A Dictionary of the Bible* (vols 1-6) (T. and T. Clark).

Heidel, A. (1946) *The Gilgamesh Epic and Old Testament Parallels* (University of Chicago Press).

Hengel, M. (2005) 'Eye-witness Memory and the Writing of the Gospels' in Bockmuehl and Hagner: 70-96.

Hick, J. (ed.) (1977) *The Myth of God Incarnate* (SCM Press).

Highet, G. (1949) *The Classical Tradition* (Oxford University Press).

Hinds, S. (1998) *Allusion and Intertext* (Cambridge University Press).

Hollis, A.S. (ed.) (1970) *Ovid:* Metamorphoses *Book VIII* (Oxford University Press).

———— (ed.) (1990) *Callimachus:* Hecale (Oxford University Press).

Holmes, R. (1982) *Coleridge* (Oxford University Press).

Honan, P. (1981) *Matthew Arnold: A Life* (Weidenfeld and Nicolson).

Hopkinson, N. (ed.) (1988) *A Hellenistic Anthology* (Cambridge University Press).

Humphreys, W.L. (1985) *The Tragic Vision and the Hebrew Tradition* (Wipf and Stock).

Humphries, M. (2006) *Early Christianity* (Routledge).

Hunter, R. (2006) *The Shadow of Callimachus* (Cambridge University Press).

Hurst, I. (2006) *Victorian Women Writers and the Classics* (Oxford University Press).

Hutchinson, G. (1988) *Hellenistic Poetry* (Oxford University Press).

Jacobson, H. (1983) *The Exagoge of Ezekiel* (Cambridge University Press).

Jaeger, W. (1961) *Early Christianity and Greek Paideia* (Oxford University Press).

James, M.R. (1924) *The Apocryphal New Testament* (Oxford University Press).

Jasper, D. (2004) *A Short Introduction to Hermeneutics* (Westminster John Knox Press).

Jenkins, P. (2001) *Hidden Gospels* (Oxford University Press).

Jenkyns, R. (1980) *The Victorians and Ancient Greece* (Blackwell).

———— (1982) *Three Classical Poets: Sappho, Catullus, and Juvenal* (Duckworth).

———— (1996) 'Leafing Through', *Ad Familiares* (Journal of The Friends of Classics) 11: 1.

———— (1999) *Virgil's Experience* (Oxford University Press).

Josipovici, G. (1988) *The Book of God* (Yale University Press).

Kearns, E. (1982) 'The Return of Odysseus: A Homeric Theoxeny', *Classical Quarterly* 32.1:1-8.

———— (1996) 'Theoxenia', *Oxford Classical Dictionary* (3rd edn): 1506-7.

Keats, J. (1977) *Letters of John Keats: A Selection* ed. J. Gittings (Oxford University Press).

189

Kennedy, D. (1977) 'Virgilian epic' in Martindale: 145-54.

Kenney, E.J. (1986) Introduction and Notes to A.S. Melville (tr.) *Ovid:* Metamorphoses (Oxford University Press).

Kenny, A. (1992) *What is Faith?* (Oxford University Press).

Ker, I. (1988) *John Henry Newman: A Biography* (Oxford University Press).

Kermode, F. (1979) *The Genesis of Secrecy* (Harvard University Press).

Kugel, J.L. (1997) *The Bible as it Was* (Harvard University Press).

Lamberton, R. (1989) *Homer the Theologian* (University of California Press).

—— and Keaney, J.J. (eds) (1992) *Homer's Ancient Readers* (Princeton University Press).

Landow, G.P. (1980) *Victorian Types, Victorian Shadows* (Routledge and Kegan Paul).

Lane, M. (2001) *Plato's Progeny* (Duckworth).

Lane Fox, R. (1975) *Alexander the Great* (Futura).

—— (1986) *Pagans and Christians* (Viking).

Law, P. (ed.) (2005) *Testament: The Bible Odyssey* (Continuum).

Lewis, C.S. (1942) *A Preface to* Paradise Lost (Oxford University Press).

—— (1969) *Selected Literary Essays* (Cambridge University Press).

Lloyd, A.B. (ed.) (1997) *What is a God?* (Duckworth/Classical Press of Wales).

Lloyd-Jones, H. (1971) *The Justice of Zeus* (University of California Press).

Long, A.A. (1992) 'Stoic Readings of Homer' in Lamberton and Keaney: 41-66.

Lord, G. de F. (1956) *Homeric Renaissance: The* Odyssey *of George Chapman* (Chatto and Windus).

Louden, B. (1999) *The* Odyssey*: Structure, Narration, and Meaning* (Johns Hopkins University Press).

Lowe, N.J. (2000) *The Classical Plot and the Invention of Western Narrative* (Cambridge University Press).

MacDonald, D.R. (2000) *The Homeric Epics and the Gospel of Mark* (Yale University Press).

Macleod, C.W. (ed.) (1982) *Homer:* Iliad *Book XXIV* (Cambridge University Press).

Manguel, A. (1997) *A History of Reading* (Flamingo).

Martindale, C. (1993) *Redeeming the Text* (Cambridge University Press).

—— (2005) *Latin Poetry and the Judgement of Taste* (Oxford University Press).

—— (ed.) (1984) *Virgil and his Influence* (Bristol Classical Press).

—— (ed.) (1997) *The Cambridge Companion to Virgil* (Cambridge University Press).

Marx, S. (2000) *Shakespeare and the Bible* (Oxford University Press).

Meeks, W.A. (1983) *The First Urban Christians* (Yale University Press).

Millar, F. and Segal, E. (eds) (1984) *Caesar Augustus: Seven Aspects* (Oxford University Press).

Mold, S. (1985) 'Handel's Music Today', *Musical Opinion*, April/May 1985: 199-201.

Momigliano, A.D. (1990) *The Classical Foundations of Modern Historiography* (University of California Press).

—— (1994) *Studies on Modern Scholarship* (University of California Press).

Murnaghan, S. (1987) *Disguise and Recognition in the* Odyssey (Princeton University Press).

Myers, F.W.H. (1908) *Essays: Classical* (Macmillan).

Neill, S. (1966*) The Interpretation of the New Testament, 1861-1961* (Oxford University Press).

Newlyn, L. (ed.) (2002) *The Cambridge Companion to Coleridge* (Cambridge University Press).

Bibliography

Newman, J.H. (1886 [1864]) *Apologia Pro Vita Sua* (Longmans, Green and Co.).
—— (1890 [1845]) *An Essay on the Development of Christian Doctrine* (Longmans, Green and Co.).
—— (1979 [1870]) *An Essay in Aid of a Grammar of Assent* ed. N. Lash (University of Notre Dame Press).
Newsome, D. (1974) *Two Classes of Men: Platonism and English Romantic Thought* (John Murray).
Nielsen, F.A.J. (1997) *The Tragedy in History: Herodotus and the Deuteronomistic History* (Sheffield Academic Press).
Nightingale, A.W. (1995) *Genres in Dialogue* (Cambridge University Press).
Nisetich, F. (2001) *The Poems of Callimachus* (Oxford University Press).
Nock, A.D. (1933) *Conversion* (Oxford University Press).
Norden, E. (1956 [1913]) *Agnostos Theos* (Wissenschaftliche Buchgesellschaft, Darmstadt).
Norton, D. (1993) *A History of the Bible as Literature* vol. 2 (Cambridge University Press).
Nortwick, T. van (1996) *Somewhere I Have Never Travelled* (Oxford University Press).
Otto, W.F. (1965) *Dionysus: Myth and Cult* (Indiana University Press).
Paffard, M. (1973) *Inglorious Wordsworths* (Hodder and Stoughton).
Page, T.E. (ed.) (1898) *Virgil:* Bucolics *and* Georgics (Macmillan).
Pagels, E. (1980) *The Gnostic Gospels* (Penguin).
Parker, R. (1996) *Athenian Religion: A History* (Oxford University Press).
—— (2005) *Polytheism and Society at Athens* (Oxford University Press).
Pater, W. (1914 [1885]) *Marius the Epicurean* (Macmillan).
Pelikan, J. (1999) *Jesus Through the Centuries* (Yale University Press).
—— (2006) (ed.) *Acts (SCM Theological Commentary on the Bible)* (SCM Press).
Poll, C. van der (2001) 'Homer and Homeric interpretation in the *Protrepticus* of Clement of Alexandria' in Budelmann and Michelakis: 179-99.
Porter, J.I. (2001) 'Ideals and ruins: Pausanias, Longinus, and the Second Sophistic' in Alcock, Cherry and Elsner: 63-92.
Porter, S.E. (1994) 'The "We" Passages' in Gill and Gempf: 545-74.
Pretzler, M. (2007) *Pausanias: Travel Writing in Ancient Greece* (Duckworth).
Prickett, S. (1976) *Romanticism and Religion* (Cambridge University Press).
—— (1986) *Words and the Word* (Cambridge University Press).
—— (1996) *Origins of Narrative* (Cambridge University Press).
—— and Barnes, R. (1991) *The Bible* (Cambridge University Press).
Price, S.R.F. (1984) *Rituals and Power: the Roman Imperial Cult in Asia Minor* (Cambridge University Press).
—— (1996) 'The Place of Religion: Rome in the Early Empire' in Bowman, Champlin and Lintott: 812-47.
Priestley, J.B. (1947) *An Inspector Calls* (Heinemann).
Pritchard, J.B. (ed.) (1955) *Ancient Near Eastern Texts Relating to the Old Testament* (Princeton University Press).
Propp, V. (1968 [1928]) *The Morphology of the Folktale* (University of Texas Press).
Rahner, H. (1963) *Greek Myths and Christian Mystery* (Burns and Oates).
Ramsay, W.M. (1903) *St Paul the Traveller and the Roman Citizen* (Hodder and Stoughton).
Rapske, B.M. (1994) 'Acts, Travel and Shipwreck' in Gill and Gempf: 1-47.
Richards, I.A. (1934) *Coleridge on Imagination* (Kegan Paul).

Bibliography

Richardson, N.J. (1983) 'Recognition Scenes in the *Odyssey* and Ancient Literary Criticism', *Papers of the Liverpool Latin Seminar* vol. 4: 219-35.

Rogerson, J. (1984) *Old Testament Criticism in the Nineteenth Century* (SPCK).

Romm, J. (1998) *Herodotus* (Yale University Press).

Rosenbloom, D. (2006) *Aeschylus:* Persians (Duckworth).

Runcie, R. (2003) 'Still yearns my heart' (Presidential Address to the Classical Association, 1992) in Stray: 226-36.

Russell, D.A. (ed.) (1964) *Longinus:* On the Sublime (Oxford University Press).

——— and Winterbottom, M. (ed. and tr.) (1972) *Ancient Literary Criticism* (Oxford University Press).

Rutherford, R. (2001a) 'From the *Iliad* to the *Odyssey*' in Cairns: 117-46.

——— (2001b) 'Tragic Form and Feeling in the *Iliad*' in Cairns: 260-93.

——— (2005) *Classical Literature: A Concise History* (Blackwell).

Ryle, G. (1966) *Plato's Progress* (Cambridge University Press).

Schein, S.L. (1985) *The Mortal Hero* (University of California Press).

Seaford, R. (1994) *Reciprocity and Ritual* (Oxford University Press).

——— (1997) 'Thunder, lightning and earthquake in the *Bacchae* and the Acts of the Apostles' in Lloyd: 139-52.

——— (2006) *Dionysus* (Routledge).

——— (ed.) (1996) *Euripides:* Bacchae (Aris and Philips).

Shaffer, E.S. (1975) *'Kubla Khan' and* The Fall of Jerusalem (Cambridge University Press).

Stanford, W.B. (1963) *The Ulysses Theme* (Blackwell).

——— (ed.) (1959) *Homer:* Odyssey Books *I-XII* (Macmillan).

Steiner, G. (1963) *The Death of Tragedy* (Faber and Faber).

——— (1984) *Antigones* (Oxford University Press).

——— (1989) *Real Presences* (Faber and Faber).

——— (1996) *No Passion Spent: Essays 1978-96* (Faber and Faber).

——— and Fagles, R. (eds) (1962) *Homer: Twentieth Century Views* (Prentice-Hall).

Stibbe, M.W.G. (1992) *John as Storyteller: Narrative Criticism and the Fourth Gospel* (Cambridge University Press).

Stray, C. (ed.) *The Classical Association: The First Century 1903-2003* (Oxford University Press).

Syme, R. (1960 [1939]) *The Roman Revolution* (Oxford University Press).

Taplin, O.P. (1989) *Greek Tragedy in Action* (Routledge).

Taylor, L.R. (1931) *The Divinity of the Roman Emperor* (American Philological Association).

Trigg, J.W. (1983) *Origen: The Bible and Philosophy in the Third-century Church* (SCM Press).

Trilling, L. (1949) *Matthew Arnold* (George Allen and Unwin).

Turner, F.M. (1981) *The Greek Heritage in Victorian Britain* (Yale University Press).

Vance, N. (1984) 'Virgil and the Nineteenth Century' in Martindale: 169-92.

Vernant, J.-P. and Vidal-Naquet, P. (1981) *Tragedy and Myth in Ancient Greece* tr. J. Lloyd (Harvester Press).

Wallace, R. and Williams, W. (1993) *The Acts of the Apostles: A Companion* (Bristol Classical Press).

——— (1998) *The Three Worlds of Paul of Tarsus* (Routledge).

Wallace-Hadrill, A. (2005) *'Mutatas formas*: the Augustan Transformation of Roman Knowledge' in Galinsky: 55-84.

Bibliography

Warde Fowler, W. (1917) *Aeneas at the Site of Rome* (Basil Blackwell).
Watson, J.R. (2002) *An Annotated Anthology of Hymns* (Oxford University Press).
Weil, S. (1957) *Intimations of Christianity among the Ancient Greeks* (Routledge and Kegan Paul).
Weinfeld, M. (1993) *The Promise of the Land* (University of California Press).
West, M.L. (1997) *The East Face of Helicon: West Asiatic Elements in Greek Poetry and Myth* (Oxford University Press).
—— (ed.) (1978) *Hesiod:* Works and Days (Oxford University Press).
White, L.M. (2005) 'Herod and the Jewish Experience of Roman Rule' in Galinsky: 361-87.
Wilder, A. (1971) *Early Christian Rhetoric* (Harvard University Press).
Wiles, D. (2000) *Greek Theatre Production: An Introduction* (Cambridge University Press).
Wilken, R.L. (2003) *The Spirit of Early Christian Thought* (Yale University Press).
Willey, B. (1949) *Nineteenth Century Studies: Coleridge to Matthew Arnold* (Chatto and Windus).
Williams, C.S.C. (ed.) (1964) *The Acts of the Apostles* (A. and C. Black).
Williams, R.D. (ed.) (1962) *Virgil:* Aeneid *Book III* (Oxford University Press).
Wilson, N.G. (ed.) (1975) *Saint Basil on Greek Literature* (Duckworth).
Winkler, J.J. and Zeitlin, F. (eds) (1990) *Nothing to do with Dionysus?* (Princeton University Press).
Winter, B.W. and Clarke, A.D. (eds) (1993) *The Book of Acts in its First Century Setting* vol. 1: *Ancient Literary Setting* (Eerdmans).
Witherington, B. (ed.) (1998) *The Acts of the Apostles: A Socio-rhetorical Commentary* (Eerdmans).
Young, F.M. (1977) 'Two Roots or a Tangled Mass?' in Hick: 87-121.
—— (1983) *From Nicaea to Chalcedon* (SCM Press).
—— (1997) *Biblical Exegesis and the Formation of Christian Culture* (Cambridge University Press).
Zeitlin, F. (1990) 'Thebes: Theater of Self and Society in Athenian Drama' in Winkler and Zeitlin: 130-67.
Ziolkowski, T. (1993) *Virgil and the Moderns* (Princeton University Press).

Index of Passages Cited

197

198

General Index

199

www.ingramcontent.com/pod-product-compliance
Lightning Source LLC
Chambersburg PA
CBHW071406100726
47908CB00004B/1072